Y0-ARB-072

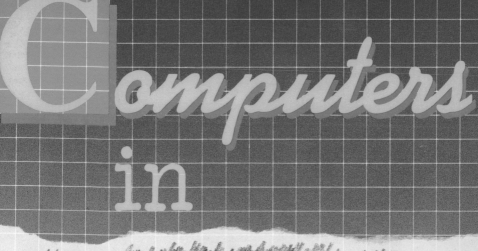

Computers in SCHOOLS

William J. Bramble and Emanuel J. Mason
with Paul Berg

m. searles

COMPUTERS
IN
SCHOOLS

COMPUTERS IN SCHOOLS

William J. Bramble
Alaska Department of Education

Emanuel J. Mason
University of Kentucky

With

Paul Berg
Alaska Department of Education

57827

The Pennsylvania State University
College of Education
Curriculum Materials Center
University Park, Pennsylvania

McGRAW-HILL BOOK COMPANY

New York   St. Louis   San Francisco   Auckland   Bogotá
Hamburg   Johannesburg   London   Madrid   Mexico   Montreal   New Delhi
Panama   Paris   São Paulo   Singapore   Sydney   Tokyo   Toronto

This book was set in Optima by University Graphics, Inc.
The editors were Christina Mediate, Stephanie K. Happer, and Susan Gamer;
the production supervisor was Charles Hess.
The drawings were done by Fine Line Illustrations, Inc.
The cover was designed by Mark Wieboldt.
R. R. Donnelley & Sons Company was printer and binder.

COMPUTERS IN SCHOOLS

Copyright © 1985 by McGraw-Hill, Inc. All rights reserved. Printed in the United States of America. Except as permitted under the United States Copyright Act of 1976, no part of this publication may be reproduced or distributed in any form or by any means, or stored in a data base or retrieval system, without the prior written permission of the publisher.

1 2 3 4 5 6 7 8 9 0   DOCDOC   8 9 8 7 6 5 4

ISBN 0-07-007151-9

Library of Congress Cataloging in Publication Data

Bramble, William J.
   Computers in schools.

   Includes bibliographies and indexes.
      1. Computer-assisted instruction.   2. Microcomputers.
I. Mason, Emanuel J.   II. Title.
LB1028.5.B635   1985   371.3′9445   84–5686
ISBN 0-07-007151-9

To our parents and our wives,
and for our children.

CONTENTS

PREFACE

In recent years educators have become increasingly aware of the need to know how to use computer technology in educational settings. The availability of computers at relatively low prices and in forms that are usable even by young children has opened educators' eyes to the potential of the technology. However, educators must increase their familiarity with this technology in order to realize its potential.

With new innovations, the people who do the initial developing often fail to recognize that practitioners require information and training. Thus, it often seems that when training materials and information are most needed, they are most lacking. Only after many users have "learned the hard way" do the needed resources become available. Educational computing has not been immune to this kind of discrepancy between the available technology and the information necessary to enable educators to use it. If training materials in educational computing had been keeping pace with the developing technology in the last few years, educational computing would be much more pervasive than it currently is.

In addition to training in how to operate and use computers, educators need an understanding of how computers relate to what we know about education. Scientific research, theory, and philosophy concerning schools, learning, and instruction cannot be overlooked when computerized education is developed and applied. A computer, in the final analysis, is an extremely capable instructional aid. Its successful use must be governed by sound educational principles. In this book, the computer is placed within the context of educational practice, research, and thought, in order to bridge the gaps between the hardware designer, the educational program developer, and the practicing educator.

This book focuses on the role of the microcomputer in education. Microcomputers are relatively inexpensive, easy to use, and capable of performing many useful functions in instructional settings. Topics covered include the history of computing, instructional hardware and software, determination of needs, development and evaluation of instructional materials, small-scale data processing, sources of assistance to educators who use computers, techniques of applying computerized instruction in the classroom, the social and economic impact of computers in society, and the future of educational computing. With this coverage, the book should be extremely useful to those interested in education and technology (parents, school board members, educational researchers and planners, and so on). The administrator who must organize and manage educational programs should find this an interesting book. However, the book should be of particular value to educators in training, as well as to experienced classroom teachers and administrators, who require some basic knowledge of instructional computing. In addition, those interested in computerized training within a business or industrial setting should also find the book worthwhile.

Technological change has occurred rapidly in recent years. Educational computing is also developing at a rapid pace. The present authors had to be cognizant of these rapid changes as the book was being developed. The manuscript was prepared on a microcomputer with word processing capabilities, so that changes resulting from new innovations could be incorporated easily.

During the preparation of the manuscript, useful insights and other assistance were provided by numerous people. The most notable contribution was by Paul Berg, an experienced educational computing specialist, whose assistance in drafting chapters in the second half of the book was critical to the completion of the project. Many of Paul's insights and conceptualizations, particularly those in Chapter 12, were extremely significant.

Ed Obie, of the Alaska Department of Education's Office of Educational Technology and Telecommunications (OET&T), provided a summary for Chapter 4 (for which he has been duly credited) and various critical comments regarding other sections of the book. Bea Tindall, also of OET&T, provided comments and ideas along the way. Critical reading of various sections and helpful recommendations were provided by Gary Anglin, Susan Mason, and William E. Stilwell. Lamar Abalahin assisted with library research. Assistance with text entry was provided by Susan Mason, Virginia Berg, and Billy Bramble. Ellen Bramble proofread much of the manuscript. Finally, the timeliness and high quality of the critiques of the early drafts provided by William H. Sanders, Indiana University; Ronald Hunt, San Jose State University; Vicki Blum Cohen, Columbia Teachers College; and John D. Davis, Sr., Northern Illinois University, were appreciated by the authors throughout the project.

William J. Bramble
Emanuel J. Mason

COMPUTERS
IN
SCHOOLS

COMPUTERS IN EDUCATION: EVOLUTION OR REVOLUTION?

Events are taking place in education that many are saying will ultimately be considered revolutionary. Despite a great deal of excitement, however, the revolution is not yet visible to everyone. What is precipitating the revolution is the fact that computers which a short time ago were available only to large institutions with highly trained technical staffs are now becoming as common as chalkboards and audiotape recorders in classrooms across the United States. How has this affected education?

Consider the following examples:

• At an elementary school in North Carolina, students previously had little opportunity for tutorial assistance in learning mathematical facts. With more than two dozen students in the class, there simply wasn't time for the teacher to give the students individual attention. Further, the task of grading daily mathematics assignments for that many students was nearly overwhelming. Today compact and sophisticated computers in the classroom give automated mathematics tutorials and drills for the students who need them. The machines that provide this instruction are tireless and infinitely patient. They score students' performance and keep records for the teacher. The teacher now has a great deal more time to directly address the special problems particular students may experience as they learn mathematics, and to provide warmth and support for children engaged in the learning process.[1]

• Students in a social studies class in Minnesota learn about how the settlers went westward from Missouri along the Oregon Trail. In their textbook, readings describe the passage of settlers over this trail during the mid-nineteenth century and briefly mention the great distance involved and the problems encountered by the travelers. Now this trip, with all its hazards and difficulties, comes alive for the students on a classroom microcomputer. Using this device and a program about the Oregon Trail, they are able to plan and participate in a trip along the trail. Along the way they are presented with problems similar to the ones that confronted the settlers. The students experience the consequences of their solutions and decisions, and may or may not make it to the end of the trip "alive."[2]

• In isolated communities in Alaska, students attend schools reminiscent of the little red schoolhouses once common throughout America. A typical school may only have two teachers, and about 20 students with a broad age range. The teachers face major challenges. During the school day, a teacher is expected to respond to a wide variety of students' needs. For example, a kindergarten student may need work with reading readiness, first- and second-grade students with basic language arts instruction, a sixth-grader with computations involving fractions, and six high school students with algebra, language arts, history, earth science, and health education. With microcomputers recently purchased by the school, and programs furnished by the state department of education, individualized courses of study are possible for the high school students; at the same time supplemental instruction in readiness and basic skills is available for the students in the primary grades, and drill and practice in computations involving fractions can be given to the sixth-grader.[3]

• Students in an elementary school in Colorado are not concerned about the card catalog in the school library. In fact, they don't use a card catalog at all, in the traditional sense. Yet they engage in a systematic process of finding books in the library, and they're good at it. At their school, library resources are now catalogued on a microcomputer. With a few simple commands, students can search for books by subject, author, or title. The computer and the student communicate in plain English. Instructions are patiently provided by the computer, and students can find books more quickly, more easily, and with far less frustration than with a traditional card catalog method.[4]

• In an elementary school in Texas, and another in New York, students use a program developed for classroom computers by a professor from the Massachusetts Institute of Technology. The program enables students to instruct the computer using simple English commands rather than complicated scientific codes. This innovative approach to education allows students to learn new concepts in mathematics by instructing the computer to form and move shapes on a television screen. Thus, the student learns by doing. Learning experientially is not a new idea, of course; it was part of John Dewey's theory of progressive education, proposed around the turn of the century. However, the computer now makes it more practical for students to experience learning individually. Instruction occurs as children initiate actions in the context of their environment, rather than in response to actions by the instructor. For the students in these Texas and New York schools the classroom environment has been expanded to include the computer.[5]

Around the country – and, for that matter, around the world – computers have captured the imagination of educators. The promise of computers in education has been recognized for several decades, but their actual use in schools was meager until quite recently. Since the mid-1970s, sales of relatively small computers called *personal computers,* or *microcomputers,* to individuals, businesses, and schools have shot skyward. For example, according to figures provided by the National Center on Educational Statistics the number of microcomputers used for instructional purposes in schools increased from about 102,000 in the school year 1981–1982 to 156,000 at the start of 1982–1983.[6] These microcomputers are comparable in size to small portable typewriters and can easily fit (with their associated hardware) on a desk top. Some are even small enough to fit in a small attaché case or a coat pocket. They are relatively reliable and inexpensive, and they are capable of an amazing variety of educational applications.

EDUCATION AND THE MICROCOMPUTER

During the 1960s computers were believed to have significant potential for education. In fact, tremendous growth in the use of computers for direct instruction was expected. But conditions were not yet right. The computers of that day were huge, costly machines, usable and affordable only by large corporations, government agencies, universities, and research centers. Large, highly trained staffs were required to operate, maintain, and program these computers. Therefore, educational uses of computers were expensive to develop and even more expensive to implement. Further, the design of the learning activities was based primarily on the programmed instruction approach, in which students progress through highly structured steps toward clearly specified behavioral goals. In this kind of instruction, correct answers are reinforced by allowing the student to progress to a new activity; typically, incorrect answers are discouraged by showing the question again with the correct answer. Mechanical or electronic devices had been designed to present materials in this way as early as the 1950s. Such devices could be produced and operated at a much lower cost than a computer. The approach had also been economically and successfully built into programmed textbooks and workbooks.[7]

Successful gains were demonstrated by the few students given computer instruction during this period; but designs emphasizing programmed instruction did not fully utilize the instructional capabilities of the computer. In addition, the proponents of computerized instruction were, of necessity, highly trained people associated with research or model demonstration projects. In sum, computers were not an efficient way to use funds for instructional materials, nor were they affordable or practical for most educational agencies or schools.

The more recent history of computers in education is quite different. The small computer — the microcomputer — is being touted as a potentially revolutionary tool for the modern educator because, in addition to its low cost, it is generally designed to be easier to use than larger machines. In fact, to use most microcomputers, the educator does not have to be a computer expert or even to know anything about programming. A few days of training will usually enable a complete neophyte to benefit from the exciting new technology. The low cost and ease of operation of the microcomputer have allowed classroom teachers, counselors, librarians, resource teachers, school administrators, and other educators to make immediate and successful use of this powerful tool.

Universities and research centers were largely caught unprepared as this revolution in the use of computers began. They were lulled by the belief that computers had been found impractical and too costly for use in education. Further, the universities were beset by a myriad of problems of their own, ranging from inability to compete with industry for computer experts to inability to maintain their existing programs in the face of dwindling funds. As a result, universities and training institutions have been slow to respond to the demands of educators for more training in instructional computing. Nowadays, educators at all levels are showing interest in learning about computers in education. Superintendents ask, "What can computers do for our school district? How can we plan our staff development so that we will be able to use computers effectively?" Teachers ask, "What should I look for in instructional software to determine if it is appropriate for my classroom?" Special education teachers ask, "What should be taken into account in using computers with physically impaired children?" University professors ask, "What do prospective classroom teachers need to know about the use of computers for instruction?"

All these questions, and many others, point to the need for more information about computers in education. This book was written to meet this need, and to point out ways to obtain additional information about this remarkable technology. This book will focus on the microcomputer and its application in educational settings.

LARGE AND SMALL COMPUTERS

Computers are electronic machines capable of reading, processing, and storing information and providing some output. Figure 1.1 shows the basic functions computers can perform.

Microcomputers are small computers. In order of increasing size, they are followed by *minicomputers* and large *mainframe* computers. The concept of size may be deceptive with regard to computers. In general, the size of a computer has to do more with its capacity than with the physical space it occupies. Some of the early computers, which were enormous machines that filled large rooms, were not as capable as many of today's microcomputers. You will see as you read further in this book that even microcomputers can store a surprising amount of information and perform complex calculations with amazing speed. Microcomputers are distinguished from larger minicomputers and mainframe computers on the basis of size, cost, complexity, amount of memory, and processing speed. More will be said about this in Chapter 2.

Figure 1.2 shows a typical microcomputer found in a school. By way of contrast, Figure 1.3 shows a large mainframe computer. The larger computer can perform larger and more complex tasks that would be impractical, or even impossible, for the microcomputer. Many instructional applications do not require such computing power. Therefore, a mainframe computer is simply not practical or justifiable in terms of cost for many educational applications.

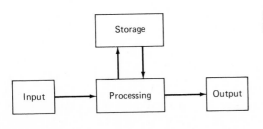

FIGURE 1.1
Basic computer functions.

FIGURE 1.2
Above: A student working at a microcomputer.

FIGURE 1.3
Below: Operations room of a modern mainframe computer.

A BRIEF HISTORY OF COMPUTERS

People often ask when the first computer was developed. That is a difficult question to answer precisely. Actually, the human mind is considered by many to be the first, and still the best, computer. The flexibility and powers of reasoning of the human mind have not yet been equalled by even the most sophisticated computers. In fact, people got along without computers for many thousands of years, and yet managed to perform calculations precise enough to build pyramids, navigate the globe, and predict the positions of the stars in the sky. Further, instances of fairly accurate census records appeared several thousand years ago. Obviously, then, computers are not necessary for such achievements. However, the usefulness of devices that aid in calculating is also obvious; and attempts to develop such devices began early in human history.

Early Developments

A variety of calculating aids were available in early civilizations. The first calculator was developed by the Chinese about 4000 years ago. This device, the abacus, is familiar to many schoolchildren (Figure 1.4). It is still in use in many parts of the world for making everyday calculations.

Before computers existed, there were two main problems in performing large-scale projects such as census studies: (1) storage and (2) summarization of the data.

To solve the first problem, several millennia ago humans invented a remarkable method of storing records and figures — writing things down. Information was first stored on clay tablets and later on parchment or paper-like substances. In this form, records were fairly permanent. They could be read and interpreted consistently by various readers and stored for later use.

Summarization of records was a problem because many classifications and calculations of data were required to combine and simplify data into concise figures. Originally, summarization was approached by brute force. That is, summaries were made by working on a problem for a long time. With some luck, the values calculated were correct. It didn't take people very long to figure out, however, that brute force was both tedious and time-consuming. It was also

FIGURE 1.4
An abacus.

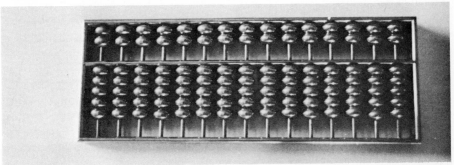

very expensive. These disadvantages led to the search for technological aids for performing calculations.

From Mechanical Calculators to Mechanical Computers

In the early 1600s in Scotland, John Napier developed a calculator to assist with multiplying, using a system of rods that could be moved about on a pattern (Figure 1.5a). About 25 years later (that is, in the middle of the seventeenth century), a Frenchman, Blaise Pascal, made another significant contribution to computation technology. When he was only about 18 years old, Pascal developed a device with gears that worked much like the mileage indicator in an automobile. It was designed to assist Pascal's father, a government official, in performing financial calculations. Later in the century, a machine invented by Gottfried Wilhelm von Liebniz improved on Pascal's device. By using repeated additions, it could multiply. It could not be made to work very accurately (the technology of the time was insufficent); but the ideas on which it was based contributed to later developments in calculating.

During the industrial revolution, inventions appeared which helped control manufacturing processes. One example is a technique developed by Joseph-Marie Jacquard, in which holes punched in cards to represent weaving patterns were used to automatically control weaving machines. This procedure is considered the direct ancestor of the punched card as a medium for storing information in more recent data processing operations.

In the early 1800s Charles Xavier Thomas, also known as Thomas de Colmar, invented the arithmometer (Figure 1.5b), a device that multiplied and divided effectively by repeated addition and subtraction, using the ideas of Leibniz. However, the work of an Englishman, Charles Babbage, was more significant to the later development of computers. In 1823 Babbage began to develop a calculation machine which he called the *difference engine* (Figure 1.6). About ten years later, he tried to develop a more sophisticated machine that operated more like a computer than a calculator. This machine he called the *analytical engine*. The two machines were steam-driven and were designed to perform their functions by converting instructions from punched cards into the precise turning of gears. Despite years of effort, neither of these machines ever worked; the technology of the time did not allow Babbage to build them with the necessary precision. However, many of the ideas incorporated in the design of Babbage's engines were later used in the design of mechanical calculators, and ultimately in electronic calculators and computers.

Lady Ada Byron Lovelace worked with Babbage. She was a skilled mathematician and is considered by many to be the first computer programmer. While she worked with Babbage on the operational procedures for the analytic engine, she developed many ideas that were basic to modern programming. Her career was shortened by illness and by popular notions of the time about the suitability of mathematics as an occupation for women.

(a)

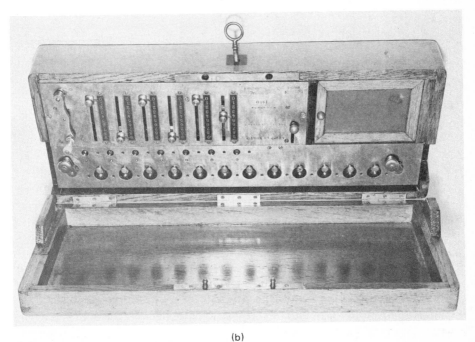

(b)

FIGURE 1.5
Early computing machines: (*a*) Napier's rods; (*b*) Thomas's arithmometer. *(IBM Corporation.)*

FIGURE 1.6
Babbage's difference engine. *(IBM Corporation.)*

Electronic Solutions to Calculating and Data Processing

The search for better ways to store and process information began almost as soon as people began to keep records and do calculations. This search has led more recently into the realm of electronics. From the late 1890s into the first quarter of the twentieth century, various advances were being made in electronics that were ultimately to have a major impact on computers. Among these were the transmission of telegraph messages by radio waves, the first cathode-ray tube, and the vacuum-tube diode. During this period, most of the developmental activity in electronics was directed toward radio and television. By 1920, sufficient progress had been made to begin the first commercial radio broadcasts.

In the late 1800s, Herman Hollerith was perfecting a method for processing data along the lines of Jacquard's punched cards. Hollerith eventually developed this technique to the point where he was able to get a contract to tabulate the data collected in 1890 by the U.S. Bureau of the Census. Hollerith's machine (Figure 1.7) used electronic impulses to read punched cards. The impulses were sent through rods on one side of the card as it was fed through the machine. If a rod encountered a hole, it touched a metal plate on the other side of the card

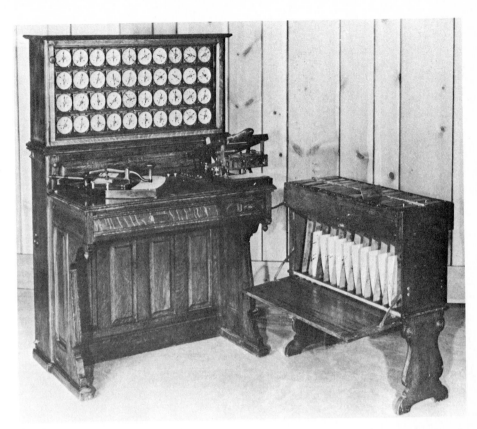

FIGURE 1.7
Hollerith's tabulation machine. *(IBM Corporation.)*

and completed the circuit. Thus, the operation was analogous to an on-off switch in which the paper in the card kept the switch off, and a hole allowed the switch to be momentarily turned on. In 1896 Hollerith formed a company that was later to become International Business Machines (IBM), a giant in the computing industry.

During and immediately after the Second World War the first electronic computers were developed. These machines had been preceded by an electromechanical computer, the Mark 1 (Figure 1.8a). The electronic computers were made with vacuum-tube circuits similar to those found in older radios and television sets. In many cases they were based on advances in electronic circuit design developed to improve weapons guidance systems and devices used to encode messages during the war. Computers were assembled using great numbers of these vacuum tubes interconnected by miles of electrical wiring. One such computer was ENIAC (Electronic Numerical Integration and Calculator),

(a)

(b)

FIGURE 1.8
First-generation computers: (a) Mark I; (b) ENIAC. *(IBM Corporation.)*

developed at the University of Pennsylvania in the mid-1940s (Figure 1.8*b*). Computers such as ENIAC worked well for complex calculations but were very expensive to build and operate. They were actually huge collections of electric components housed in large indoor areas. They consumed enormous amounts of electricity and produced tremendous amounts of heat. Probably the least desirable aspects of these *first-generation* computers were their large size and their enormous consumption of power. Almost as soon as these machines had

FIGURE 1.9
Second-generation computer system. *(IBM Corporation.)*

been developed, scientists and engineers began to search for a smaller replacement for the vacuum tube.

By 1947, Bell Laboratories had developed such a replacement, the transistor. *Second-generation* computers using transistors instead of tubes appeared by the late 1950s (Figure 1.9). Transistors were roughly ½₀₀ the size of vacuum tubes, used only a small fraction of the electrical power, were more reliable, and operated much more quickly. They made computers more practical for industrial, governmental, and research use. First-generation computers had been commercially available from companies like IBM, Remington Rand, Monroe, NCR, RCA, and UNIVAC, among others. In only about five years, these computers had become obsolete, and were being replaced by faster, smaller, and more reliable and efficient second-generation computers that used transistorized circuitry.

Computer developments since the appearance of the transistor continued in the direction of miniaturization, a trend accelerated by the American space program. *Third-generation* computers were marked by an almost incredible degree of miniaturization. A single tiny silicon "chip," about the size of the nail on your little finger, can now contain much of the major electronic circuitry of a computer and can represent circuits that would once have required thousands of transistors (see Figures 1.10 and 1.11). Further, when they are manufactured in large quantities, these chips are quite inexpensive.

Many observers say that *fourth-generation* computers began to appear in the mid-1970s, with the introduction of small computers that were practical and affordable for individual people to own and use at home and at work. They see *fifth-generation* computers coming in the very near future — computers that are capable of thinking and making decisions much as human beings do.[8]

Growth in both the number and the use of computers in recent years has been phenomenal. Because of the tiny silicon chips, computers are now com-

FIGURE 1.10
Above: Comparison of vacuum tube, transistor, and microprocessor chip. Chip (on the right) contains the equivalent of 2,000 transistors or tubes.

FIGURE 1.11
Below: Comparison of a microprocessor chip to some familiar objects.

mon components of such items as dishwashers, microwave ovens, automobiles, and airplanes. They make these items "intelligent," as the computer people like to say. Actually, they make the machines able to control themselves to a greater extent, so that the user has less responsibility for operating the system. Computers are also an essential feature of space vehicles such as the space shuttle. They are found as well in our schools and offices; in fact, it is estimated that about 80 percent of the jobs in the United States today involve computers in one form or another.[9]

A by-product of miniaturization of computer components is the practicality of making computers of varying size and complexity. Huge computers have

FIGURE 1.12
Typical microcomputer set-up in a school.

been developed which can store and rapidly process millions of pieces of information and work on a large number of problems simultaneously. Somewhat smaller, often special-purpose, minicomputers are commonplace in many office environments. However, probably the type of computer receiving most attention today is the microcomputer or, as it is sometimes called, the *personal computer*. Personal computers are small enough to fit on a student's desk (Figure 1.12) and yet have as much computing capability as many of those huge first-generation computers mentioned earlier. Chapter 2 will have more to say about microcomputers' capabilities and their component parts.

Table 1.1 (page 16) summarizes many of the major developments leading to the computer as we know it today.

COMPUTERS IN EDUCATION

The First Try at Educational Computing

By the middle 1960s, most colleges and universities and many larger school districts had large computer systems. These computers were used primarily for administrative and research purposes. However, a group of forward-looking educators seized the opportunity to use these machines to develop computer-assisted instruction. A few were able to obtain special funding, usually from governmental agencies, to purchase computers specifically for instructional purposes. In some cases special equipment and laboratory programs were developed. Most of these developments had roots in the reinforcement approach to

TABLE 1.1
A SUMMARY OF THE HISTORY OF THE MODERN COMPUTER

Year	Event
About 2600 B.C.	Abacus
1617	Napier's rods
1647	Pascal's machine arithmetique
1673	Leibniz's multiplying machine
1801	Jacquard's automatic weaving machine
1820	Thomas de Colmar's arithmometer
1823	Babbage's difference engine
1834	Babbage's analytic engine
1890	Hollerith's card-tabulating machine
1944	Mark I automatic sequence controlled calculator
1945	ENIAC
1949	Development of transistors
1951	Purchase of first commercial computer
1951 to 1959	First-generation computers (vacuum tubes)
1960–1965	Second-generation computers (transistors)
1965 to present	Third-generation computers (integrated circuits; silicon chips)
1975	First commercial availability of microcomputers

learning, known as *operant conditioning.* They were fairly simple in design but demonstrated some of the instructional potential of computers.

Development of the PLATO system (Programmed Logic for Automatic Teaching Operation) was started at the University of Illinois in 1959 with funds from the National Science Foundation. The project was later supported by Control Data Corporation. PLATO is a system for developing and presenting instruction using large computers and special terminals.[10] Ultimately, a large amount of courseware was produced for this system. Much of this software has been made available for use with microcomputers.

During the mid-1960s, an experimental program was set up by Professor Patrick Suppes and his colleagues at Stanford University. Elementary school students could receive instruction in the form of tutorials and drill and practice using special terminals connected to a large computer. This project showed a great deal of promise as regarded computers' ability to respond to the unique learning styles of individual students.[11]

At the Lincoln laboratory at the Massachusetts Institute of Technology (MIT), the Lincoln Terminal System was developed for on-the-job training applications in industrial and military systems. The terminals included computer components and visual and audio displays. The researchers at MIT indicated that this approach to on-the-job training could be an effective solution in terms of cost.

Considerable excitement was generated by these and similar projects at the time. Proponents of computer-assisted learning made exciting predictions about the future of instructional computers, the development of instructional software, and the number of students who would benefit. The educational literature abounded with articles about computer-assisted instruction (CAI), and educators enthusiastically looked forward to instructional applications of computers.

A few school systems did provide computer-assisted instruction; but surprisingly few students and teachers actually had experience with the technology at that time. The machines available for CAI were simply too cumbersome, too limited, or too expensive — or all three. Further, educators were just beginning to learn about CAI and often did not make optimal, or even appropriate, use of it. Finally, there was diminishing federal support for educational research and development. The result was a decline in CAI in public education by the mid-1970s.

While the optimism of the 1960s no longer existed in public education, computers were being used for training in business, industry, and government.[12] Many of the barriers to computer-based education in schools were not as pronounced in these areas. For example, hardware was too expensive for many school districts to afford; but many larger businesses and the government already had it available. Thus, advances in the application of computer-assisted instruction through much of the 1970s occurred outside of the formal educational establishment. This pattern continued until the appearance of low-cost microcomputers.

The Second Try at Educational Computing

The first of the microcomputers became available to the public toward the end of the 1970s. Suddenly, names of computer companies like Apple, Atari, Radio Shack, and Commodore became familiar to most people. Neighborhood computer stores opened. Video games became the rage at local arcades and on home computers. For the first time computer manufacturers had a product that was affordable for widespread use in homes, schools, and businesses. This product was priced, designed, and packaged for the masses of people who did not have training in computer science. Interest in the new microcomputers soared. Computer clubs were formed, and programming contests were held. Some teenagers were able to turn their ability to design microcomputers or software into wealth nearly overnight. One of the better-known examples was the highly successful Apple computer, developed by two young computer hobbyists.[13] Thousands of people were using microcomputers on an everyday basis at home and at work by 1981.

These new computers had some extra features that made them more attractive for educational use. For example, they could provide displays of color graphics on a television screen. They could also store and retrieve large amounts of information quickly, using special peripheral devices called *floppy disks.* Further, small, low-cost printers could be used with microcomputers to print instructional materials tailored to individual needs.

Microcomputer developments have prompted increasing optimism about their importance in society. For example, the U.S. House of Representatives Committee on Science and Technology said in a 1978 report:

> While a great many people were still debating whether or not the horse would ever be replaced, society's leaders failed to plan properly for the impact that the technology of the car would have on our civilization. The proper question . . . now . . . is not whether [a microcomputer revolution] is coming, but how to handle it when it does come.[14]

In the years since that statement was made, the microcomputer has become more prominent in education and society. Although the microcomputer has not yet reached its full potential in education, interest in this technology is increasing rapidly. Among those using microcomputers, optimism about their expanded use is apparent. The title of a 1981 article by Professor Seymour Papert, "Society Will Balk, but the Future May Demand a Computer for Each Child," illustrates this optimism.[15] Whether there is necessarily a computer in every child's future is still debatable. But as new developments in hardware are announced almost daily, that is becoming increasingly probable.

The availability of sophisticated, low-cost computing equipment is only part of the story for educators. Methods of utilizing this equipment must also be considered. While there are many useful products available in education, we are just beginning to learn how to make fuller use of the range of options offered by the technology. Computers have been used for drill and practice, tutorials, and testing and are effective at these activities. They can give students individualized instruction with the kind of patience and detail that teachers do not usually have time to provide.[16] We are now seeing educational uses of computers in problem solving, creative writing, graphics and art, engineering design, and many other areas.

A point to emphasize here is that while hardware has improved dramatically, software has a long way to go before the full potential of computers for instruction is reached. Not enough high-quality software is available to meet current needs. Also, microcomputers are not as good as they could be from an educational point of view. Improvements that would enhance the educational capabilities of microcomputers would include more natural devices for input than the keyboard, input devices for physically impaired students, more convenient ways of displaying output, and greater compatibility with other media such as videotapes and videodisks.

BEFORE GOING ON . . .

While it is not a necessity, the reader will gain more from this book if a micro-computer can be made available for some "hands-on" experience. If a computer is already available, then the reader is all set. If not, now is the time to buy, borrow, or find one that may be used once in a while. Ways to do this might include making a visit to a microcomputer dealer, a school library, or a nearby university with a microcomputer laboratory. Also, a visit to a classroom at a time when students are engaged in computer-assisted learning can be a useful experience for someone starting to look into educational computing.

SUMMARY

The presence of computers in education — and in society in general — is definitely on the increase. Because of this, everyone will need to know more about computers. If you are an educator or are planning a career in education, if you are a parent concerned about how computers relate to your child's education, or if you are simply an interested bystander observing educational processes, you need to know more about the use of computers in education.

Early work on devices to assist with calculations provided the basis for modern electronic computers. Other advances that assisted in the development of computers included the idea of using holes punched in cards to store information, and improvements in technology and electronics. The first generation of computers, built with vacuum tubes, became available commercially in the early 1950s. By 1960 they were replaced with the second generation, which used transistor circuitry. In the mid-1960s these computers were replaced with the third generation of computers, using silicon chips. Many people say that the fourth generation began with the appearance of the microcomputer, and that the fifth generation will bring us computers with the ability to think and solve problems — that is, to approximate the kind of intelligent behavior now attributable only to people.

Today's microcomputers utilize integrated circuits which have made them smaller, faster, more reliable, and less expensive. They are described as *small* computers only in terms of their physical size; their capability is large when compared with that of large computers available a decade or two ago. The microcomputers most often used in schools are small enough to fit on a desk top. While they are not very capable when compared with modern large (mainframe) computers, they are easy to operate, are inexpensive, and have enough computing capacity to perform many of the operations required in an educational setting.

NOTES

1 Bingham, M. (1981). Pinging to success the North Carolina way. *Electronic Education,* 22–24.

2   Minnesota Educational Computing Consortium. (1981, February). *Oregon Trail, Elementary* (Vol. 6), 23–37.

3   Alaska Department of Education. (1982, June). *Educational Telecommunications for Alaska Project: Final Report* (Vol. 4).

4   Malsam, M. (1981). A computer first for an elementary school: Microcomputer replaces card catalog. *Educational Computer Magazine, 1*(3), 40–41.

5   Nelson, H. (1981). Learning with Logo. *onComputing, 3*(1), 14–16.

6   Fast Response Survey System. (1982, September). *Instructional use of computers in public schools*. National Center for Educational Statistics.

7   Snelbecker, G. E. (1974). *Learning theory, instructional theory, and psychoeducational design*. New York: McGraw-Hill.

8   Markoff, J. (1983). Computers that think: The race for the fifth generation. *InfoWorld, 5*(30), 25–26.

9   Kearsley, G. P., Hillelsohn, M. J., & Seidel, R. J. (1981–1982). Microcomputer-based training in business and industry: Present status and future prospects. *Journal of Educational Technology Systems, 10,* 101–108.

10   Congress of the United States, Office of Technology Assessment. (1982). *Informational technology and its impact on American education*. Washington, DC: Office of Technology Assessment.

11   Coburn, P., Kelman, P., Roberts, N., Synder, T., Watt, D. N., & Weiner, C. (1982). *Practical guide to computers in education*. Reading, MA: Addison-Wesley.

12   Mason, E. J. (1982). Microcomputers in training programs. *Viewpoints in Teaching and Learning, 58*(3), 58–65.

13   An example of this is given in: *Time*. (1983). Updated book of Jobs, *121*(1), 25–27.

14   U.S. House of Representatives, Committee on Science and Technology. (1978). *Computers and the learning society*. Washington, DC: U.S. Government Printing Office.

15   See: Papert, S. (1981, September). *Electronic Education,* 4–6.

16   Northwest Educational Laboratory. (1981). *Applications of technology to the teaching of the basic skills* (Report). Portland, OR.

SUPPLEMENTARY READINGS

Bell, T. E. (1983). My computer, my teacher. *Personal Computing, 7*(6), 123, 125, 127.

Bernstein, J. (1981). *The analytic engine*. New York: Morrow.

Blair, M. (1980–1981). Get out your computer: A revolution is on the way. *Computing Teacher, 8*(2), 50–51.

Deken, J. (1981). *The electronic cottage*. New York: Morrow.

Doerr, C. (1979). *Microcomputers and the three Rs: A guide for teachers*. Rochelle Park, NJ: Hayden.

Edwards, J. (1977). *Elements of computer careers*. Englewood Cliffs, NJ: Prentice-Hall.

Electronic Learning. (1981, September–1982, June). *The computing primer: EL's guide to computing for the absolute novice* (Parts I–V).

Emmet, A. (1983). American education: The dead end of the 80s. *Personal Computing, 7*(8), 96–101, 103, 105.

Evans, C. (1981). *The micro millenium*. New York: Washington Square.

Goldstine, H. (1972). *The computer from Pascal to Von Neumann*. Princeton, NJ: Princeton University Press.

Gress, E. The future of computer education: Invincible innovation or transitory phenomenon? *Computing Teacher,* 1981, *9*(1), 39–42.

Horn, C., & Poirot, J. (1981). *Computer literacy: Problem solving with computers.* Austin, TX: Sterling Swift.

Hughes, E. (1981). What's in the box? Taking the mystery out of computers. *onComputing, 3*(2), 22–34.

Kaplan, J. (1981). Starting over. *Educational Computer Magazine, 1*(2), 26–27.

Kelman, P. (1982, January–February). What if they gave a computer revolution and nobody came? *Classroom Computer News,* 10, 54.

Morrissey, W. J. (1981–1982). Overcoming educators' fears about computers. *Computing Teacher, 8*(2), 50–51.

Moursund, D. (1982). *Administrator's guide to microcomputers.* Eugene, OR: International Council for Computers in Education (ICCE).

Moursund, D. (1982). *Introduction to computers in education for elementary and middle school teachers.* Eugene, OR: International Council for Computers in Education (ICCE).

Nelson, H. (1981). Computerized homes: Fact or fiction? *onComputing, 2*(4), 20–28, 86–91.

Papert, S. (1980). *Mindstorms: Children, computers and powerful ideas.* New York: Basic Books.

Press, L. (1981). Getting started in personal computing. *onComputing, 2*(4), 8–17.

Rice, D. R. & Moscow, D. K. (1981). The microcomputer in the schools of the 80s: Dawn of a new age. *Educational Computing Magazine, 1*(4), 44–46.

Stewart, G. (1981). How should schools use computers? The debate heats up. *Popular Computing, 1*(2), 104–108.

Taylor, R. P. (Ed.) (1981). *The Computer in the school: Tutor, tool, tutee.* New York: Teachers College Press.

Toffler, A. (1980). *The third wave.* New York: Morrow.

MEET THE COMPUTER

This chapter introduces the parts of a computer. At this point, we begin to think of a computer not as one thing, but rather as a system of things. A *system* may be defined as a "group of items or actions that work together to perform certain functions."[1] Since what is usually called a *computer* is really made up of a number of different parts (often in the same cabinet), it can more accurately be called a *computer system*. In this chapter, the reader is introduced to the major parts of a typical computer system and given a nontechnical overview of what each of these parts does. The objective of the chapter is to provide enough information, in everday language, so that even someone who is unfamiliar with electronics and other technical subjects can understand these devices well enough to use them. The discussion pertains to the kind of small computer one might find in a school or educational setting, but much of what is said also applies to larger computers.

WHAT IS A SYSTEM?

Overview of a System

Imagine that we are hovering in a helicopter over a large manufacturing plant. Let us suppose that this factory makes clothing. Figure 2.1 shows how the plant appears from above. (However, numbers were added to assist with locating things.)

There is a long rectangular building at the top of the figure, indicated by the number 1. This building has two functions. First, it is where the actual manufacturing is done. The fabric is cut and sewn here, zippers and buttons are added, and so on. The second function carried on in this building is control of the factory. Although they cannot be seen from our perch above the plant, the manager and the line supervisors maintain control of the manufacturing processes from offices and desks in this building. Therefore, it can be said that both the processing and the control functions of the plant are housed in this building. It is easy to understand why this building is very important to the plant.

To the right there is a fenced-off area, identified by the number 2, that contains what look like power lines. This is the plant's power supply. It has transformers that convert the electric power sent from the local power company into the voltages and wattages that are needed to operate the factory.

Toward the left side of Figure 2.1 we see rectangular shapes representing buildings arranged in two rows of six buildings each and identified by the number 3. In these buildings raw materials are stored temporarily until they are processed in the factory. At any given time the contents of these buildings may be changing. In one building we might see huge bolts of denim. Another might contain large boxes of thread and buttons. If these buildings did not store the raw materials for processing, the plant could not operate. Some of these buildings also contain another thing the plant needs: they store the patterns for the gar-

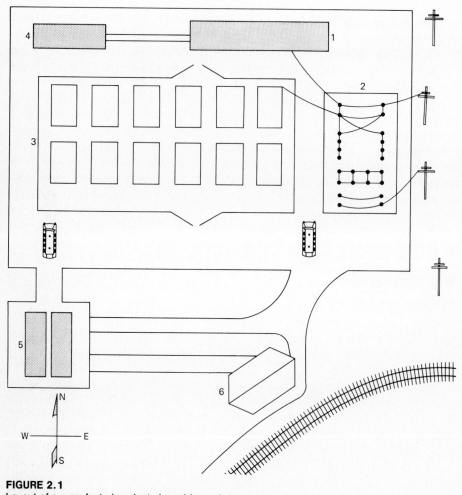

FIGURE 2.1
Layout of a manufacturing plant viewed from above.

ments being produced. Thus, when the factory switches from blouses to blue jeans, the correct patterns must be available so that the machines can be set up properly. In this way, the patterns are like instructions for the machines in building 1. When styles change, so must the patterns. Finished products are also stored in these buildings.

Just north of the small buildings is a larger one identified by the number 4. In this building the operating rules and procedures of the company are kept. These are very rarely changed. For example, they contain procedures for determining how the company assigns responsibility for delivery of raw materials from the warehouse to the factory; job descriptions; and company policies for determining the number of vacation days a worker can accrue each year. There is an important difference between the kinds of storage represented by building number 4 and that represented by the buildings in area 3: information and materials stored in building 4 do not change very frequently, but the contents of the buildings in area 3 are constantly changing. Further, in area 3 stored materials are constantly being removed and replaced; but the information and materials in building 4, although available for use at all times, cannot be removed or altered.

Directly to the south of the main plant building and outside the plant grounds are two large buildings identified by the number 5. These buildings are for long-term storage of finished products, patterns not currently being used, company records, and the like. The advantage of this external storage facility is that things not currently being used can be kept until they are needed without taking up valuable space within the compound of the main plant. This company uses buses to carry materials from this peripheral storage area to the main plant. Two of them are on the road between the main plant buildings and the outside storage facility. The buses are also used to carry materials between the plant and the train depot.

To summarize, we have observed the following parts of a manufacturing plant:

- There is a central processing building where the factory is managed and the raw materials are processed into garments.
- A power supply provides electricity at the necessary current and voltage levels to run the plant.
- Storage areas inside the main compound hold information about operating the plant, and raw materials and patterns for the garments currently being manufactured:

     Materials and patterns that support current operations of the plant are kept in a temporary storage area. The contents of temporary storage can be easily changed to reflect new functions and products.

     Relatively permanent company policies and operating procedures are kept in a long-term storage area so that they will be available while the plant is operating.

- Old company records, patterns not currently being used, and anything else not required for current operations are kept in long-term storage outside the main plant area.
- Buses provide transportation between the areas of the plant, and to and from the depot and external storage areas.

It will be seen that the computer has many similarities to this manufacturing plant.

A Computer System

In Figure 2.2 the components of our factory have been renamed; their new labels represent their functions. With these labels, we can easily see the similar-

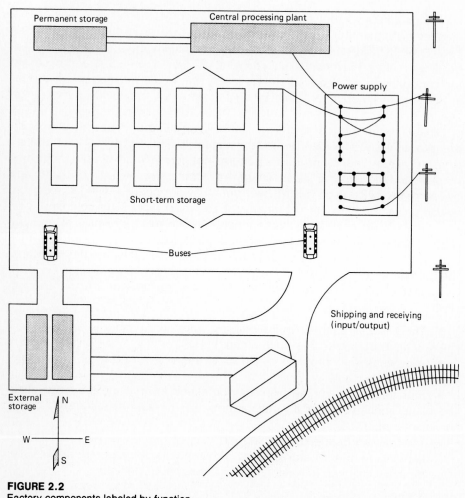

FIGURE 2.2
Factory components labeled by function.

ity between the manufacturing plant viewed from the helicopter and the computer system diagrammed in Figure 2.3. It is not too great an oversimplification to say that the computer is like a small manufacturing plant which processes information and data. More accurately, it receives, stores, processes, and provides information or data.

Some words of clarification about Figure 2.3 are in order before going on.

FIGURE 2.3
Opposite page: A basic computer system.

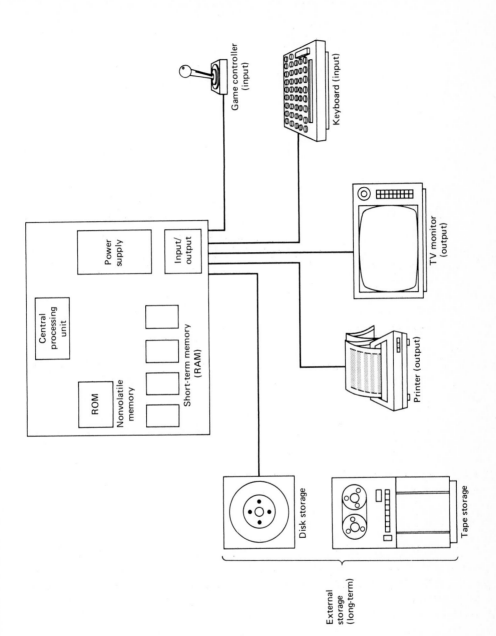

Game controller (input)

Keyboard (input)

Central processing unit

Power supply

Input/ output

ROM

Nonvolatile memory

Short-term memory (RAM)

TV monitor (output)

Printer (output)

Disk storage

Tape storage

External storage (long-term)

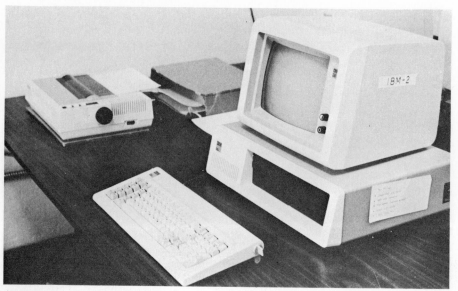

FIGURE 2.4
Typical educational computer system.

First, the central processing unit, power supply, and memory apparatus are usually out of sight in an enclosure. Second, the input and output devices shown here will not necessarily appear with every computer system. Further, other devices that we have not discussed may also be used to input and output data (e.g., paper tape readers, card readers and punchers, and optical scanning equipment). The devices shown are the ones most frequently seen in school and instructional microcomputer systems.

Compare the actual computer system shown in Figure 2.4 with the drawing in Figure 2.3. Can you identify all the parts in the photograph? The keyboard, disk drive, TV monitor, and printer are easy enough to find; but where are the central processing unit, power supply, short-term memory, etc.? They are hidden from sight in the box behind the keyboard, or in a separate container. Although these parts are usually hidden from view, they are important for the educator to know about. That is because they determine the capability of the computer and because people who work with computers and those who sell them often refer to these parts. For this reason, we will next describe the inner workings of a computer.

INTERNAL COMPONENTS OF A COMPUTER

The purpose of the discussion that follows is to give enough background to facilitate utilization of computers in instructional settings. One need not become a programmer or an engineer to understand enough about how a microcomputer works to use one. Further, in keeping with our fundamental interest in educational applications, we have tended to focus on the kinds of computers found most often in instructional settings. This means that we are primarily interested in microcomputers. However, much of the information in this section would also apply to larger computers. Finally, we will provide an overview of only the major internal components of a computer. There are other parts, but knowing about these is less necessary for the average reader. Those who are interested in a more detailed account of the innards of computers and computer architecture are directed to some of the supplementary readings listed at the end of this chapter.

Central Processing Unit

In our factory, there was one large building from which operations of the factory were controlled and in which the actual processing of raw materials into garments took place. It was called the *central processing plant* in Figure 2.2. There is a device with an analogous function in the computer; it is called the *central processing unit* (CPU). The CPU contains an arithmetic logic unit which can add and subtract, compare values (i.e., *X* is larger than, smaller than, or equal to *Y*), and perform other kinds of mathematical or logical operations. It also contains the control unit, which ensures that operations are performed in the desired sequence on the appropriate data; and it keeps track of where to get data for processing and where to return them. There are also several special locations in the CPU, called *registers*. These registers may be thought of as temporary storage places. The actual processing is done with these registers. One register, for example, is called the *accumulator*. If the instructions received by the CPU say that one number should be added to another, the first one would be placed in the accumulator register and the second would then be added to it. This total must be stored somewhere. If it is not, it will be lost when some new number is moved into the accumulator to be processed. The control of the sequenced movement of numbers into and out of the accumulator register, and from and to storage locations in other parts of the computer, is part of the control unit's responsibility.

From the discussion so far, it should be relatively easy to see that the CPU is the part of the computer that does the major work. There are several different brands of CPUs found in the microcomputers usually used for educational purposes. They are identified by numbers like 6502, Z80, 9900, 8088, and 6809, representing different manufacturers and design features. However, the exact number or name of a CPU should be less important to the reader than what the computer system will be able to do.

Permanent Memory

In our overview of the manufacturing plant, we discussed a small building (in the upper left-hand corner of the compound) that provided long-term storage of the policies and procedures which the plant required to operate efficiently.

The computer has an analogous need for specific instructions on how to operate. The computer uses a type of memory to store these instructions that can retain them even when the power is turned off, because these instructions must be available for reuse immediately when the machine is switched on again. One example of such instructions might be the kinds of characters that will appear on the screen. Computers do not naturally send roman letters and arabic numerals to the screen on a TV monitor. This is done by placing the necessary instructions for character display in permanent memory.

Some computers are designed to serve only one purpose and therefore have all their instructions in permanent memory. Such a computer would not give the user much latitude in determining what it can do, since it already has instructions for its operation built into it. For example, let's say that a particular microcomputer installation has been designed to maintain library records for a school district. The administration may want teachers and students to have access to these records at any time during the school day. To save the cost of hiring a computer operator to run the machine, the computer could be designed with the necessary instructions to run itself. When the machine is turned on, the following message would appear on the TV screen:

```
****************************************************
      Welcome to the Library Index File System!
****************************************************
DO YOU WISH TO:

      (1)   LOCATE A TITLE
      (2)   SEARCH A SUBJECT
      (3)   SEARCH AN AUTHOR
      (4)   RESERVE A BOOK
      (5)   OBTAIN HELP WITH USING THIS SYSTEM

      SELECT A NUMBER FROM 1 TO 5:
```

The teacher or student would make a choice and then would be given further instructions about what to type until all the desired information is displayed on the screen.

Computer people call permanent memory *read-only memory,* or ROM. This term is used because information in this type of memory can only be "read" by the computer; that is, it cannot be added to or changed. Another term that is used for permanent memory is *nonvolatile memory,* because information in permanent memory is not lost when the computer's power is turned off. Computers that do not have ROM must be given complete operational instructions every time they are turned on. That is, they must be told how to do everything, including how to inform the computer user that the computer is ready to receive instructions. Obviously, the instructions in ROM have a lot to do with what the computer is capable of doing and how it operates.

Temporary Memory

In our factory, the twelve buildings where fabrics and patterns were stored temporarily while awaiting processing served a function similar to that of temporary memory in the computer. The function of temporary memory is to provide the computer with data and instructions that it will require for current operations. If permanent memory can be said to be nonvolatile, then temporary memory is volatile. That is, information stored in temporary memory is lost when the computer's power is turned off. In fact, the computer's temporary memory must receive a continuous flow of electricity while the computer is on. The slightest interruption will have consequences on what is stored.

Why have such a delicate kind of memory? The answer is that temporary memory makes the computer infinitely flexible in terms of its function. The function of the computer can be almost completely determined by the information in its temporary memory. Since temporary memory is sensitive to changes in electric current, instructions stored in it can be changed easily at any time. This allows the same machine to be used for a wide variety of applications: typing practice, simulation of chemistry experiments, management of students' records, storage of class grades, and so on.

Since what is in temporary memory can be read as instructions or altered to contain new instructions at any time, this kind of memory is called *random-access memory,* or RAM. When data or programs are put into a computer, they go into RAM. If there is any interruption of power to RAM, these data or programs are lost.

Both ROM and RAM are important, then: ROM contains the kinds of instructions the computer will always need, regardless of what it does; and the contents of RAM can be changed to suit changing needs. Since for every application, a computer should be capable of displaying characters that can be recognized by the user, sets of characters (e.g., letters and numbers) are usually stored in ROM. On the other hand, the capability of changing instructions that are stored in RAM allows the same computer to be used on one occasion for one purpose, and then on another occasion for a very different purpose.

Input-Output Control

Our manufacturing plant had roads for sending raw materials into the factory and for bringing finished products out. The computer also has paths for input and output of data, and devices for controlling this input and output. The paths are actually sets of wires and connectors, called *buses,* that tie together the components of the computer system. A computer can be connected to a number of different kinds of devices. Signals to and from these devices must be controlled if the computer is to operate properly. Typically, the user does not have to be concerned about the devices that control these signals. Their programming and operation are more the concern of those who design computers.

Questions involving input and output that are more important for educators to ask involve the actual peripheral device or devices that they wish to use with the computer. A computer professional should be able to determine whether a given application is possible with a given computer. For example, an educator who wishes to print pictures in color using a special color plotting device might need to have special equipment and programming installed in the computer. Because of the possibility of unforeseen complexities, it is a good idea to see the computer running with any special peripherals before assuming that is is capable of doing what is required.

Chips

If one were to look inside a small computer, one would see several rectangular blocks (Figure 2.5). They usually appear to be made of dark plastic, about ¼ inch thick, 1 inch or so wide, and from 1 inch to 3 or 4 inches long. (Some are larger; others may be smaller.) Each of these rectangular blocks contains a silicon chip similar to the ones discussed briefly in Chapter 1. What are *chips?*

A *chip* is actually a very small piece of silicon, about the size of an adult's smallest fingernail. On it, the complete electronic circuitry for some device is placed. The advent of the silicon chip has been one of the major reasons why extremely powerful computers can now be produced in small packages rela-

FIGURE 2.5
View of the inside of a microcomputer showing an assortment of chips.

FIGURE 2.6
An integrated circuit (IC) with a silicon chip mounted on it.

tively cheaply. As we noted in Chapter 1, a single silicon chip can contain the circuitry equal to 1000 or more transistors. For example, the circuitry that today is found on the CPU chip would have filled a room in the early days of computers, only about three decades ago.

The rectangular blocks that you would see mounted on a board inside a computer are not the chips themselves. Rather, they contain the chips; and their "feet" are mounted into sockets in the computer board (see Figure 2.6). The rectangles are known as *integrated circuits* (or ICs). Computer specialists sometimes refer to the kind of CPU chip used in a small computer as a *microprocessing unit,* or MPU. The central processor, RAM, ROM, and input-output devices are all ICs. The electronics of these complex chips is called, not surprisingly, *microelectronics.* Microelectronics technology has enabled computer designers and manufacturers to reduce size and costs considerably while maintaining very high standards and reliability.

SOFTWARE AND PROGRAMMING

We have used the word *program* a number of times in this chapter. A program is a set of sequential instructions for the computer. The sequence of instructions that tell the computer what to do can be considered analogous to teaching. In a sense, the computer "learns" to perform complex activities by having the necessary instructions placed in its memory. Even with the necessary hardware, a computer is incapable of intelligent action unless it is programmed. Programs in general are referred to as *software.* Since software is so essential to the operation of the computer, a computer system is not considered complete if it does not include both hardware and software.

Once a program is written, it may be placed in ROM when the computer is manufactured, or it may be placed in RAM temporarily while the computer is in operation. Some programs are quite long and complex, and it would be desirable to be able to store them outside RAM permanently so that they do not have to be typed in every time they are needed. Such storage is possible using several kinds of devices that will described later in this chapter.

Programming is a very technical and complex skill. Fortunately, not all computer users need to become skilled programmers. Sophisticaticated programs that let the computer take care of its own technical needs, yet are highly flexible and can be adapted to the user's needs, are becoming available for many of the popular microcomputers. However, it helps to know something about programming, in order to understand the kinds of demands one can reasonably make upon a computer. Therefore, we will cover programming and computer languages briefly later in this book (Chapter 9). The reader who is interested in learning to program is encouraged to seek the training necessary through courses and the many excellent programming texts on the market.

BITS, BYTES, AND WORDS

Computers use binary numbers, 1s and 0s, to form symbols. Each binary number, whether it is a 1 or a 0, is called a *bit*. It might be useful to think of the 1s and 0s as electric light switches. When the light is on, the condition is called 1; when the light is off, it is 0. Eight bits grouped together form a *byte* (pronounced *bite*). Bytes can be used as coded representations of letters, numbers, and other symbols. Table 2.1 shows one coding approach, the ASCII (pronounced *ask-key*) system. (The initials stand for American Standard Codes for Information Interchange.) With this approach, any letter of the alphabet, any number, and many special characters can be represented by the 8 bits in a byte. The reader may have noticed that people speak of computers as having "48K," "64K," etc.. This is a way of referring to the amount of internal memory a computer has. The K stands for *kilobytes*. As is indicated by the prefix *kilo-*, a kilobyte is 1000 bytes. However, the true value of a kilobyte is 1024 bytes, because of the binary number system that is used in computers (2 raised to the tenth power is 1024).

In many of the microcomputers available in the late 1970s and early 1980s, and in many of the current models, a *word* and a byte are both 8 bits. The trend is for longer words, and 16- and 32-bit microcomputers are now common. Longer words permit greater flexibility and processing speed; but these advantages may entail higher costs of hardware and programming.

The subject of memory capacity and word length can become complex rather quickly. What the typical educational computer user needs to keep in mind about memory is that the more kilobytes there are in a computer's memory, the more instructions and data it can hold. To get a rough idea of what *memory size* means, assume that a typical page of double-spaced typewritten text contains about 1500 (1.5K) characters. Then a 48K microcomputer would be capable of holding about 32 such pages in its memory, and a 64K computer could store about 43 such pages. Beyond this, most users need not involve themselves with the intricacies of bits, bytes, and computer words unless they

TABLE 2.1
SAMPLES OF BINARY CODE EQUIVALENTS OF LETTERS AND
NUMBERS IN ASCII CODE

ASCII	Number or symbol	ASCII	Letter
011 0000	0	100 0001	A
011 0001	1	100 0010	B
011 0010	2	100 0011	C
011 0011	3	100 0100	D
011 0100	4	100 0101	E
011 0101	5	100 0110	F
011 0110	6	100 0111	G
011 0111	7	100 1000	H
011 1000	8	100 1001	I
011 1001	9	100 1010	J
011 1010	:	100 1011	K
011 1011	;	100 1100	L
011 1100	<	100 1101	M
010 0001	!	110 0001	a
010 0010	"	110 0010	b
010 0011	#	110 0011	c

Note: The eighth bit is not shown, because it is reserved for a special use called *parity.* See a text on microprocessor programming for a discussion of this, and a complete listing of ASCII codes; e.g.: Zaks, R. (1980). *Programming the 6502.* Berkeley, CA: SYBEX.

get involved in programming. As was indicated earlier, however, it is now possible to utilize existing programs for a great many applications, particularly in education. The result is that the need to become a skilled programmer in order to use computers is not as pressing as it once was.

COMPUTER LANGUAGES

Computer programs are not written in everyday language. As you would probably guess by now, computers have their own *machine language.* Actually, computers "understand" symbols formed by combining 1s and 0s into binary numbers. It is difficult for people to program or communicate with computers using this kind of language. For this reason, programs have been written to translate computer languages into ones more like those that people use, and also to translate human-like languages into binary symbols for the computer. These higher-level languages have unique rules and features, which must be learned by the programmer. However, they have made programming much less difficult.

A number of higher-level languages have been developed for use with microcomputers. Currently, BASIC (Beginner's All-Purpose Symbolic Instruction Code) is one of the most common. What can be coded in BASIC as $Y = X + 1$ might require something like 000000110000100100000001 in machine language. It is clear from this example that instructions for the computer would be less difficult to prepare in BASIC than in machine language. Before the programmer is able to use a particular high-level programming language like BASIC, however, the computer must contain that translation program. We will look more closely at programming languages in Chapter 9.

EXTERNAL PARTS OF A COMPUTER SYSTEM

Look again at the computer system shown in Figure 2.4 — or, better, look at a real computer system if you can. You immediately see a number of things, but not the CPU, RAM, ROM, etc. Those things are usually out of sight inside the computer, and (as we have noted) a user does not have to be directly concerned with them. In fact, most of the microcomputers that have been developed for educational applications are designed to be operated very simply. This is done by programming the computer (in ROM, of course) to take care of its own technical details.

In the system pictured in Figure 2.4, the inner workings of the computer are mounted on a board in the container behind the keyboard. If we take this box away from the remaining devices in the picture, plug it into an electrical outlet, and turn it on, we will quickly find how unexciting and useless an operating computer can be without devices for communicating with it.[2] Thus, it should be fairly obvious that when a price for a computer is advertised, one must realize that there will be additional costs for other devices that must also be purchased to make the computer useful.

Monitor and Keyboard

Now let us assume that you have connected the television monitor to that seemingly dull computer. Eureka! You can now see that the computer is doing something. Maybe it is showing the name of its manufacturer across the top of the screen or blinking a light in one corner; or perhaps the screen lights up with color patterns. Now you have a computer that can communicate with you. However, you still cannot communicate with it. By the way, computer people usually refer to the television monitor as a CRT (for *cathode-ray tube*). They tend to think of it as a device that displays communications from the computer, and not so much as a television set. With slight modification, however, a regular television set can be used as a monitor.[3]

We next connect the typewriter-like keyboard, and this lets us ''talk'' to the computer. The computer user can type information on the keyboard that is transferred into the computer. One's typing ability necessarily influences how well one can communicate with a computer through a keyboard. For this reason, many people feel that different methods of communicating with a computer are necessary, particularly for young children, people who do not type well, and handicapped people.

So far we have covered these essential components of a computer system:

- The computer itself, consisting of several internal components, including a central processing unit, random-access and permanent memory, and an input-output device to allow communication with external devices and the user.
- At least one input device (the keyboard is probably the most common).
- At least one output device (often a television monitor).

As was mentioned earlier, what is in RAM memory is lost when the power is turned off, and therefore RAM memory is said to be *volatile.* Do you think that information going into the computer from a keyboard, or out to a CRT, is volatile or nonvolatile? If you said *volatile,* you are correct. This is because what comes from the keyboard goes into RAM, and much of what is displayed on the screen is determined by what is in RAM. Devices have been developed for storing information for long periods outside a computer until it is needed, and for making lasting forms of computer output. We turn to those devices now.

External Storage

Small computers, like those found in educational settings, usually use any of three kinds of external storage: (1) cassette tapes, (2) floppy disks, and (3) hard disks. As would be expected, each has certain advantages and disadvantages. Table 2.2 contrasts the three.

TABLE 2.2
RELATIVE COSTS, CAPACITIES, AND SPEED OF TRANSFERRING INFORMATION INTO THE COMPUTER OF TYPICAL DISK AND CASSETTE TAPE SYSTEM

External memory device	Cost (approximate)	Capacity	Speed
Cassette tape recorder-player	Inexpensive	Depends on length of tape (may be impractical to have more than RAM available memory of computer, i.e., 4– 64K)	Often more than 2 minutes
Floppy disk 5¼-inch	Higher cost than cassette	90 to 800K	Often complete disk read in less than 1 minute
8-inch	Higher cost than 5¼-inch disk	300 to 1000K	Often complete disk read in less than 1.5 minutes
Hard disk	Most expensive	1000K to 20,000K	Much faster than floppies (often about 5 to 10 times)

Note: Figures in this table are only approximate. Speed is based on loading the equivalent of a typical microcomputer's available RAM into memory (about 30K). Prices, costs, and capacities will vary between manufacturers, applications, operating systems, and so on.

Compared with other methods, *cassette tape* is a relatively inexpensive way to store programs and data. Audio cassette recorders costing from about $25 to $100 are commonly available in classrooms. They can be used to record data from a microcomputer on cassettes that are easy to use and inexpensive. Compared with floppy-disk and hard-disk storage, cassette tape recorders tend to be relatively slow. However, if the teacher plans to change the program in a machine only once or twice a day, this might not be a problem.

A *floppy disk* is a thin circular sheet of plastic, or Mylar, encased in a plastic, cardboard, or heavy paper cover. Floppy disks are now widely used in two sizes, 5¼-inch and 8-inch (Figure 2.7). Some microcomputers can also use a 3-inch diskette; and other sizes may eventually be tried. Data can be stored on a disk in a manner that is electronically similar to the way information is placed on plastic recording tape. The amount that can actually be stored depends on how the information is arranged (some people say *formatted*) on the disk. Although an 8-inch floppy can usually hold more than the 5¼-inch, the disk drive costs more. As Table 2.2 shows, compared with the other forms of external storage, the floppy disk (which reads and records data on the diskette) is relatively fast and moderately priced. It is also fairly easy to use.

In contrast, the storage capacity of the *hard disks* designed for school and institutional use is much greater than that of most floppies. Current capacities of hard disks range from 35 to 250 times those of the 5¼-inch floppies. A hard disk is actually a rigid aluminum plate covered with a magnetic coating. The plate is mounted in a protective container with the necessary mechanisms and circuitry to read data and transmit it to the computer. A hard-disk system is expensive compared with a floppy-disk system. In fact, it may be the most expensive component of a microcomputer system. But if large storage capacity is needed, hard disks may be more economical than floppy disks despite their higher price. Where very large data files are involved, hard disks may be the only way to store the files, since most small computers are designed to work with no more than four to six floppy-disk drives at a time. Further, hard-disk systems can oper-

FIGURE 2.7
Two sizes of floppy disks.

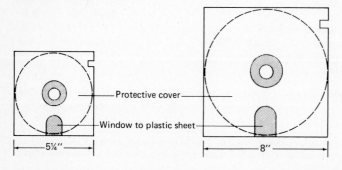

Protective cover

Window to plastic sheet

5¼″   8″

ate much more rapidly then floppy-disk systems. However, most instructional applications do not require such large storage capacity or speed, and because of their cost, hard-disk storage devices are not found in schools as often as floppy disks and cassette tape recorders.

External storage is one field that is sure to change in the coming years. We have not discussed all the devices that are currently available, and even more will be developed. Videodisks and lasers are two approaches that are being studied.[4] Also, a different concept in storage, called *bubble memory,* is considered by some to be a hopeful advance.[5] This kind of memory has many of the characteristics of RAM, but the information in it is not lost when the power is turned off. Whatever happens in this changing field, it is probable that storage capacities will increase, stored data will be accessed faster, and cost per unit of storage will decrease in the next few years.

Printers

Printers connect directly to the computer and print on paper. Computer people call printed computer output *hard copy.* Printed computer output has certain advantages over output that appears on a CRT screen. For one thing, it is more transportable. Unlike a CRT screen, printed output can be carried easily from one place to another and folded and placed in a briefcase or an envelope. Also, there are no electric power requirements for using printed output; and printed output is more permanent than a screen image. Finally, it is easier to deal with long messages and files in printed form, because only about 20 to 25 lines of text can ordinarily be displayed on a CRT screen. For these reasons, a printer is often considered to be an important part of a microcomputer system.

Two of the more popular ways for printers to place symbols on a page are the dot matrix and the daisy wheel. There are other ways to place a printed image on a paper, such as with laser beams, ink jets, and thermal techniques; however, because of cost, and for other reasons, printers using these techniques are not commonly found in school microcomputer systems. In addition, techniques have been developed for changing standard electric typewriters into printers.

Daisy-wheel printers use plastic or metal shapes that hit an inked ribbon to place a mark on paper. The complete set of symbols for the printer are arranged on the ends of what look like spokes of a wheel (or petals of a daisy, if you prefer) attached to a hub (see Figure 2.8*a*). This hub is mounted inside the printer and can easily be removed to change type styles.

Dot-matrix printers, on the other hand, use a matrix of electronic impulses that hit against an inked ribbon to create images. Each letter, number, or symbol is formed by a unique combination of dots. The more dots there are in the printing matrix, the clearer the image. (See Figure 2.8*b*.)

The speed and quality of printers vary. Typically, the slowest component of a computer system is the printer, by a wide margin. For example, while many

This is an example of daisy wheel printing.

(a)

This is an example of dot matrix printing.

(b)

FIGURE 2.8
Daisy-wheel and dot-matrix printing: (a) example of daisy wheel (left, Qume; right, Dataproducts Corporation) and daisy-wheel print; (b) dot-matrix mechanism (Dataproducts Corporation) and an example of dot-matrix print.

microcomputers can process at rates of half a million or more characters per second, most printers can produce only between 15 and 250 characters (or symbols) per second. Dot-matrix printers tend to be faster and less expensive to purchase and maintain than daisy-wheel printers. However, the print quality is not as good with a dot-matrix printer.

Usually, faster printers cost more, but there are exceptions. Flexibility in the kinds of paper or forms a printer will accept can also affect price. For example, a printer that can accept 13-inch-wide paper might be expected to cost more than one that takes an 8½-inch sheet. Some printers require special paper, such as paper with a heat-sensitive surface or with holes along the side for tractor feed. These characteristics will also affect price.

Computers Talking on the Telephone? Communication Devices

Computers can communicate with each other using regular telephone lines and a device called a *modem* (see Figure 2.9). *Modem* stands for *modulator-demod-*

FIGURE 2.9
A simple electronic mail system in which two microcomputers communicate with each other through a central computer.

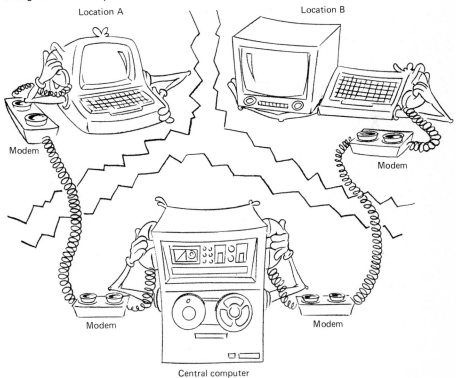

Location A

Location B

Modem

Modem

Modem

Modem

Central computer

(a)

(b)

FIGURE 2.10
Two kinds of modems: (*a*) direct connect modem; (*b*) acoustic coupler modem.
(*Novation, Inc.*)

ulator. To put it simply, this device converts the digital signals (1s and 0s) that a computer creates to audio signals that can be carried by telephone. Conversely, it can translate audio signals into the digital impulses that computers use. Thus, modems make it possible for computers to "talk" to each other. Figure 2.10 shows two modems.

Computers that can communicate with each other provide a number of benefits over those that cannot. For example, they can share programs, databases, and computing capacity. Business and industry have begun to use this capacity to offer training programs to sales and service staff at distant locations.[6] In addition, electronic mail services are now offered by commercial companies which allow subscribers to send messages to each other from local computer terminals. In this kind of application, there is a central computer system which receives the message and stores it until it is "picked up" by the addressee using his or her own computer equipment. Other services made possible by modems are offered on a subscription basis by large information service companies such as SOURCE and CompuServe (see Chapter 6). These services include access to a variety of databases. For example, one of these companies advertises that its subscribers can get up-to-the-minute stock market information; make airline reservations; shop for the best prices for merchandise; obtain programs for their home computers; read reviews of books, movies, and other forms of entertainment; and get the latest news. The ability of computers to share information is one of the most exciting areas for potential development in technology. We will have more to say about this potential later in the book (see, especially, Chapters 6 and 12).

SIZES OF COMPUTERS: CAPACITY

Now that we know something about hardware, memory, and the like, we can begin to discuss intelligently what we mean by the term *microcomputer*. As we suggested earlier, it is not enough to say that a microcomputer is a "small" computer. A small computer is not necessarily one that takes up little room in the conventional sense; and a big computer does not have to be compared to an elephant or a truck. Terms describing size refer to the computer's *capacity*. One index of capacity is memory; the more memory a computer has, the larger it would be considered. Because of modern microelectronics technology, a computer considered "large" in this sense by today's standards takes up less physical space than many "small" computers of a decade or two ago (Figure 2.11).

Processing speed is also considered part of a computer's capacity. Some computers process data faster than others. Generally, the smaller-capacity computers are slower than the larger ones. The reasons for this are complex, and beyond the scope of this book. Some applications — such as search, sort, and large-scale data analyses — must be done on a large-capacity computer because the time required to do them on a small computer would be unreasonably long.

In Chapter 1 we said that computers can be classified by size into three broad

FIGURE 2.11
The shrinking size of computer memory. *(IBM Corporation.)*

categories. The largest computers are called *mainframes*. The smallest, or least capable, of the true computers are called *microcomputers*. They usually are sold with from about 8K to 256K of internal memory. Microcomputers are the size most often found in educational settings. Between mainframes and microcomputers, with a range of about 256K to 600K of internal memory, are *minicomputers*. It should be stressed, however, that this classification system is changing as technology advances. That is, as computers of all sizes are designed with increased capacities, what is considered a microcomputer will probably change. In fact, 32-bit microcomputers with 1 million bits of RAM have been projected as standard in the next few years.[7]

It might be misleading to characterize present microcomputers as less capable than larger computers. They are very capable and useful devices. In fact, some of the most recently available microcomputers, with the right configuration of peripheral devices, are more capable, faster, and more reliable than the larger computers that were available only a few years ago (Figure 2.12). Further, the

1970 — 32K programmable memory   1984 — 128K programmable memory

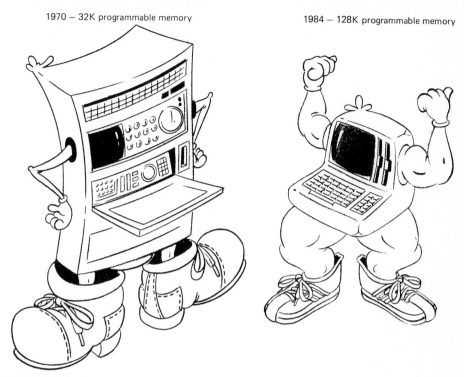

FIGURE 2.12
Physical size of a computer does not indicate computing capability. Modern microcomputers have more operating speed and capacity than many of their mainframe predecessors.

simplicity of use that has been built into many microcomputers allows them to be used by people who do not know much about computers.

SUMMARY

In this chapter we discussed the parts of computers in general, focusing on microcomputers in particular. Microcomputers are the type most likely to be used in educational applications because of the balance they offer between capability, price, and ease of use. What is usually called a *computer* is really a *computer system,* containing a number of components that work together.

Internally, the computer has a central processing unit, permanent and temporarary memory, and a component that allows communication with the outside. Permanent memory (ROM) is used to store instructions that the computer will need every time it is used. Temporary or random-access memory (RAM) holds data and information that may be required by the computer only for specific uses.

Externally, there are devices for communication between the user and the computer. For example, the keyboard lets the user put instructions and data into the memory of the computer. The printer and television monitor allow the computer to display what is in its memory. An external device called a *modem* allows one computer to communicate with another by telephone. Since computers lose everything in random-access memory (RAM) when the power is turned off, disk drives and cassette tapes are often used to store data and instructions so that they can be reused.

A program is a sequence of instructions that tells the computer what to do. We saw that without the instructions in programs, computers are not very useful. Several high-level programming languages are available for use with microcomputers. These high-level languages make the task of programming a computer less difficult than it would otherwise be in machine language. Computer programming is a complex skill. However, with the proper software, the microcomputer user need not be an expert programmer.

NOTES

1 Wanus, S. J., Wagner, G. E., & Lambrecht, J. J. (1981). *Fundamentals of data processing* (2nd ed.). Cincinnati: South-Western Publishing Co., 1981.

2 We are stretching the point a little by separating the computer from the other devices, because for most machines the manufacturers, recognizing the uselessness of the computer alone, include some of the external devices in the same enclosure as the computer circuitry. For example, some manufacturers package the computer in the same cabinet with the keyboard, the CRT, or both. Some even place a whole computer system — with keyboard, disk drives, CRT, and printer — in a single cabinet. The Osborne I computer was the first completely portable computer system on the commercial market. In a single case it contained a 64K microcomputer, a keyboard, two disk drives, and a CRT. It weighed 26 pounds and could be stored under an airline seat. At present, smaller packages are available that have even more features and greater capacity than the Osborne I.

3 The modification is usually in the form of a small box about the size of a cigarette case that connects by wire to the television on one end and the computer on the other. It is called an *RF modulator.*

4 Onosko, T. (1982). Vision of the future. *Creative Computing, 8*(1), 84, 86, 91, 92. Freiberger, P. (1982). Apple Computer puts big effort into R&D division. *InfoWorld, 4*(21), 1, 4.

5 Freiberger, P. (1982). Teleram 3000 ushers in year of portable computer. *InfoWorld, 4*(24), 1.

6 Kearsley, G. P., Hillelsohn, M. J., & Seidel, R. J. (1981–1982). Micro-computer-based training in business and industry: Present status and future prospects. *Journal of Educational Technology Systems, 10,* 101–108.

7 Sanders, D. H. (1983). *Computers today.* New York: McGraw-Hill.

SUPPLEMENTARY READINGS

Adams, C. K. (1978). *A beginner's guide to computers and microprocessors — With projects.* Blue Ridge Summit, PA: TAB Books.

Chips for the making. (1982). *Popular Computing, 1*(3), 54–56.

Davis, M. (1983). The chip at 35. *Personal Computing, 7*(7), 127–129, 131.

Frederick, F. J. (1980). *Guide to microcomputers.* Washington, D.C.: Association for Educational Communications Technology.

Hughes, E. M. (1981). A beginner's guide to memory. *onComputing, 3*(1), 18–26.

Hughes, E. (1981). What's in the box? Taking the mystery out of computers. *onComputing, 3*(2), 22–34.

Kosel, M., & Carlstrom, G. (1978). *Elementary, my dear computer.* Lauderdale, MI: Minnesota Educational Computing Consortium.

Osborne, A. (1980). *An introduction to microcomputers: Vol. 0. The beginner's book.* New York: OSBORNE/McGraw-Hill.

Vles, J. M. (1981). *Computer fundamentals for nonspecialists.* New York: AMACOM.

Zaks, R. (1980). *Microprocessors from chips to systems.* Berkeley, CA: SYBEX.

CHAPTER 3

INSTRUCTIONAL USES
OF COMPUTERS

CHAPTER CONTENTS

Many people are impressed with computer technology but cannot see how it can be used effectively in education or understand what computers can do that teachers cannot. One of the most valuable characteristics of computers is their ability to perform many routine functions in a school or classroom. This can free the educator to do other tasks. Some things computers can actually do better than people. For example, the computer with its peripheral components can process information, make calculations, perform logical operations, and store, retrieve, and display information. Computers can do these things very rapidly and accurately. Computers can store large amounts of information in their memories and even larger amounts of information in long-term storage (i.e., on tape or disk). They can print information on electronic display screens called *cathode-ray tubes* (CRTs) or on paper. Let's look at these functions in terms of two kinds of tasks that computers can perform for educators.

First, consider *testing of students.* A large number of test items can be stored on disks. Programs can also be stored that enable the computer to select a group of test items from a large pool, present them to a student, score the test, store and analyze the scores, and print the test results for the student and teacher. As the test is administered by the computer, the student can get immediate feedback about his or her performance on each item and on the entire test, and a permanent record of the test score can be kept for the teacher. While teachers can perform all these tasks themselves; the savings in time and energy, the timeliness of the feedback, and the record keeping provided by the computer offer substantial advantages. Moreover, tests need not always be given after instruction. Question-and-answer drills, for example, are instructional. With proper identification of instructional objectives and an appropriate presentation strategy, effective drill and practice instruction can be done by computer. This type of computer instruction has been shown repeatedly to be effective in a variety of course areas. Drill and practice instruction does not strain the power of even a small computer. Such instruction can be highly effective while consuming a minimum of the teacher's time.

Second, consider *simulations of experimental situations.* This is another example of how computers can be applied to instruction. Many scientific experiments are too costly, too time-consuming, too dangerous, or simply too complicated to be done easily in classrooms. For instance, experiments in animal genetics or weathering of materials may take years or even generations to carry out in real life. And if dangerous radioactive or explosive materials, complicated electronic measurements, or elaborate laboratory procedures are required, experiments may be impractical for the regular classroom. However, experiments like these may be simulated on computers. Computer software can be developed that allows students to make choices, set the conditions for the experiment, and receive valid data about the results of an experiment given the chosen conditions. Thus, experiments can be simulated in animal breeding, chemical analysis, retail sales, investments in stocks and bonds, animal and plant ecology, and military encounters, to name just a few of the many possibilities. Students may actually benefit more from a computerized simulation than they would from observing an experiment conducted in real life, because they can participate in the experiment by changing the conditions or variables.

In this chapter we will discuss these and other instructional uses of computers. We will begin by looking at computer hardware and what it can do in instructional settings. Then, a few of the ways computers can be used in education will be considered. This should help the reader to understand how to utilize the capabilities of microcomputers in educational settings.

INSTRUCTIONAL USES OF COMPUTER HARDWARE

The focus is on the microcomputer in this section, although many of the features identified apply to larger computers as well. Table 3.1 lists common devices for input, output, processing, and data storage, along with the functions performed by each. More important, some of the ways in which these components can be used in education are shown. Different instructional needs may, of course, call for different hardware. However, as shown in Chapter 2, at least one input and one output device will be needed to use with any computer. Depending on the application, other devices may be required as well — perhaps additional input devices (game paddles, a graphics pad, and a light pen, for instance), a communications modem, or a long-term storage device (such as a disk drive).

Let us now consider some illustrative situations. In every case, a teacher is using computers to provide instruction. However, a different hardware configuration is used for each application.

• A fourth-grade teacher wants to provide drill and practice in basic mathematics facts. She has located an appropriate set of educational software on floppy diskettes. The software presents items on a CRT, asks the student to make a response on the keyboard, and stores responses on the disk. The teacher can review computer-generated reports of the student's responses, and summaries can be displayed on the screen. The software is available in forms that will run on either of two widely available brands of computers. For this application, the teacher will need to have only one computer with the appropriate software, a CRT, and a disk drive.

• A junior high school science teacher uses microcomputers in her laboratory for experiments in which temperature changes that result from combining various chemicals are measured and the amounts and types of chemicals used are related to the heat generated. Results of the experiments are saved on disks and printed for students to use in later work outside the class. In this instance the teacher chooses the following computer components: (1) microcomputer with keyboard, (2) electronic heat sensor that is able to communicate with the computer, (3) disk drive, (4) color monitor, and (5) dot-matrix printer.

• A fifth-grade teacher wants to provide beginning instruction in writing computer programs in a standard computing language. He has already completed some preparatory activities introducing basic concepts in computing.

TABLE 3.1
ROLES PLAYED BY COMPUTER COMPONENTS IN INSTRUCTION

Component	Function	Educational use
Keyboard	Input of alphabetic, numeric, and special characters, and mathematical operators	Entry of data and educational programs by students and teachers
Paddles, light pens, touch-sensitive panels, "mouse" devices	Alternative devices for responding that provide faster or easier input of data under certain conditions, or for people who cannot type on a keyboard	Facilitates data input for young children and handicapped persons; permits data entry analogous to writing
Graphics pad	Input of lines, shapes, and color images	Facilitates development of graphics and special visual effects to enhance educational programs.
Modem	Connects computer to telephone line to allow communication with other computers	Facilitates sharing software and data within a school system
Disk drive or cassette tape player	Reads and stores data on floppy disks or magnetic tapes	Permits relatively permanent storage of data, records, and programs
Display screen (television set or CRT)	Electronic visual display of output	Displays program results, students' performance, records, data, etc.
Printer	Provides durable display of output from the computer	Permanent copies of records, reports, computer-prepared student worksheets, program listings, etc.
Speaker	Provides auditory output	Enhances instruction with sound and music

These were done without the use of computers. In the next phase of instruction, the students will be using a set of printed materials and experimenting with short, simple programs on small desk-top computers. For this application the teacher chooses an inexpensive microcomputer with a small amount of memory, a keyboard, and a CRT. Since the equipment is inexpensive, he can obtain twelve machines — enough to provide a good deal of access time for each student.

• A preschool teacher wants to provide instruction in the recognition of geometric shapes, color, and letters. Since the children do not already know their numbers and letters, a keyboard would not be a useful input device. Instead, during instruction a letter, shape, or colored square is presented to the students, and they are asked to select a matching figure by directing a blinking square (cursor) to an answer square directly below the figure. For this application the teacher has chosen a microcomputer with a CRT and a joystick. (A joystick is an input device that utilizes a bar or buttons and is commonly used for playing computerized games.) The joystick was chosen because younger children often find a standard typewriter keyboard frustrating. Since the educational software is available on a disk, a disk drive is also required for this application.

These illustrations show that the nature of the application affects the hardware components. Now we shall make a more detailed study of the kinds of tasks computers can assume in instructional settings.

COMPUTER-AIDED LEARNING

At one time, people involved in instructional computing tended to group educational computer applications into two main categories: *computer-assisted instruction* (CAI) and *computer-managed instruction* (CMI). Historically, CAI consisted of drill and practice or tutorial presentations. *Drill and practice* involves the repeated presentation of questions, checking of answers, and provision of feedback on the correctness or incorrectness of the responses. Its purpose is to reinforce and aid in the memorization of facts and concepts. *Tutorial sessions* sometimes contain question-and-answer segments; but they are designed more to present and illustrate material. Thus, tutorial sessions present, explain, and introduce concepts; in drill and practice, on the other hand, instruction is generally provided by repetition and reinforcement.[1]

In CMI, students do not necessarily receive direct instruction from the computer. Rather, the computer's function is to keep records of students' progress, provide prescriptions and schedules for instructional activities, and perhaps provide testing and diagnosis of learning problems.[2]

Nowadays the distinction between CAI and CMI is probably not as useful as it once was. That is, some drill and practice or tutorial software may incorporate aspects of CMI functions, such as keeping track of the student's progress. In this chapter we will use the term *computer-aided learning* to refer to any and all uses of computers for instruction. However, the reader should be aware that other, similar terms have been proposed, such as *computer-based education* (CBE) and *computer-based instruction* (CBI).

Table 3.2 presents eight instructional uses of computers. In each instance, the primary purpose of each use is denoted by an X in the appropriate column of the table. An application may primarily benefit the teacher, students engaged in

TABLE 3.2
BENEFITS OF USING COMPUTERS IN VARIOUS INSTRUCTIONAL APPLICATIONS

Computer application	Aid to teacher	Individual instruction	Group instruction
Development of instructional materials	X		
Maintaining students' records, administering and scoring tests, designing learning experiences for individual students	X		
Group presentations and demonstrations	X		
Presentation of facts and principles with tutorials		X	X
Reinforcement of learning through drill and practice		X	
Computerized games, simulations, and problem solving		X	X
Instruction in computers and programming		X	X
Creative and occupational uses of the computer—e.g., music, art, writing, business		X	X

group learning, or students engaged in individual educational activities. Often, of course, an application will have benefits in two or three areas; but here only the primary benefit for each type of application has been indicated.

The first three applications listed in Table 3.2 primarily benefit the classroom *teacher*. Computers can be used to develop instructional worksheets, puzzles, handouts, and so forth. They can be used to test students, to keep records, and (in more sophisticated applications) to provide prescriptions, schedules, or learning activities for individual students. The computer can be used to demonstrate calculations, graphs, and displays to a group or an entire class. In group applications, however, special equipment may be necessary. For example, large projection screens would enable a group of students to see the visual output better than a small CRT; similarly, audio output may have to be amplified to a greater degree than is necessary for a single user. Further, a computer network might be set up in a classroom so that students can communicate with each other and with the teacher. Certain adaptations in software design are necessary for group instruction. There are courseware developers who specialize in courseware for group use.[3]

Individual instruction may be enhanced by introduction of facts and principles during computerized tutorial sessions. Facts and principles can be reinforced through repeated exposure during computerized drill and practice sessions. Individual learning can also be facilitated by computer simulations and problem solving in practicing computer programming, and in creative applications of computers.

Table 3.2 suggests that the computer can also facilitate *group instruction* by providing group presentations of tutorial instruction, problem-solving activities, and activities in which groups design creative applications of computers involving graphics, art, engineering, etc.

Let us now look at these different tyes of computer-aided learning in turn.

Development of Instructional Aids

Teachers often have difficulty finding the right type of paper-and-pencil activities for a particular instructional objective. Worksheets obtained from commercial publishers may not precisely fit a lesson plan, or the teacher may want to produce materials tailored for an individual student or small group. In such situations a computer with the right software can be a welcome aid.

For example, computers can generate worksheets of mathematics problems complete with answer keys for the teacher. The worksheets can be designed according to specifications, printed, and then reproduced as necessary. Computers can also generate word lists for spelling tests in which key letters are omitted. Students are then asked to complete the words by filling in the missing letters. Also, by means of computer graphics, graphs and other kinds of displays can be printed on worksheets complete with questions.

The Minnesota Educational Computing Consortium (MECC) has developed an instructional materials generator that creates scrambled word puzzles based on a word list from an instructional unit.[4] The teacher has only to enter the desired word list. The words are then arranged vertically, horizontally, and diagonally by the computer. It enters random letters into the spaces in the puzzle which are not taken up by the words and prints the puzzle and instructions on a worksheet. (See Figure 3.1.) In this way, a worksheet tailored to lesson plans and students' needs can be produced with a minimum drain on the teacher's time.

There are many ways to use computers to generate teacher-made learning activities. Some teachers prefer to develop their own programs for this. Others use software packages that permit easier authoring of drill and practice exercises, tests, and other educational materials. (This type of use is discussed further in Chapter 7.)

Record Keeping, Testing, and Instructional Prescription

Computer-managed instruction (CMI) usually includes some or all of the following features:

Ability to maintain records of students' progress
Capability for administering and scoring tests
Provision of assignments for individual students
Prescription of remedial assignments for students who need them
Ability to alert teachers to instructional tasks that may be necessary on a scheduled basis or when certain conditions are met in the classroom

The extensive record keeping involved in coping with a vast array of individ-

COLORS

```
. . . L A V E N D E R .
Y A R G I . E . . . . E
. . . O E E A Q U A L .
. . L T R . . . . P . .
. E I G . K . . R . . .
T H . S N . W U O D . .
W . . I C O P R E . . .
. . P E L A A R B . . .
. . U L . N R L . . . .
. L E . G . A L . . . .
B Y . E . C . . E . . .
. . . . K . . . . T . .
```

IF YOU WISH, YOU MAY INSERT A DITTO
MASTER AT THIS TIME. PRESS THE RETURN
KEY WHEN YOU WANT THE PUZZLE TO PRINT.

COLORS

```
C F E L A V E N D E R F
Y A R G I R E N T P L E
F T J O E E A Q U A L K
J G L T R D Q Y M P M T
R E I G E K U E R Q J V
T H C S N N W U O D U M
W X R I C O P R E X Q X
I O P E L A A R B X F U
F L U L H N R L J Z Q M
G L E Y G V A L G S N F
B Y R E U C K H E V C X
F X N Q K K A L I T A P
```

THERE ARE 14 WORDS HERE — CAN
YOU FIND THEM?.

HERE ARE THE WORDS TO LOOK FOR:

AQUA	BLACK
BLUE	GRAY
GREEN	LAVENDER
ORANGE	PINK
PURPLE	RED
SCARLET	VIOLET
WHITE	YELLOW

FIGURE 3.1
Computer-generated word game. *(Minnesota Educational Computing Consortium.)*

ual students' needs is so time-consuming that a teacher can have difficulty keeping up with it. The amount of information to be recorded and related to other data is an enormous task. However, computers are very adept at storing, analyzing, relating, and retrieving information. A number of student management systems have been devised for large and small computers.

One particularly comprehensive computer-managed instructional system is Comprehensive Achievement Monitoring (CAM), developed by the Hopkins Independent School District in Hopkins, Minnesota.[5] This system was designed for use where a careful specification of curriculum and instructional objectives by the school district has been completed or is planned. A pool of test items is generated for each objective and forms the basis of a testing system.

For students enrolled in courses managed by CAM, a set of objectives is assigned for each course or for each portion of a course. At critical points in the instruction, tests are constructed from the item pools to measure students' achievement. Tests are administered and answers recorded in a way that facilitates rapid processing of the test results. Students respond on standard answer sheets or precoded cards. The test results then become the basis of a computerized report for each student. Reports can also be produced for each classroom and each school. Because microcomputers are relatively slow when handling large amounts of data and have only small memories available, additional processing can be done on a larger computer to provide summaries for the school district and analyses of the test items.

The CAM system permits very close tracking of students' progress. The classroom teacher can follow every student's progress on the instructional objectives selected for that student. Remedial prescriptions are possible when students have problems mastering particular objectives. The students' rate of progress and achievement level can be monitored by the teacher for use in the classroom and for conferences with parents. The school and district can obtain convenient summaries of students' performance. In addition, analyses of test items that can be helpful in revising tests and improving instructional materials can be provided.

Of course, CMI systems such as CAM have some disadvantages. The school or school district may have to go to considerable effort to develop a detailed set of objectives for the curriculum that will be agreeable to all. Banks of test items have to be developed; a large amount of clerical record keeping and data entry is required; and the cooperation of a large portion of the district staff is essential for full implementation. If a school system can overcome all the hurdles, however, a system like CAM can have many advantages.

Group Demonstrations and Presentations

Demonstrations are excellent ways to introduce concepts to students. Science teachers particularly can use demonstrations to illustrate such things as chemical reactions, anatomical structures, and variations in plant growth.

Sometimes actual demonstrations and experiments are performed in areas such as genetics, chemistry, biology, and physics. But these can be difficult, time-consuming, and expensive. Some phenomena are hard to demonstrate experimentally because of the size of the components required; others are difficult to observe because they change very slowly or because they are dangerous.

Teachers have therefore used films and videotapes as alternatives to real-life demonstrations. There are many advantages to film or videotape demonstrations. For example, costly, complicated scientific phenomena can be filmed once, and the cost of the demonstration can be considered in terms of the many classrooms that will eventually view the product. The stages of a genetics experiment can be filmed or taped over a period of time. A historical film can be made in the location in which the events happened. Special camera techniques can enhance observation of microscopic phenomena. Movement, color, animation, and other techniques can make instruction come alive.

However, films and videotapes in their conventional forms are constrained to a linear presentation. That is, they start at the beginning and run straight through to the end. Of course, a teacher can skip a portion of a film or videotape, or stop the action. But what if a student says, "I understand what I just saw, but what would happen if the situation were changed slightly? Would the result be the same?" The ending on the videotape or film cannot be changed at that point to fit new conditions. Further, for practical reasons, a large variety of solutions cannot be shown; but many situations may be needed to ensure that students understand the basic relationships involved. This is where the computer can be an extremely handy tool for the teacher.

We can illustrate the use of computers for classroom demonstrations and experiments through two examples.

First, suppose that a science teacher wants to demonstrate the transmission of blue and brown eyes in humans. Eye color — here, blue versus brown — is basically controlled by a single pair of genes, one gene contributed by each parent. The tricky part of the problem has to do with the fact that blue eyes are a recessive trait. This means that any of the following genetic combinations will result in offspring who show the dominant trait, brown eyes:

Brown — blue
Blue — brown
Brown — brown

Only the combination blue — blue will produce blue eyes in a child. This principle can be very nicely illustrated in the classroom using an appropriately programmed microcomputer. Students can ask questions, such as "What proportion of the children of a blue-eyed father and brown-eyed mother will have blue eyes?" And, "Is a blue-eyed child possible with two brown-eyed parents?" If the programming is adequate, they can receive answers to many such questions and then be shown how the transmission mechanism for eye color applies. Alternatively, if students are limited to questions about the mechanism, they could attempt to discover for themselves the genetic principles that account for transmission of eye color.

The teacher could also use the computer as a demonstration tool for group instruction on this topic. Questions would be addressed to the students in a group lesson, and the students' answers would be typed in at the keyboard by the teacher. The computer would be connected to a large video monitor or a projection screen so that all the students in a group could see the demonstration. In this case, the students would not run the program themselves but would participate in the demonstration in a group setting.

For a second example of a classroom demonstration, consider a lesson on the operation of a small business such as a food stand. A group of students could identify the raw ingredients needed for the food to be sold; the equipment and labor costs; and the costs of other materials, site rental, advertising, and so on. They could suggest the prices that they believe people would be willing to pay for the products and the probable sales volume that would result. The computer could then show the profit level for each single item and estimate overall profits. The computer could also estimate the effect of changing the various input parameters, such as amount of advertising, amount of labor, and type of equipment. Students could gain a good understanding of the principles involved in operating a small business from this kind of experience.

Introduction of Facts and Principles through Tutorials

Computers can be used to convey content and direct instruction to groups or individual students in the form of tutorials. Tutorials are, however, typically used in individual instruction.

Tutorial instruction usually proceeds through several steps for each principle:

Description and explanation
Illustrations and examples
Questions and remediation (if necessary)

A fact or concept is defined and described, and an illustration or example is given. The student is then asked one or more questions to determine whether he or she knows the fact or understands the principle. If the student does not demonstrate mastery, assistance is given. The student is then retested, or run through the tutorial sequence again to facilitate reaching mastery. The feature of tutorials which differentiates them from other forms of individual instruction (such as drill and practice) is that presentation of the basic descriptions and illustrations forms the substance of the learning activities. In some courseware, instructional materials are used other than the computerized tutorials.

A shortened example of a sequence from a tutorial in mathematics is shown in Figure 3.2. This sequence is intended to teach students the concept of *squaring a number*. Notice how the tutorial tends to follow the sequence described above. A description and an explanation are given; an illustration is presented; the student is asked a question to which he or she provides an answer. If the answer is incorrect, remediation is presented (as in the case of ``8'' for the square of 4 in the example shown). When a sufficient number of correct answers have been given, the session is concluded and the student proceeds to another segment of the tutorial. Each segment typically focuses on one fact, concept, or principle.

Tutorials are quite common in commercially available educational software and have been found effective in a wide variety of subject areas. Tutorials may also be produced by teachers to fit special classroom needs.

```
(Frame 1)
              SQUARING A NUMBER

YOU CAN OBTAIN THE SQUARE OF A NUMBER
BY MULTIPLYING THE NUMBER BY ITSELF.
THUS, 2 SQUARED IS THE SAME THING AS

          2 X 2

AND 2 SQUARED IS EQUAL TO 4.   SOMETIMES
WE SAY IT THIS WAY,  "THE SQUARE OF 2
IS 4".

IF YOU WANT TO OBTAIN THE SQUARE OF
ANOTHER NUMBER, MULTIPLY THE NUMBER BY
ITSELF.   THE SQUARE OF 3 IS 3 TIMES 3,
OR 9 (3 X 3 = 9).
----------------------------------------
(Frame 2)

NOW LET'S SEE IF YOU CAN FIND THE SQUARE
OF 4.   ENTER YOUR ANSWER BELOW:
            (student enters 8)
----------------------------------------
(Frame 3)

THAT WAS A GOOD TRY, BUT IT WAS NOT
CORRECT.   REMEMBER TO MULTIPLY 4 TIMES
4 TO GET THE RIGHT ANSWER.   TRY AGAIN.
THE SQUARE OF 4 IS
            (student enters 16)


----------------------------------------
(Frame 4)

THAT'S BETTER! NOW LET'S TRY ANOTHER
PROBLEM.   WHAT IS THE SQUARE OF 6.
THINK ABOUT IT CAREFULLY AND THEN GIVE
YOUR ANSWER BELOW.
            (student answers 36)


----------------------------------------
(Frame 5)

VERY GOOD! YOU ARE ON THE RIGHT TRACK
NOW!


            :
            :
          etc.
----------------------------------------
```

FIGURE 3.2
Example of tutorial instruction.

Drill and Practice

One thing computers are extremely good at is the tireless interactive presentation of questions to give students the opportunity for extensive practice. When large computers first became available for experimentation, drill and practice was a logical first step for instruction. A considerable amount of drill and practice instruction has since been developed; in fact, to many people CAI means drill and practice.

From the student's perspective, drill and practice consists of the following sequence, which is repeated until the student demonstrates mastery:

Presentation of an item
Student's response
Reinforcement

The principles of learning underlying drill and practice draw heavily from the operant-conditioning approach to the psychology of learning. Basically, the idea is that when a response occurs and is reinforced, it will tend to occur again. Thus, a reinforcer is a condition, event, or stimulus that encourages the repetition of behavior. Most computerized drill and practice uses some method to inform the student that an answer is correct or incorrect immediately after the response is given. If the response was incorrect, the item may be readministered or the whole set of items may be repeated until the student reaches the criterion level of performance. (*Criterion level* means some proportion of correct answers considered to be indicative of mastery, such as 80 percent or 90 percent.)

When the student can perform at the criterion level for an exercise, he or she has completed the lesson. The student then proceeds to the next phase of instruction, either on the computer or in some other way. Directions and a short example are usually presented at the beginning of the lesson. If the student experiences problems in the midst of a lesson, some programs provide help in the form of an additional explanation. However, drill and practice emphasizes learning through repeated exposure to questions. (Tutorials, on the other hand, tend to emphasize explanation, demonstration, and illustration; a smaller portion of the student's effort is taken up by answering questions.)

An example of drill and practice items for addition is presented in Figure 3.3. In this exercise, the computer generates all possible combinations of single-digit numbers. The instructions in the first frame concern procedures for completing the drill. The assumption is made that single-digit addition had already been introduced. Notice that the exercise begins with easier items, which students are more likely to answer correctly, and then proceeds to more difficult items.

If the computer keeps a record of the student's answers, a drill can be terminated when a specified level of performance is reached. In some drills, however, the computer simply presents items until the student decides to stop or runs out of time. Each time the student gives an answer to a question, the computer immediately provides feedback about whether or not the answer is correct. When the student responds incorrectly, the correct answer is automatically shown. When a correct answer is given, the student may receive a word or two of praise from the computer for answering correctly.

(Frame 1)   DIRECTIONS

THE FOLLOWING ARE ADDITION PROBLEMS.
WHEN EACH PROBLEM APPEARS ON THE SCREEN,
TYPE YOUR ANSWER ON THE KEYBOARD.   IT
WILL APPEAR ON THE LINE NEXT TO THE
"EQUALS".   IF YOU MAKE A MISTAKE IN
TYPING YOUR ANSWER, USE THE BACK ARROW
KEY AND TYPE IN THE ANSWER YOU
WANTED.   WHEN YOU FEEL YOU HAVE THE
RIGHT ANSWER, PRESS THE "RETURN" KEY
AND THE COMPUTER WILL SCORE YOUR
ANSWER.

****

WHEN YOU ARE READY TO BEGIN, PRESS
THE "RETURN" KEY.   WHEN YOU WANT TO STOP
PRESS THE ESCAPE (ESC) KEY.

(Frame 2)   1 + 2 =

(Frame 3)   2 + 2 =

(Frame 4)   4 + 1 =

(Frame 5)   5 + 3 =

(Frame 6)   4 + 2 =

                          :
                          :
                        etc.

FIGURE 3.3
Drill and practice in the
addition of one-digit numbers.

Branching in Drill and Practice   The type of drill and practice exercise that was shown in Figure 3.3 is quite simple. Drill and practice is sometimes made more effective with the technique of branching. Branches are points in the program where at least two alternative paths can be followed, depending on the student's response. Branching allows programs to be tailored to the needs of individual students. Drill sequences which are unnecessary, or for which the student has already demonstrated mastery, are not selected. Rather, drill sequences most appropriate to the student's performance at the moment are followed. Branching is used in a great variety of ways; and some applications of branching are far more sophisticated then what we have just described.

The following example illustrates the concept of branching. Suppose that an instructional unit on calculating the amount of interest earned by a savings account involves the following three objectives:

1   Knowledge of definition and use of the terms *interest, principal,* and *rate*
2   Understanding of the basic concepts and relationships of simple interest and compound interest, and of formulas for calculating earned interest
3   Ability to solve problems in calculating earned interest given the type of interest, principal, rate, and time period

To master objective 3, a student must have previously mastered objectives 1 and 2. Similarly, mastering objective 2 assumes mastery of objective 1. Thus, a student is assumed to progress through the instructional sequence in the following order:

1 ———————————— 2 ———————————— 3

Knowledge of terms	Understanding of	Ability to solve
and definitions	concepts and	problems
	relationships	

The drill sequence for this unit would then require items for all three objectives. Instruction would be presented so that the items for objective 1 would come first, then items for objective 2, and finally items for objective 3. That is, instruction would progress from simple to complex, from knowledge of terms and definitions to understanding of concepts to problem solving.

So far, our illustration is an example of a linear instructional program. A problem frequently encountered in linear instruction is that students who fail to master items for objectives 1 or 2 do not progress to more complex objectives. Branching offers a solution to this problem because it allows for alternative routes based on information available at given points in the sequence. In our example, performance on each of the three objectives can be measured, and remediation can be provided if progress is not satisfactory.

An instructional sequence involving branching is shown in Figure 3.4. Here, the boxes represent kinds of instruction. In the simplest case, a student could go from the start to the end of the instructional sequence, receiving instruction on objectives 1, 2, and 3. For this student, the instruction would be linear. However, as is shown in Figure 3.4, a progress check is made immediately preceding and following instruction on each objective to determine whether additional instruction is required. Progress checks are represented by the diamonds, and remediation loops by the arrows. Until a student demonstrates satisfactory performance on each step of the instruction, he or she does not proceed to the next step. After instruction on the third objective and satisfactory performance on the test items for that objective, an overall performance check is made. The results of this check determine whether the student completes the lesson or engages in additional remediation study. It is conceivable that a student could go from the first assessment of the first objective to the final evaluation without

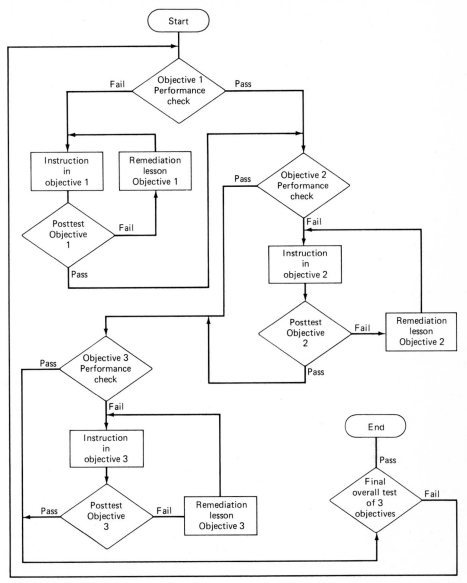

FIGURE 3.4
Illustration of a simple branching program of instruction. Students are given different activities depending on their performance.

receiving any instruction if all the preinstructional questions are answered correctly. On the other hand, a student might gain partial understanding sufficient for satisfactory completion of the three posttests but not sufficient to pass the overall assessment. Such a student would be routed through the instruction again.

This is a very simple illustration of branching. However, it does illustrate the power of the technique. As was noted earlier, very sophisticated applications have been developed; and a thorough discussion of branching techniques is beyond the scope of this chapter. Readers who are interested in more detailed consideration of this important topic are encouraged to consult additional sources.

In Conclusion: Computerized Drill and Practice   To summarize, drill and practice is a very common form of instruction. It involves the presentation of a set of items that are designed to match specified instructional objectives. Further, some of the programming may allow the teacher to tailor the type and number of activities in a lesson. In addition, students can proceed at their own pace through the learning activities. The basic format involves three steps:

1   Presentation of the item
2   Response from the student
3   Reinforcement

Sequencing is important in drill and practice. Branching may be used to enhance drill and practice, and to administer remediation activities when performance is not judged to be satisfactory.

Simulations, Games, and Problem Solving

Simulations, games, and problem solving are three different kinds of computerized instructional activities. However, although they are distinct in design and operation, they do share several traits; accordingly, they are often grouped together. For example, they use more of the power and capacity of computers than tutorials or drill and practice. Further, they are more obviously suitable to instruction in cognitive tasks on a higher level than knowledge of facts and definitions or simple understanding of concepts and principles.[6] Simulations, games, and problem solving give greater opportunities for introducing affective objectives and, if properly designed, can provide intrinsic motivation for learning.

These types of applications can be more difficult and costly to develop than drill and practice. The teacher must be sophisticated in using problem-solving activities that involve the computer. Moreover, knowledge about how to develop these types of applications is not yet well established. However, these approaches have the potential to significantly alter educational practices. (For this reason, simulations, games, and problem solving will be covered again in Chapter 10, in greater detail.)

Simulations   As we mentioned earlier in this chapter, simulations enable a teacher to present artificial versions of real-life situations that are too costly, time-consuming, dangerous, or complicated to recreate in a classroom. In this sort of instruction the computer is able to simulate the conditions of an experiment or situation. The student can set conditions and make decisions, and the computer will show or demonstrate their implications. One well-known computer simulation, the flight simulator, has been used for years in training pilots to fly commercial and military aircraft. The simulator includes an exact replica of the cockpit and controls of a given type of aircraft. The mock-up is connected to a computer system that is programmed to give a trainee seated in the cockpit the experience of the in-flight movements of aircraft and visual effects which result from adjustments to the controls and instruments. Flight simulators work quite well and provide valuable training before actual flights, without risking aircraft or life.

There is considerable flexibility regarding how computers can be used in simulations. They can control mechanical movement (as flight simulators do), or graphics displays, or text shown on a CRT screen. The success of these applications depends on the imagination and skill of the persons developing them. Of course, costs are a concern in simulations as well as real-life experiments, particularly when complicated mechanical or scientific equipment is required.

To help convey an idea of the range of possibilities for computer simulations, some applications are listed below:

Illustrating chemistry, biology, or physics experiements
Predicting outcomes of sports events
Recreating historical events
Cooking and meal planning
Running a small business
Identifying characteristics of election campaigns and voting trends
Illustrating social science experiments
Designing manufacturing processes
Demonstrating aspects of health and physical fitness
Helping with career selection and planning

The reader might try to think of some interesting simulations for a few of these areas. The brief descriptions of examples that follow are provided to illustrate instructional simulations.

• *Balloon flight:* This simulation is part of a ninth-grade general science course developed by the Alaska Department of Education.[7] In the simulation, the student attempts to complete a balloon flight over a given course. The student can make in-flight adjustments, much as a real-life balloonist would. The computer then makes adjustments in the balloon's flight based upon the student's input. The simulation is designed to illustrate several instructional objectives concerning the properties of gases.

• *Odell Lake:* This simulation was developed by the Minnesota Education Computing Consortium (MECC). It provides instruction to students in several objectives related to a food chain and an ecosystem. The student plays the part of several different species of fish. Each fish encounters various aspects of its environment, including other fish, mammals, birds, insects, and even humans. In every encounter, it must make choices which affect its survival. The object is to survive. While elementary students are enjoying the game-like presentation of the program, they are learning concepts that might seem dull in a textbook.

• *Oregon Trail:* This simulation was also developed by MECC. The activity is designed to simulate the westward travel of American settlers in the mid-1800s over the Oregon Trail. The objective of the game is to survive and arrive safely at the end of the trail. A student "traveling the Oregon Trail" is allocated an amount of money to spend on various provisions. The student makes decisions along the trail, and even shoots at bandits and wild game. By completing the simulation, the student learns some history, geography, and economics, and something about survival in the wilderness.

More and more simulations are becoming available from commercial sources. As long as simulations are not too costly to produce, package, and market, and as long as they can take advantage of the capabilities of microcomputers to present realistic training, educational software producers will show increased interest in them. Thus, over the next few years even more of this kind of software should become available.

Games   Microprocessors and microcomputers are well known for their ability to present games. The popularity of computer games is unprecedented. Alien spaceships attack, rockets flash across the screen, strange creatures attempt to devour other creatures. In arcades across the country, these machines gobble a mountain of coins; and many of the games have been programmed to run on home computers as well. While these games may be entertaining, their educational value is doubtful. However, a number of attempts have been made to harness the motivational powers of games for educational purposes by presenting instructional problems in game format. The student performs a task of educational value in order to do well in the game.

One popular educational game is Hurkle (also available from MECC). In this game a small friendly creature, called a *Hurkle,* hides on the screen by becoming invisible. It is the task of the student to find the Hurkle by guessing. The Hurkle may hide on a horizontal or vertical number line or on a two-dimensional grid. The purpose of the game is twofold. First, by playing the game a student learns about numbers, number lines, and a two-dimensional coordinate system. Second, the student learns something about strategies for problem solving, since the objective of the game is to find the Hurkle with the fewest possible guesses.

In another well-known game, MasterType, the student receives instruction in typing skills. Letters and numbers appear in the four corners of the screen.[8]

These characters must be typed within a given time in order to divert a mock disaster on the screen. The student's errors, speed, and other performance characteristics are reported on the screen at the end of each lesson.

Games can be fun. In well-constructed games, students can learn without really knowing that they are learning. However, games do have drawbacks. Sometimes they seem contrived and uninteresting because of poor design or conceptualization; in such cases, the time required to master the objectives may exceed the ability of the game to keep the student interested. In addition, some instructional objectives do not easily fit a game format, and other, more appropriate instructional strategies must be found.

Problem Solving   Interest in computerized instruction has shifted, in the past few years, away from relatively simple applications such as drill and practice and tutorials and toward problem solving. Many people in the field insist that the most important applications of computers in education are in problem solving.

Computers were developed to help solve a diverse range of complex problems. Some computers are capable of making calculations with such speed and accuracy that they can solve in a matter of seconds problems which might require a lifetime to work out by hand. By comparison, drills, tutorials, and for that matter most instructional applications seem very simple.

When used as a tool for problem solving, the computer can serve as an extension of the human mind — but not as a replica of it. Computers as we know them today do not develop strategies for solutions on their own. They only carry out instructions providing them with such strategies. For example, to calculate the distance of a star from the earth, one obviously does not simply ask the machine a question like, "How far is Alpha Centauri from the earth?" The programming necessary to solve this problem must provide detailed step-by-step instructions for the computer. Thus, strategies for solutions must first be derived by people and then programmed into the computer. Further, in order to create such sets of instructions, one must understand key elements of the problem and the nature of the solution. If our example is used for instruction, then, the student must determine what measurements are needed and how to use them to find a solution, and must be able to express the relationships involved in the form of precise mathematical statements. Finally, the student must know how to provide the detailed programming instructions to the computer.

A great deal of understanding and conceptualization is required before one can write a computer program to solve a problem. However, if the student is able to engage in problem solving of this sort, a considerable amount of learning takes place in addition to programming. In fact, as Seymour Papert points out in his book *Mindstorms*,[9] the act of instructing a computer to perform tasks and solve programs can be very instructional to a student. Another way to look at this is to recognize that teaching something to another person usually increases one's own understanding of it, and that programming is very much like teaching a computer.

There is a great deal of enthusiasm for the problem-solving approach to instruction using modern computers; and this approach will become increasingly prominent in the next few years. But there are barriers to be overcome if the approach is to realize its potential. For instance, either students and teachers will need a greater degree of programming skill, or programming languages and methods of placing information in a computer will have to become simpler and more natural. Because problem solving as an instructional technique calls for considerable "computer sophistication" on the part of students, and because experience with this technique is very limited, it is not known whether the approach is equally effective for all students or effective only for the more capable ones.

One of the most interesting and popular approaches to learning by programming computers is LOGO, a language developed by Papert and his colleagues at MIT. This language enables students to program computers using a simple set of commands and graphics. LOGO, which is described in greater detail in Chapter 9, has been successfully implemented in a number of school systems around the country. In the next decade other "natural" languages and simpler hardware will be developed which should facilitate instruction using the problem-solving approach.

Instruction in Computers and Programming

Studying computers and programming was formerly reserved for only a few college students. Today, with easier access to computers and simpler programming languages, programming instruction of one sort or another is being offered not only to high school students but even to elementary school students. As society becomes more sophisticated technologically, it is likely that basic literacy in computing will be considered necessary for virtually everyone. Of course, not every student will need to be an expert programmer. Several levels of literacy have been proposed. These range from awareness of what computers are and what they can do to sophisticated problem solving with computers.

For teachers who provide instruction to students in computer programming, the following steps are suggested:

1 Determine a set of reasonable objectives for the particular group of students.
2 Select a set of strategies and activities appropriate for that group.
3 Select an appropriate computer language or languages.
4 Select hardware, software, and instructional materials.
5 Obtain sufficient materials and resources for the students to do the necesary research and complete the task.

One effective approach is to allow the student access to computer hardware for actual programming and for the procedure of correcting and refining programs known as *debugging*. However, some activities should precede actual experience with computers, particularly for younger children. For example, some teachers ask elementary students to describe a familiar task such as walking to school, playing a game of cards, or making a particular kind of sandwich. The students are asked to describe the task in sufficient detail so that someone who does not know anything about that task (or perhaps a robot) could perform it from these instructions. By trying to instruct another person to perform a task, the student comes to understand the level of detail necessary in programming. If the teacher serves as the robot and interprets instructions literally, the demonstration can be humorous and entertaining as well as instructional.

When students reach the stage of actually writing and debugging programs, access to a computer becomes essential. One of the nice features of microcomputers and other data processing systems is the immediacy with which a program can be tested and corrected if there are problems with it. This contrasts with the experience of the authors of this book, who developed programs on large computers as graduate students in the late 1960s. In those days, computer programs were submitted to the computer center on punched cards, and output was not available until 24 to 48 hours later. Debugging even modest programs often required days or sometimes weeks. Today students can enter programs on a microcomputer or terminal and receive almost immediate feedback; usually, students can make corrections and retry a program several times per hour.

As computer programming is offered to students with greater frequency, teachers will need to become familiar with the techniques of programming. For those teaching advanced topics in computer programming, more extensive coursework is required. In the future, teachers of programming can look forward to simpler programming languages and simpler ways to communicate with computers, and even to instructing computers by voice. Experts are now beginning to talk about communicating with computers by means of brain waves. If and when we reach that point, users of computers will probably not need to learn computer languages as we know them today. However, for the immediate future, programming and instruction in programming will continue to be important.

Fostering Creativity with the Computer

Computers are used today for an amazing variety of tasks. To name a few, automobiles and many other machines are designed with the aid of computer graphics. Music, poetry, visual art, and motion picture sequences are created by computers. Within many professions and occupations, groups of people who utilize computers have evolved. These people must be skilled in the area in which they work (art, music, engineering, writing, etc.) and in using computers.

Recently, creative uses of computers have begun to find their way into instructional programs. For example, there is a computer program that allows students to "paint" pictures on a screen. At the bottom of the screen are "pots" of different colored paints. A small point of light serves as the "paintbrush." The brush is controlled by a joystick similar to that used in computer games. Using the joystick, the student puts the paintbrush into a pot of paint of a particular color, then moves the brush to the desired location, and proceeds to "paint" a picture on the "canvas" of a color CRT monitor.[10]

Word processing also has tremendous potential for instructing students in creative writing. Computers are commonly used in word processing. In this application, what is typed on a keyboard appears on a CRT screen. It can be corrected, edited, stored, and even sent to another computer station electronically. When it is ready, any number of copies can be printed. The tedium of producing successive drafts is reduced, and students can focus on perfecting their writing by revision.

COMMENTS ON MIXING COMPUTERS AND EDUCATION

We have just discussed several kinds of instructional applications of computers. The enormous potential for computers in education should be clear; and it is far greater than anything that could have been predicted even a few years ago. But *potential* is one thing; *achieving* it is quite another. The degree to which computers will realize their potential in education depends to a large extent on teachers.

Care must be taken with the selection of software and instructional approaches, just as with selection of textbooks. Different types of instructional objectives are best taught with different methods. Sometimes teachers will be fortunate enough to have a variety of ready-made software to choose from. But there are few exhaustive field studies and research efforts to guide teachers as they select computerized instructional materials. Hence they will have to know what factors to look for in selecting good software.

When selecting computer-based instruction, teachers will need to deal with the issue of how to integrate the instruction into the curriculum. The role of teachers and students may vary somewhat from traditional roles, and certain adjustments may be required. Generally these changes tend to be in the direction of greater autonomy for students and a more managerial or supervisory role for the teacher.

Some experts argue that the power and capacity of the computer is not tapped in drill and practice or tutorial instruction. They say that for these applications the computer is simply a "page turner." However, the evidence to date is that these forms of instruction are effective. Instruction time is often reduced, and students' motivation is increased. The present authors feel that these applications are appropriate for microcomputers.

People sometimes worry about the implication of using computers in education. One of the fears most commonly expressed by teachers is that computers may take over a significant portion of the teaching process, driving them from the profession. This fear has not been substantiated by experience. When computers are used properly in schools, they open greater opportunities for learning while freeing teachers from the more mundane aspects of instruction.[11] However, the use of computers and other technologies in schools may mean that teachers will have to upgrade their own skills to avoid obsolescence. Another common fear is that computers are impersonal and will dehumanize education. This is not likely to happen if teachers know how to ensure that motivation, encouragement, and suitable social experiences are included in an educational program.

SUMMARY

Different needs in educational uses of computers will require different hardware. A variety of ways to utilize computers in instructional settings were discussed. These include:

Development of instructional materials

Maintenance of records, testing, and prescribing individualized education

Presentation of demonstrations and instruction to groups

Provision of facts and principles through tutorial instruction

Drill and practice

Presentation of instruction involving complex relationships by use of problem solving, simulation, and games

Consideration of the computer and computer programming as a topic of study

Enhancement of creativity

Only a limited amount of research is currently available on the effects of computers and computerized education. However, much of the available evidence suggests that computerization enhances learning and increases motivation.[12] Teachers can use computers for some of the more routine aspects of teaching such as drills and record keeping, so that they will have more time for working with individuals or groups of students.

As we gain experience with computers, we may find that not all students benefit equally from this form of instruction. Group instruction techniques for use with computers are in their infancy, and methods of facilitating social development of students in computer-based education are not yet well established. A major challenge facing education today, therefore, is to determine just how and where to use emerging electronic technologies and to make the necessary adjustments in educational practices.

NOTES

1 Drill and practice is based on the principles of reinforcement, which were developed from considerable research on the psychology of learning. Good reference sources for this approach are: G. E. Snelbecker. (1974). *Learning theory, instructional*

theory, and psychoeducational design. New York: McGraw-Hill. Hill, W. E. (1977). *Learning.* New York: Crowell.

2 Baker, F. B. (1978). *Computer managed instruction: Theory and practice.* Englewood Cliffs, NJ: Educational Technology Publications.

3 EduPro of Palo Alto, California, has a series of educational microcomputer programs designed for group use. The series is called *Microgroup.*

4 Word Find is the name of the program described here. It is available on *Elementary* (Vol. 2) and *Teacher utilities* (Vol. 1) from Minnesota Educational Computing Consortium, 2520 Broadway Drive, St. Paul, MN, 55113-1118.

5 Kosel, M., & Horn, M. (1973, April; rev. 1977, November). *CAM—How to use it.* Rodel, L. J. (1979, March). *CAM coordinator's manual.* St. Paul, MN: MECC.

6 See, for example, the discussion of analysis, synthesis, and evaluation in: Bloom, B. S. (Ed.). (1956). *Taxonomy of educational objectives. Handbook I: Cognitive domain.* New York: McKay.

7 Individualized Study by Technology (IST). (1981). *General science.* Produced under contract by Northwest Regional Laboratory, Portland, OR, for the Alaska Department of Education.

8 *MasterType: The typing instruction game.* (1981). By Bruce Zweig; produced by Lightning Software, Palo Alto, CA.

9 Papert, S. (1980). *Mindstorms: Children, computers, and powerful ideas.* New York: Basic Books.

10 The program is Picture Painter, produced by MicroLab, Highland Park, IL. It was reviewed in: *Creative Computing.* (1982). *8*(1), 44.

11 Mason, E., Smith, T., Gohs, F., & Cohen, D. (1981). *Evaluation of the IST courses.* FY 81 Pilot Study, Alaska Department of Eduction.

12 Bell, T. E. (1983). My computer, my teacher. *Personal Computing, 7*(6), 120-123, 125, 127.

SUPPLEMENTARY READINGS

Boe, T. (1982). Integration of computer methods in the science laboratory. *AEDS Monitor. 20*(7,8,9), 18-20.

Dershem, H. L., & Whittle, J. T (1980). Using computer games to challenge elementary school students. *Computing Teacher, 7*(5), 32-34.

Minnesota Educational Computing Consortium. (1982). *Using the Computer in the classroom.* St. Paul, MN: MECC.

National Council of Teachers of Mathematics. (1980-1981). NCTM recommendations for the 1980s. *Computing Teacher, 8*(2), 54-55.

Perry, T., & Zawolokow, G. (1982). CAI: Choosing hardware and software. *Apple Orchard, 3*(1), 22-24.

Robyler, M. D. (1981). Instructional design versus authoring courseware: Some crucial differences. *AEDS Journal,* 173-181.

Rowe, N. C. (1981, November-December). Some rules for good simulations. *Educational Computer Magazine,* 37-40.

Spivak, H., & Varden, S. (1981). Classrooms make friends with computers. In J. L. Thomas (Ed.), *Microcomputers in the schools.* Pheonix, AZ: Oryx.

Steele, C. (1983). Learning packet teaches graphics and animation to elementary school students. *The Computing Teacher, 10*(5), 63-65.

GETTING STARTED

CHAPTER CONTENTS

In a few short years, computers have gone from being rare in schools to being commonplace.[1] This mirrors the effects of technology on society in general. Most skilled or professional occupations currently involve computers or micro-processors in some way. Many of our daily activities — including shopping in neighborhood markets and even using the telephone — involve the use of computers. There is no doubt that to prepare the citizen for the future, schools will have to provide students with education about computers.[2]

This chapter will discuss the steps an educator might go through to begin using microcomputers: analyzing needs, planning, selecting a system, gaining support, and purchasing the system. The material in this chapter was designed to be useful both for readers who have no experience with computers and for readers who are in settings where computers are already being used but may be considering expansion of or improvements in their present system.

STARTING WITH NEEDS

Planning should not start only with consideration of the hardware that may be available. Rather, it should begin with the needs of the school or educational program to which computers might be applied. Once these needs have been identified and analyzed, the degree to which computers can offer solutions may be determined. In this section we consider how to go about determining needs.

Identifying Needs

Schools, like many other elements of society, operate with limited funds. Purchases must be made wisely. Although the price of computers has come down considerably in recent years, they are still costly. A well-designed study of needs can be essential if expensive errors in terms of time, money, and personnel are to be avoided.

Needs assessment ought to focus on some aspect of a program. For example, a study of needs might center on a classroom and be carried out by the teacher; or a committee might study schoolwide needs. Actually, the committee approach is probably better — for several reasons. First, it would allow a more coordinated approach. (For example, with coordinated scheduling, the same pieces of equipment can be used for two or more activities — such as music education, school finance, and the library — even though the needs may be very different.) Second, a committee approach would tend to create a group of people who can provide a broader base of expertise than a single person. Third, broader involvement of personnel in planning will most likely lead to a wider base of support within the school community.

One common approach to studying needs is to compare the current situation with what might be more desirable. Using this method, discrepancies between what is and what ought to be are studied.[3] Table 4.1 shows an example of such a study. Basically, the method involves collecting information with which to

TABLE 4.1
OUTLINE OF A COMPUTER NEEDS STUDY FOR ADULT EDUCATION IN A SCHOOL DISTRICT
Program or School: <u>Adult Education Program, XYZ School District</u>

Level	Present conditions	Desired conditions

1 Area(s) of concern
  Adult education
	Evening adult education classes
	Limited resources
	Limited access by many
	  potential students to courses
	  because of the times they
	  can be offered
		More general availability
		  of courses

**2 Goals and objectives of
  each area of concern**
	Increased awareness of the
	  effects of technology on
	  society
		Greater capacity for
		  individualization to
		  relate to each
		  participant's
		  occupation

3 Activities to meet objectives	Offer class two nights per week
	  (fall and spring semester)
	Discuss applications of
	  technology
	Show films and give
	  demonstrations
		More "hands-on"
		  computer experience
		  for students
		Activities involving
		  specific occupations
		  represented by
		  participants

make rational decisions. The following three levels are studied, each one in terms of what is currently being done and what would be more desirable:

1 *Areas of concern:* Since computers can be applied to virtually anything from art, science, or language classes to management of athletic programs, it is a good idea to identify areas of direct concern. For example, a high school that does not offer a business education program would probably not emphasize instruction in accounting. On the other hand, such a school might want to have an individualized accounting course available to those few students each year who wish to learn something about the subject.

2 *Goals and objectives for the areas identified:* Here we are concerned with major goals and objectives of the program. For example, let us say that a foreign-language department has the goal of offering students high-quality training in foreign languages. One objective that might come under this goal would be for the students to recognize and use a working vocabulary of at least 2000 words in the language at the end of the first year of study.

3 *Activities to meet the objectives:* Here, what is being done and what is desirable would be addressed. For example, the foreign-language department might currently be doing a number of vocabulary activities, such as flash cards, weekly examinations, and contests. However, more opportunity for individual and group study of vocabulary might be desirable.

To illustrate the use of this procedure and the form in Table 4.1 for identifying educational needs, we will consider a school district's adult education program. Under *Areas of concern* in Table 4.1, adult education has been listed. According to the entries in the second column, courses are offered in the evenings, with limited resources. Further, these courses offer limited access to potential students because of the times when they are offered. The school district wants to make the courses available to more people in the future. The current goal of the program is to increase adults' awareness of the role of technology in society. A greater degree of individualization of the program is desired, so that participants may become able to explore the relationship of technology to their own jobs. The school district offers early evening courses during the fall and spring semester. The courses are well attended. However, to meet the desired objective of greater participation, the courses would have to be structured so that people could take them at alternative times.

In Table 4.1, there are certain discrepancies between what is desired and the current situation. Computers might be used to resolve these discrepancies. Computers are capable of making individualized instruction available whenever people want to take it. Further, the simulation capabilities of computers would make hands-on experience possible. In addition, because computers allow a student to work at his or her own pace, a degree of individualized tailoring of instruction would occur naturally.

Determining Which Needs Can Be Met by Computers

Once *what* is needed has been clarified, consideration may be directed to *how* computers can help to meet those needs. Although the modern microcomputer is not very expensive in terms of what it can do — when compared with machines that have been available over the last few years — it is still not so inexpensive that its cost-effectiveness can be assumed in all situations. Many things can be done better without a computer. For example, putting a complete dictionary on a computer so that students could find definitions electronically would be more expensive in terms of time and resources, and no more efficient, than giving each student a copy of the latest unabridged edition. Further, sometimes computerized learning is not exactly the learning that is desired. (To get a sense of this, you need only consider whether you would rather fly with a newly licensed pilot who had been trained only on a computerized flight simulator, or with one who has spent some time learning to fly in real airplanes.) Thus, it is important to determine how and when computers will be utilized in regard to the identified needs.

No potential source of information should be overlooked. Colleagues in other schools and professional groups can provide useful information. A variety of magazines and publications can also be of assistance. Many of these publications are listed in this book (see Chapter 8, for example). Also, people who use computers — such as teachers who use microcomputers at another school, or experts in computerized instruction at a nearby university or the state department of education – might be consulted. A local computer store will probably be of assistance in locating computer users' clubs; and its staff might have suggestions about how a school's needs can be met. (However, at this stage one should not get carried away by the urge to buy.)

Once the needs are known, consideration should be given to whether and how computers can be part of the ways that needs will be met. Table 4.2 (page 78) shows some typical areas of application of microcomputers in schools; it also indicates which personnel need access to the equipment if a given implementation is to be successful. For example, if a teacher wants to provide individualized drill in multiplication, then each student who is to receive the drill must have access to the computer. This does not mean that any one student should have access to the computer at all times, but rather that the computer can be used by only one student at a time. Table 4.2 also gives estimates of the random-access-memory (RAM) requirements for such applications. These estimates are based on the experience of the authors and others.[4] One should keep in mind, however, that certain computers require more space for their disk operating systems or software-based programming language. These estimates are therefore highly variable between computer systems. For example, let's say that we have a microcomputer with 48 kilobytes (48K) of memory. If the BASIC programming language must be loaded into memory to run a program written in BASIC, and the language takes up 10K of memory, only 38K will remain available. Further, if the program itself requires 10K of memory, it cannot be run on a system with less than 20K (that is, 10K for BASIC and 10K for the program). It is very likely that additional space in memory will be required for the computer to actually perform the program.

Figure 4.1 (page 79) shows the amount of memory required for various purposes by a computer programmed to provide drill in arithmetic. The computer is programmed to generate multiplication examples for the student. When the student's response to each example has been typed at the keyboard, the computer either presents a new example if the answer was correct, or gives the correct answer and presents the item again. It stores in its memory the number of correct responses the student has made. Additionally, at the bottom of the screen, it shows the percentage of correct responses. It can be seen in Figure 4.1 that the program requires a minimum of 32K of memory. Although the program itself takes up only 10K, the remainder is needed for the disk operating system, the necessary work space, and the language (BASIC).

MAKING A PLAN

Using what has been learned in the needs study, planning can begin to meet those needs for which microcomputers can be of assistance. At this stage, it is wise to consider whether additional expertise would be helpful. If a few microcomputers with fairly standard applications will suffice, then a teacher with some

TABLE 4.2

TYPICAL APPLICATIONS OF COMPUTERS IN SCHOOL SETTINGS WITH MEMORY AND ACCESSIBILITY REQUIREMENTS

Application	Accessibility	RAM memory	Special hardware and peripherals
1 Instruction			
a Drill, CAI, programming	Single student	16–48K	None
b Problem-solving, tutorials, simulations, graphics programming, testing	Single and small groups of students	16–48K	Color graphics, color CRT
2 Administration			
a Payroll	Office staff	48–128K	Tractor-feed high-speed printer
b Finance	Office staff	64–128K	High speed printer
c Planning	Office staff	48–64K	Printer
d Maintenance	Administrators, maintenance staff	64–128K	Printer
e Students' records	Guidance and teaching staff	64–256K	Printer
f Word processing	Clerks, typists	64–128K	High-quality printer
g General administration	Clerks and administrators	64–128K	Printer
3 Library card index	Students and teachers	48–128K	
4 Special education			
a In school			
(1) Individual educational programs (IEP)	Teachers and program committee	64K	Printer
(2) IEP management	Regular and special education teachers	64K	Printer
(3) General educational applications	Single student	16–48K	Voice synthesizer, hard disk storage, unique input-output devices
(4) Adaptive programming	Student and teacher	32–64K	Unique input-output devices, e.g., light pen, pressure-sensitive panels, toggles, voice synthesis

b Homebound
    (1) Adaptive programs
    (2) Monitoring progress
    (3) Testing
    (4) Communications
	Each student and teacher	32–64K	Printer, modem, unique input-output

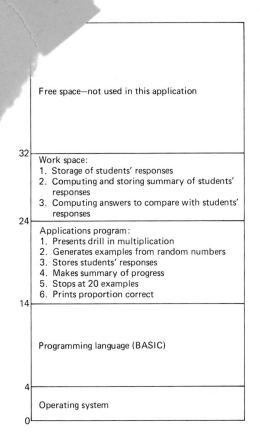

Free space—not used in this application

32

Work space:
1. Storage of students' responses
2. Computing and storing summary of students' responses
3. Computing answers to compare with students' responses

24

Applications program:
1. Presents drill in multiplication
2. Generates examples from random numbers
3. Stores students' responses
4. Makes summary of progress
5. Stops at 20 examples
6. Prints proportion correct

14

Programming language (BASIC)

4

Operating system

0

FIGURE 4.1
Distribution of memory in a 64K computer. (Numbers are only illustrative and do not apply to any particular computer or application.)

familiarity with microcomputers, or a hobbyist, might help. On the other hand, more complicated applications may require additional assistance. For large-scale computing applications, assistance from a well-qualified professional computer consultant is essential.

Let us now look at several important aspects of planning.

Begin with What Is Available

Planners should consider any existing systems in the school or district. If, for example, there is a minicomputer in the district that is currently being used for testing students, it might be worthwhile to determine the costs of using that system on a part-time basis. If the terminals and software that would be required already exist, this might be a better alternative than purchasing new systems. On the other hand, it might be much cheaper to start new with microcomputers. The existing system might require too great an expenditure to equip and maintain it to meet the needs that have been identified. It has been found that even a free computer can be more expensive than purchasing a new one that would meet recognized needs more precisely.[5]

Hardware and Software Considerations

Software has already been developed for a large variety of microcomputer applications. A list of many of these applications is given in Table 4.3. If an application is on this list, software for it that will run on some machine probably exists. Quality varies, however. For unique applications, software does not exist and must be written. This will be expensive in terms of staff time, the cost of a consultant, or both.

Some people say that computer *hardware* should be selected only after the machine requirements for running specific programs have been determined. In other words, one should go shopping for the best software to meet the recognized needs, and then select a machine that will run the software. Others say that anyone getting ready to purchase computers should look at the peripheral devices a system will be capable of operating. A high degree of flexibility in adding peripherals will permit greater expandability and a longer useful life for

TABLE 4.3
USES OF COMPUTERS IN EDUCATIONAL SETTINGS

Teaching and learning	Administration	Support services
Drill and practice	Personnel records	Guidance records
Testing	Payroll records	Students' records
Tutorials	Payroll preparation	Vocational information
Word processing	Word processing	College information
Computer-managed instruction (CMI)	Attendance records	Test score files
	School calendar planning	Food services records
Computer programming	Long-term planning	Library search and retrieval
Computer literacy instruction	Statistical analysis	
Low-incidence courses	Budget planning	Library loan records
Instructional simulations	Fire inspection records	
Educational games	Bus scheduling	
Class demonstrations	Mailing lists	
Music writing	Class scheduling	
Homebound instruction	Files maintenance	
Problem solving	Accounts (payable and receivable)	
Special education programming		
Special tutoring	Staff assignments	

the computer. Still others recommend finding the newest, most advanced com-
put system on the market, arguing that such a system will not become obso-
l re established model. The present authors take the posi-
op for a package of hardware, software, and peripherals
ed needs, work well together, permit expansion of the
ue to be useful for some time.

Whether to select a standard machine for the school or district is an important consideration. There are some advantages to having everyone use the
same kind of computer. Among these are software compatability and a pool of
users who can share their knowledge and experience. Further, if everyone uses
the same kind of machine, a group can use funds more effectively by purchasing
only a few of the peripherals and software that will be used infrequently, and
then sharing these as they are needed. Another advantage is that if one component or machine breaks down, another can be borrowed and used in its
place, so that scheduled activities are not disrupted. Finally, if everyone uses the
same equipment, discounts for large purchases may be possible.

However, there are advantages to having several different kinds of machines
in a school. Different kinds of computers would expose the students to different
operating systems, different kinds of peripherals, and variations in the configu-
rations of computer systems. Further, some machines were designed with certain applications in mind. Although they are capable of doing other things, it is
sometimes difficult and costly to implement those other applications on them.
For example, systems designed primarily for home use are sometimes outfitted
to display 30 to 40 characters per line on the screen. Word processing, on the
other hand, is easier when the image on the CRT screen can be made to appear
like a typed page. Thus, while word processing is possible on a computer producing a 40-column display, 70 or 80 characters per line would be preferable.
There are devices that will change the 40-column display into 80. However, they
add to the cost of a system. A similar situation exists with graphics. Not all microcomputers have a built-in ability to place pictures on the screen. Some have
better graphics than others. Some computers will produce excellent graphics on
a CRT but will not print them on a printer. Thus, to gain flexibility of application,
it is often useful to have more then one kind of computer available.

Large versus Small Computers for Instruction

Although this book is primarily about microcomputers, larger computers may
already be available in a school. Often schools that use large central computers
will do so on a time-sharing basis. A time-sharing system is one in which a reasonably large computer is shared simultaneously by many users, often for different purposes. The district may own the computer or rent time on it, and one
or several terminals may be located in the school. A terminal usually looks something like a microcomputer and may in fact be a microcomputer outfitted with
a modem. When time is rented on a large computer, a fee is usually charged

each time the computer is used. There are also costs for telephone lines, connection fees, special software, and so on.

The major advantage of accessing a time-sharing system is that it does not saddle the district with any of the maintenance headaches associated with owning a large computer. Further, the computer company may have a large library of high-quality software available to subscribers. Another consideration is that since the central processor and memory in such a system are usually larger than in a microcomputer, the user might be able to do more things (such as handling larger databases). Finally, the cost of setting up a terminal might be less then the cost of setting up a microcomputer system for a particular application.

However, there can be disadvantages to time sharing. First, the expense of installing, maintaining, and using telephone lines is often greater than the cost of purchasing microcomputers. Second, when the time-shared system breaks down or otherwise becomes unavailable for use, it does so for all users of the system. Thus, a temporary replacement system cannot be borrowed from the teacher in the next room or the media center, as is possible with microcomputers. Third, many terminals do not have the graphics or sound capabilities of many microcomputers, and these features are extremely useful for instructional programming.

Another problem for some time-sharing applications is security of the information that is stored. Since the terminals are all connected to the same computer system by telephone lines, everyone will have access to whatever the system stores. Most shared systems are protected by passwords and codes. Although these protection systems have not proven completely effective in the past, they provide enough security for most educational applications.

Coordination of Needs and Plans

It is important that any plans made ultimately reflect recognized needs. Further, these needs should be matched with various hardware and software combinations in order to determine the best alternatives. One way to do this is to list the needs and then identify how computers can help, what equipment would be needed for implementation, and whether any known software exists to support implementation.

Table 4.4 shows an attempt to match needs with computerized solutions. Areas of expected application of computers are listed in the first column, followed by the identified need for each area. The specific hardware functions that could be applied to the needs are identified in the third column, followed by an indication of whether or not software is available for that function.

Studying the Alternatives

On the basis of data like those listed in Table 4.4, it is possible to identify the characteristics of the system which are needed. Let us look at this sample situation to see how that is done.

TABLE 4.4
SYSTEMATIC ANALYSIS OF RECOGNIZED NEEDS

Area of application	Need	Computer system functions	Availability of software
1 Instructional			
a Mathematics drill	Individual practice	Provide instruction	Yes
b Spelling drill	Individual practice	Provide instruction	Yes
c Business arithmetic	Simulation	Provide instruction	Yes
d Science stimulation	Graphics demonstrations	Provide instruction	Yes
2 Administration			
a Word processing	Typing, forms	Print (high-quality)	Yes
b Payroll	40 employees biweekly	Print checks and records	Yes
c Accounting	$800,000 budget	Keep entries and disbursements	Yes
d Inventory	2 schools, motor pool	Inventory and dispositions	No
e Mailing	School mailings	Make labels	Yes
3 Guidance			
a Students' records	Index by students	Store and retrieve	Yes
b Occupational data	Index by career	Store and retrieve	Yes
c College data	Index by location, tuition costs, subject	Store and retrieve	Yes
4 Special Education			
a Mathematics drill	Individualization	Provide instruction	Yes
b Homebound instruction	Two-way communication between home and school	Send and receive tests, lessons, assignments	Yes

Starting with the column headed *Availability of software,* we find that software packages already exist for nearly every need. This is ideal. In real life it often does not turn out that way. If we were to look at the advertising for these software packages, review them at a computer store, or look at one of the many software atlases or magazine reviews, we would find a description of the hardware required by each. For example, we can guess from Tables 4.2 and 4.4 and the software packages we have identified that for basic instructional needs, 16K to 48K of RAM would suffice. On the other hand, needs for internal computer memory go as high as 256K for some functions requiring larger databases (such as students' records). Only the instructional and special education needs require graphics. Only the homebound instruction application requires modems. In addition, a printer that is capable of producing high-quality documents for the administrative area would be desirable, while the other functions could probably be satisfactorily served with a less expensive printer.

Probably not all needs can be optimally matched with available hardware and software. Therefore, before going any further, planners should set priorities. For example, instructional applications are often performed most satisfactorily by

TABLE 4.5

ANALYSIS OF ALTERNATIVES FOR MEETING NEEDS FOR COMPUTERS IN EDUCATIONAL SETTINGS

Option	Hardware and peripherals	Software availability	Expandability	Price
1 A single system for all requirements; brand W has most general capabilities	Brand W computer comes with 128K RAM, keyboard, green screen CRT. Purchase: dot-matrix printer 1 letter-quality printer (for admin) 1 5MB hard disk 1 5¼″ floppy disk	Word Processor Index File School Finance Student Records PILOT language Planning & forecasting CMI Vocational Guidance	Can add: Modem Color monitor Sound Color graphics PASCAL language	$4500 per system (includes 7 dot-matrix printers) $1750 letter-quality printer
			Total for 7 systems = $31,500 (+$1750)	
2 Two kinds of systems: **a** Instructional (4 systems)	Brand X computer comes with 48K RAM, color graphics, standard keyboard, game paddles, BASIC Purchase: Color monitors, 5¼″ floppy disk, cassette tape recorder, sound synthesizer, printer	Pilot Classroom management	Can add: 16–80K RAM Hard disk Modem Color plotter Graphic tablet	$1550 × 4
			Cost of four systems = $6200	
b Guidance and administration (3 systems)	Brand Y computer comes with 128K RAM, built-in black and white or green screen CRT, 96-keyboard, 10-MB hard disk Purchase high-quality printer, 5¼″ floppy	Word processor Spread sheet Index file Finance programs Scheduling resources Students' record Vocational guidance	Can add: Modem Printer buffer Remote terminal system	$5100 × 3
			Cost of 3 systems = $15,300 Total for 7 systems = $21,500	

TABLE 4.5
CONTINUED

Option	Hardware and peripherals	Software availability	Expandability	Price
3 Three kinds of machines:				
a Instructional (4 systems)	Same as brand X	Same as brand X	Same as brand X	$6200 for 4 systems
b Administrative (2 systems)	Same as brand Y	Same as brand Y	Same as brand Y	$10,200 for 2 systems
c Guidance (1 system)	Brand Z computer comes with 64K RAM, green screen CRT, standard keyboard, disks Purchase: dot-matrix printer	Word processing Vocational file Database management system	Modem Remote terminal Graphics Additional memory to 256K	$2750 for one system
			Grand total for 7 systems = $19,150	

systems that may not have the characteristics of the best business systems. Setting priorities will help establish which characteristics of systems to emphasize.

At least three options are available:

1 Choose the same computer for every application.

2 Settle on two or more kinds of computers, at least one with high-quality graphics for instructional use and another with greater memory for applications requiring large databases.

3 Purchase different systems for each application.

Suppose that a school system analyzed these three options and determined that its needs for seven microcomputers could best be met by three different kinds of computers. Four of one kind were selected for instructional uses, one of a second type for the guidance program, and two of a third type to meet administrative requirements. The school system was able to reach this decision by analyzing the costs and capabilities of each of the three options. This analysis is summarized in Table 4.5.

Table 4.5 shows that the first option is most expensive. Brand W computer has the most capabilities. Because of this, it is the most expensive of the four systems that were considered (brands W, X, Y, and Z). However, none of the recognized needs requires so much computer capability. For example, the instructional system requires only 16K to 48K and graphics, whereas the administrative system has less need for graphics but much more need for additional memory. Further, option 1 requires purchase of an additional letter-quality printer to meet administrative needs. Therefore, option 1 is inefficient in terms of cost, because more computing capability is being purchased than is needed.

Using two kinds of systems — option 2 — represents a somewhat better use of funds. A less expensive computer system (brand X) can be purchased for instruction, and a more capable computer can be obtained for administration and guidance. The total cost for seven computers is lower than in option 1.

The third option utilizes three different computer systems for guidance, instructional, and administrative needs. This solution provides enough computer power for each need and gives flexibility for later expansion. Further, option 3 can be provided at a considerably lower cost than options 1 and 2.

The column headed *Expandability* in Table 4.5 should be given particular attention. A desirable system will be capable of being expanded to serve future needs. One of the most expensive kinds of errors that can be made in planning is not to provide for the future, and then to have to discard a whole system because it is incapable of doing what is required.

Special Equipment

Software vendors often list the minimum system necessary to run a particular piece of software. To realize the full potential of the software may require additional hardware. For example, the manual for one program that produces mailing labels says only that the program will run on a particular brand of computer. It does not say that the user will need to purchase a printer and the equipment necessary to connect a printer to the computer (such as cables and connectors) in order to make mailing labels. Sometimes, information about system requirements is omitted because it would appear to be common sense (obviously, you need a *printer* to *print* mailing labels). But occasionally such information is omitted because it would make the package seem more expensive. For example, some programs require special cards inserted into slots in the main computer board (memory expansion card, disk emulator, CPU emulator, special buffer, 80-column card, etc.). The cost of some of these cards can be substantial, in some cases exceeding the price of the software and even that of the computer.

Figure 4.2 shows the kind of description of hardware requirements typically found in a software manual. Usually this information is located in the first few pages or in an appendix. This information should be used to estimate the actual cost of purchasing software to go with the computer system.

Speed and Obsolescence

Many people are understandably awed by the rapid development of new technology in recent years. They fear that any computer purchased today will be obsolete by tomorrow morning. It is true that innovations have been occurring in this field almost daily. However, it is not true that all these innovations nec-

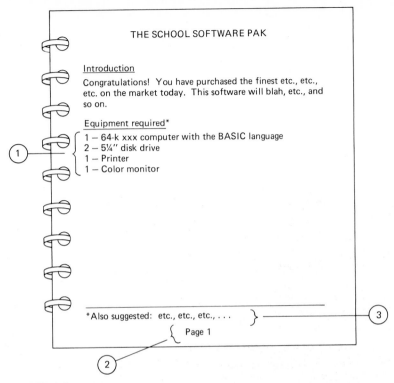

THE SCHOOL SOFTWARE PAK

Introduction

Congratulations! You have purchased the finest etc., etc., etc. on the market today. This software will blah, etc., and so on.

Equipment required*

1 — 64-k xxx computer with the BASIC language
2 — 5¼" disk drive
1 — Printer
1 — Color monitor

*Also suggested: etc., etc., etc., . . .

Page 1

FIGURE 4.2
The equipment required to operate a software package should (1) indicate the most desirable system configuration, (2) appear early in the documentation of software manual, and (3) indicate additional hardware requirements.

essarily affect every application. For example, a new way of programming graphics does not necessarily affect the quality of an existing word processor. Even a design for a faster keyboard does not make present keyboards obsolete, since an existing keyboard may already carry information five to ten times faster than most people can type it.

In a field where time is calculated in milliseconds and microseconds, the processing speed of equipment is sometimes not a factor worthy of consideration. When machines interact with people after relatively few processing steps, as in many instructional applications, users would have difficulty telling whether a particular computer was fast or slow relative to other machines. However, speed may be a factor to consider when there are going to be many processing steps, as in the alphabetizing of a mailing list. Some computers can do this kind of thing much faster than others, and innovations for faster processing might be worthy of consideration in such applications.

Second Thoughts

When people make plans, they often replay alternatives in their minds, even after the decisions seem obvious. This would not be unusual for someone planning to introduce new applications of microcomputers in an educational setting. Such second thoughts can sometimes be helpful in last-minute planning, and once in a while they can help to avoid disaster. For example, in our discussion of planning, we have not yet considered whether people will accept new ways of doing things with microcomputers. This is an important but complicated issue. Any change in established procedures will require the generation of interest and effort. Therefore, the development of enthusiasm and willingness to participate among teachers, students, and parents should be a part of each new plan for introducing microcomputer applications in schools.

The length of time students can be expected to profitably work at a computer terminal or microcomputer might also provoke some second thoughts. Although this is influenced by the nature of the tasks being performed on the computer, there is mounting evidence that 30 minutes to 1 hour per day, preferably in 10- or 15-minute units, may be optimal for intensive individualized instruction from a computer.[6] Computers cannot be expected to provide complete educational programs, at least not at present.

It is also a good idea to reconsider whether there are any less expensive, or more traditional, methods that could meet the needs that have been identified. The novelty of computers can be exciting, and often perceived need for a computer is based more on emotion than on reason. For example, although a computer is a great aid in doing calcuations, it can offer a real benefit over a calculator only when a large number of repetitious calculations must be performed. Adding or multiplying a couple of numbers is done more quickly, more easily, and less expensively on a calculator. Applications like placing all the words in a dictionary on the computer sound impressive, but are they necessary? You can probably look up a meaning in a dictionary more quickly than you could set up the program in a computer, type in the necessary commands, and wait for the definition to appear on the CRT screen. Besides, using a dictionary will probably not go out of style for some time, and it is a good skill for students to learn. (On the other hand, when a dictionary program is part of a word processing program, it can be extremely useful for checking spelling and definitions while a document is being prepared.)

It is good to have second thoughts about the options and priorities at this stage. From this point on, planners are beginning to think about specific hardware and software, and to some degree they should be committed to the idea of implementing a computerized solution for the needs that have been identified.

SELECTING AND DESIGNING A SYSTEM

To this point, we have analyzed needs, studied applications, developed options for meeting the needs, and done some rethinking. Now it is time to decide on the system that will be used. In this section some guidelines and suggestions for successfully navigating this stage are provided.

Getting Necessary Information about Products

Just about every computer will process data. Computers differ in how quickly they will do this, how many and what kinds of peripheral equipment they will operate, what kinds of pictorial images (or graphics) they will produce, how much software is available to run on them, and other characteristics. Even if a particular computer is not designed to do something, it can probably be made to perform that function if one is willing to pay for designing the necessary software, peripherals, and interfaces.

Asking the right questions is important in getting information about microcomputers. Simply asking whether a computer can perform a particular function may produce no useful information. For example, a question like, "Can this computer produce three-dimensional line drawings of various shapes when the required dimensions are given?" will almost invariably bring the response, "Of course!" Buying a computer is different from buying a car because what a car can do is well known: it can provide transportation. To be sure, a computer also has definite functions that make it a computer (such as the ability to transfer binary data from one memory location to another with lightning speed); but people do not ordinarily buy computers for those functions. Rather, computers are usually bought because they are capable of doing many useful things with the proper software and peripherals. For example, the same computer that can be made into an instrument for synthesizing music can with other software be turned into a sophisticated system for monitoring the scheduling and maintenance of a school system's buses. Children can use a computer to play games, and with the right software the same machine will monitor the functioning of a school building's heating and air conditioning. Thus, the proper question about a computer should not be "Will it . . . ?" but rather, "How can I get it to . . . ?" (See Figure 4.3.)

Keeping this point in mind will help planners extract information from advertising brochures and the persuasive arguments of salespersons. Advertising and sales information about equipment or software packages can be useful, but one should not rely solely on these sources. Local people should be sought out who use computers in applications similar to those being considered. Microcomputer magazines can also be helpful resources. Finally, it would be worthwhile to contact one or several of the agencies that have been set up specifically to help schools implement microcomputer applications. (Many of the sources and resources that could be helpful to those beginning to use computers are discussed in Chapter 8.) Another place to go for information might be the state department of education. Many departments of education have organized offices of instructional computing or instructional technology to assist local schools in purchasing and using educational technology.

FIGURE 4.3
Most computers will be able to do anything a computer can be reasonably expected
to do, but they must be properly programmed.

A Sample Guidesheet for Specific Concerns

In addition to the equipment itself, there are a number of specific concerns that must be addressed. Among these are space and environmental needs, costs, expandability, training required for users, reliability, service, languages and programs available, documentation, and display capabilities (including graphics and character sets). Table 4.6 is an example of a guidesheet that might be used to help determine the adequacy of a potential system. Such a sheet could be filled out for each system being considered.

Each aspect of the hardware would be described under *Characteristics*. The column headed *Comments* should contain any notes that relate to the capability of the equipment in terms of what is needed. A point system (the third column in Table 4.6) might be devised to indicate the quality of each item regarding the identified needs. The rating system might be designed so that a low number would be assigned to an unfavorable characteristic or an unimportant one, and higher numbers to each item that is more favorable and important, using a scale from 1 to 10. Zero would indicate that the machine has no capability in a particular category. The ratings would be placed under *Points,* and the scores on each sheet totalled. With this method, the best system for the identified needs might be the one with the highest total score. However, ratings for single items are important. Further, care should be taken not to attach too much importance to small differences, since ratings of this type may be imprecise or subjective.

The items on the checklist in Table 4.6 may, of course, be augmented or arranged differently as the need arises. In the column headed *Characteristics,*

TABLE 4.6
GUIDESHEET FOR SELECTING MICROCOMPUTER SYSTEMS

Item	Characteristics	Comments	Points (1–10)

1 Computer
  a RAM
  b CPU
  c Expansion capability
  d Other			

2 CRT			

3 Keyboard
  a Number of keys
  b Standard layout
  c Special keys
  d Calculator keyboard			

4 Printer			
5 Alternative input devices			
6 Graphics capability			
7 Sound capability			

8 External Storage
  a Tape
  b Floppy disk
  c Hard disk			

9 Character sets			
10 Telecommunications devices			
11 Expandability			
12 Operation system			
13 Programming languages			
14 Software			
15 Other considerations			

only those that would affect planned applications should be listed. Some of the items in the list might require clarification. For that reason, explanations are given below.

   1 *Computer:* This includes all items that constitute the computer itself — that is, the CPU, RAM memory, capability for expansion of memory, special processors, etc. Processing speed might also be a consideration. All microprocessors execute instructions very quickly by human standards. However, when an extraordinarily large amount of data must be processed (as in an inventory program), processing speed can become an important consideration.

2 *CRT:* Monitors, or CRTs, for displaying computer output on a screen come in two basic types. One provides a full-color display, the other only one color (usually white, green, or amber on a black background). Full-color displays are particularly useful for educational programming. However, single-color displays are useful for text-oriented applications such as word processing. Further, green and amber displays are considered more restful to the eyes for applications requiring watching the screen for a long period of time (i.e., more than 1 hour). Degree of resolution (detail) may also be important.

3 *Keyboard:* Computer keyboards are arranged much like those found on typewriters. However, differences may occur in the placement of certain keys (e.g., return or shift keys, or numbers and special symbols). In addition, some computer keyboards include a calculator-like keyboard of ten or twelve keys to facilitate entry of numerical data. Many keyboards are designed with special-feature keys that are programmed during manufacture to represent frequently used words in programming (e.g., PRINT, SAVE, LIST, RUN,); and many have keys that users can program to fit their own needs. Word processing is best done on machines with keyboards like those on typewriters. Such keyboards will have raised plastic keys of the proper size and shape for typing. Other keyboard surfaces are available. For example, some computer keyboards have smooth, touch-sensitive plastic surfaces. This kind of keyboard is most desirable in environments where there is potential for damage to conventional keyboards because of dust (e.g., a wood shop classroom), dampness (e.g., a home economics kitchen), or the presence of young children.

4 *Printer:* Special considerations with regard to printers include capability for producing graphics, inverse printing, and colors. Some printers are fairly good at plotting lines, graphs, and pictures. Some have special foreign-language character sets that would be useful to foreign-language classes. Printing speed varies considerably from one machine to another.

5 *Alternative input devices:* Input devices include game paddles, joysticks, and light pens as alternatives to the keyboard. Such alternatives can be particularly useful with young children and handicapped students. Another hand-held device known as a *mouse* is particularly useful for moving a cursor on a screen.

6 *Graphics capability:* For many educational applications, graphics capability is essential. Some computers do not handle graphics easily or are not capable of producing color images. Such computers would be less satisfactory for teaching mechanical drawing, for example, than ones with better graphics capability. Simulations, especially in science, tend to require color graphics.

7 *Sound capability:* Some computers can produce a variety of sounds and music. This can be extremely helpful for training applications. Sound can enliven instruction, and it can be used to make simulations more realistic. Also, with the proper programming, a computer that can produce sound can be used in music and language instruction and in the instruction of the visually handicapped.

8 *External storage:* The greater the variety of external storage devices available for a computer, the more possibilities there are for using the computer to store and retrieve information. Applications such as maintenance of students' files and school financial records are best done with large storage devices like hard disks. On the other hand, the capability to store and retrieve programs on cassette tape provides an inexpensive method of data storage suitable for many classroom applications.

9 *Character sets:* Special character sets are essential for foreign-language and certain mathematics instruction (e.g., special symbols, accent marks, square root symbols, Greek letters).

10 *Telecommunications devices:* Capability for telecommunications permits computers to communicate with each other through telephone lines. If a multi-user system is envisioned, or if several computers must be able to communicate and exchange information, telecommunications capability using modem equipment must be possible.

11 *Expandability:* The system should be capable of being expanded to meet future needs. Expandability might involve videodisk or videotape interfacing, connection to sound-producing equipment, laboratory devices for monitoring experiments, etc.

12 *Operating system:* The operating system of a computer consists of programs partly or completely in ROM that determine how the computer will work. It is important to know whether the operating systems of programs and computers are compatible.

13 *Programming language:* The more languages a computer can use, the more software there tends to be for it. Many languages are available for use with microcomputers. BASIC (Beginner's All-Purpose Symbolic Instruction Code) is a language most microcomputers can use. Pascal is a more sophisticated language than BASIC. It requires more advanced programming skills to be used effectively. PILOT (*P*rogrammed *I*nquiry *L*earning *or* *T*eaching) is one of a group of languages specially designed for course authoring. (Computer languages are discussed in Chapter 9.)

14 *Software:* The larger the pool of existing software, the more possibilities there are for using the computer. If software cannot be found for the desired applications, then it will have to be written. This can bring added headaches and be a potential source of frustration. When an existing software package is purchased, one can be reasonably sure of its cost, reliability (at least by reputation), and equipment requirements. High-quality software is difficult and time-consuming to develop. The cost of custom-designed software cannot be overestimated, even if the development will be done by teachers and students and the school does not expect to incur any direct costs. Therefore, a good idea would be to search for as many suitable software packages as can be found for each application. The versatility, cost, and availability of these programs should cer-

FIGURE 4.4
Software must be compatible with the system on which it will operate.

tainly contribute to the selection of a system. Many experts advocate selecting software first and then locating a machine that will run it. (See Figure 4.4.)

15 *Other considerations:* Among the other concerns are (a) the resources that will be required; (b) documentation; (c) reliability; (d) warranties; and (e) choosing a dealer. We will complete our list by looking at each of these.

a *Resource* needs that are often overlooked have to do with personnel, time, space, and actual, total dollar costs for all aspects of the system — including hardware, software, training, etc. The degree of training required to operate the system in the ways that are proposed should be carefully evaluated. Before any equipment is purchased, one should know where it will be placed, whether the environment the computer needs can be provided at that location, and whether the computer will be accessible to those who use it. Computers are extremely sensitive to static electricity and also humidity. Carpets that produce static electricity when walked upon should be avoided. A room in a damp basement would not be suitable for a computer (but not all basements are damp). Any requirements for special furniture, outlets, power supplies, grounding, etc., should be identified. It might help to have someone who knows about computers look at the proposed setting before the equipment is put in place.

b The quality of the *documentation* that comes with the system should be evaluated. Can it be understood by those who will need to use it? Does it go far enough in explaining all the features of the computer and how to use the software and the operating system? Many software packages include documentation in the program. This feature can be useful when people will be using the software who have not had a chance to study the manuals (users of a computerized library index system, for instance). However, placing the documentation in the program may require a larger memory to run the program.

c *Reliability* refers to *dependabilty*. To put it another way, how long can the system be expected to operate without a breakdown, and how long would it take to repair? This kind of information can sometimes be found in reviews in magazines and other publications.

d *Warranties* vary greatly. Some computer companies honor warranties only if the computer was purchased from a dealer authorized by them. Some warranties are for a period of 90 days from the date of purchase; others are in effect for 1 year or more. Watch for conditions placed on a warranty (for instance, that the computer can be transported only in the carton provided by the factory) which could void the warranty if violated.

e The quality of the *dealer* should be evaluated — particularly the dealer's past service. Services provided by a dealer include assistance with installation, repair, system expansion, ordering of special components and software, demonstrations of systems and software, technical information about products, and training programs for customers. Ask to speak to others who have used a particular dealer. A full-service, high-quality dealer is preferable to one who offers scanty service at a slightly lower price.

Some Final Considerations

We have left some things until last because they do not directly concern choosing an alternative, although they should be part of the selection process. These include training of personnel and users, accessibility, maintenance, and security.

Training Although microcomputers have been designed for simplicity of use (some people call them *user-friendly*), it cannot be assumed that anyone will be able to sit down in front of one, turn it on, and operate it without some training and reading of manuals. (See Figure 4.5.) This is true even for people who are

FIGURE 4.5
Nobody told me about the four books I would have to read before I could make this computer work!

OUT

IN

Miss Kilobyte
Computer teacher

experienced with computers. Each piece of hardware and software comes with its own documentation, including printers, disk drives, special expansion cards, and programs. At least one person should be designated who will read the manuals and become familiar enough with the operation of the machine to assist others in getting started. It is probably not necessary for this person to become an expert programmer. Rather, he or she should concentrate on becoming familiar with the operation of the computer and its peripherals. Further, this person should be responsible for creating a library-like setup, so that the manuals and documentation can be made available to those who will use the equipment.

There is a tendency among educators to look upon anything technical, or mathematical as related, no matter what the subject. Consequently, many mathematics teachers have found themselves charged with the responsibility for activities involving the school's instructional computer. A considerable number of mathematics teachers have enjoyed and willingly accepted this assignment; but one should not assume that mathematics teachers are the only choice. Further, the area of interest of the person taking this responsibility during the selection process must be expected to have an impact on the decisions that are made. For that reason, it is preferable to have a diverse group of teachers and staff involved in selection and training. Another benefit of a diverse group is that it is bound to have an effect on the extent to which the machines are eventually used.

Location and Access   If the system is to have several different kinds of users (such as students in a classroom and a staff in a central office), the location of the machine must be considered. (This was noted under item 15, *Other considerations,* on page 94.) Most microcomputer systems with all their peripherals can easily fit on a desk or table, and so space alone is not likely to be a major consideration. More important considerations are the length of time required by each application, the time of day when specific tasks must be accomplished, the storage of software packages when they are not in use, the number of people the system can serve at one time, the amount of disturbance the presence of the computer might cause to other activities going on in the same space, and the accessibility of the computer to those who will need to use it. Attending to these issues will be part of the selection and design phase.

Security and Maintenance   Finally, security and maintenance are factors that should be considered as part of the selection and design process. Vandalism and theft are problems in schools, and there is no reason to believe that a computer system would be immune. Further, while microcomputers have been designed to require very little maintenance, there are occasional user-level adjustments and practices that can help to keep them operating well. The person who has been given the primary responsibility for setting up the computer could also be given responsibility for user-level maintenance and security.

Two points should be clear. First, someone needs to be in charge. Second, this person will have much to do with such concerns as training, access, storage, and security, and should not be weighted down with so many other responsibilities that these tasks become impossible.

GAINING SUPPORT

Innovations often do not gain acceptance immediately, even when they offer obvious benefits. We are reminded of two business education teachers arguing over whether their school should purchase a word processing program for the computer they were already using to teach inventory record keeping. One argued that a word processing program could augment teaching in the typing classes, since with such a program the computer could display a page on a CRT pretty much as it would look on paper, and students could format letters, tables, and other kinds of documents; learn to set tabs, margins, and so on; and correct their own mistakes. The other teacher was against the idea, arguing simply that "typing on a computer is not typing."

The traditional organization of schools encourages doing things in the old and accepted ways. This organization was well established before educational computers were even thought about. Further, individualization of instruction — something computers can do well — is a relatively new idea in public education. For these reasons, in schools in which there has been little or no interest in educational computing, some efforts will probably be necessary to gain acceptance for computers through publicity and training.

Generally, as familiarity with the equipment increases, so does acceptance of it. It is worth noting that about six months after the discussion described above the teacher who had been opposed to the idea of teaching word processing on a computer attended a workshop on business computers. Shortly afterward, she completely changed her mind, arguing that business education programs which did not emphasize the new technology were going to have difficulty placing their graduates in the work force. This story illustrates why it is important to include training of teachers in any plans for introducing new applications of microcomputers.

Like any other kind of training, computer training for teachers should be designed to fit identified needs. However, teachers in a school are bound to have different backgrounds and therefore different needs for such training. One way to approach this problem would be to offer training initially at two levels. The first level would focus on operating the equipment and software. The second would go into more depth, covering such topics as specific software applications, software evaluation, programming, user-level maintenance, and course development. If no one is available who has the expertise to offer such a course, then it might be approached as a group study project.

Training for teachers should have four goals:

1 The training should demonstrate to teachers the advantages to be gained by using the computer.
2 As part of the training, teachers should be able to operate microcomputers and see them being used by students.
3 The training should emphasize any compatibilty between doing tasks by computer and using traditional methods. (For example, even though a computer may be useful for presenting certain aspects of an algebra program, the students will still use the same textbook and in all likelihood will need more explanation and more practice than students who have been taught with traditional media.)
4 The training should interest teachers in computer applications in the classroom.

When ways to gain support are being considered, parents and students should not be overlooked as allies. Students seem to enjoy working with computers. Further, it is not unusual for some of them to know a considerable amount about computers. Many will have computers at home, and may be able to program them. Others have been reading about them, hearing about them in the media, and seeing them all around — at supermarket checkout counters, in banks, and in other public places. They are also keenly aware of computers through electronic games and toys. Not only can parents provide support for bringing computers into the schools, they will often demand such training. Parents may be familiar with the increasing importance of computers in their work and can probably be called upon to strongly advocate experience with computers for children in the schools.

Finally, to increase acceptance of computers a wide group of school staff members should be involved in planning, as we noted earlier. A single microcomputer in a classroom can be used for many things when the students are gone for the day. The administration can develop bus schedules on it; the cafeteria manager can use it to keep information about menus and ordering; the guidance counselor can use it to maintain a file of students' grades and scores — and these are just a few of the after-school uses of a computer system. Since these tasks may not need to be done during regular school hours, the additional uses need not tie up the computer and prevent students from using it for instruction. Recognizing these kinds of applications can bring increased support for a proposal to obtain microcomputers for a school or to expand existing facilities. (However, one should be aware of the danger that administrative priorities may eventually take over a machine meant for instructional uses, and that administrative uses may conflict with after-hours needs of students.) In sum, it can be said that computers have so many applications in schools that it is no longer as difficult as it once was to gain support for a request for educational computers.

PURCHASING A SYSTEM

Let us assume that you have gone through considerable planning and study to determine which microcomputer system to purchase and have finally made a decision. The next step (assuming that the administration has approved the funding) is to arrange for the actual purchase. Teachers should work closely with the school administration on this matter. There are probably local procedures and arrangements that have been devised for the purchase of equipment and materials for the school. Further, there may be reason to contact the state department of education: for example, state funds may be available if the purchase qualifies for some special program.

Purchasing a New Computer

Two important aspects of purchasing a new computer system are (1) getting the system that is actually wanted and (2) getting the best price. Most vendors do not want to take advantage of buyers, but it is the buyers' responsibility to determine which system is best for their own needs.

Getting the best price can be greatly simplified if there are state or district contracts with set prices. This can eliminate much shopping and uncertainty, and one can deal directly with an authorized vendor who has a reputation for good service. When there are no state or district contracting lists, some shopping may be appropriate. The dealer should be willing to set up a system in the store, or in the school itself, and to demonstrate the operation of the machine and the software packages of interest. It is often possible to get better prices from mail-order houses than local dealers, but the same degree of customer service cannot be expected from a mail-order business.

Many districts have a policy of advertising for bids on large purchases. This requires preparing a *request for proposals* (RFP) which specifies needs. (Sometimes these are *requests for bids*.) The RFP is made available to vendors, who then make written replies called *proposals.* A proposal in this sense is actually an offer to sell products that will meet the specifications in the RFP at a stated price. Proposals from different vendors can be compared and the best offer chosen. The procedures for handling RFPs can be worked out with the people who do the purchasing for the school district.

Purchasing a Used Computer or a Kit

Buyers of a used computer should look for the same kinds of features and characteristics to match their needs as would be provided by a new computer. If a used computer cannot do what is needed without considerable additional expense, then it probably is not a bargain. For a used system, as for a new system, the seller should be willing to demonstrate that the system will operate with the needed software.

Money can be saved sometimes by purchasing a used computer. However, used computer equipment might be difficult to return, repair, or sell. It does not usually come with any warranties, and it may not be eligible for service contracts. Further, specialized parts may be difficult to obtain if the computer has not been made for a few years. On the other hand, used computers of newer vintage do not depreciate in value very rapidly if they are in good condition. Given these various considerations, purchasing a used computer can be a more complicated proposition than buying a new one.

Sometimes a computer will be cheaper in kit form. However, kits take a long time to put together, and they do not always work without adjustment when they are completed. Thus, the same caution given for software applies to hardware: if you can avoid doing it yourself, do so.

SUMMARY

Purchasing a computer system or systems for use in a school requires considerable planning. One must begin with actual educational needs and make sure that computers can meet them, at least in part. There are many unhappy stories about people who purchased computers and then went searching for uses for them. This kind of error is avoidable with proper planning.

Ten steps have been suggested for planning for computers in the classroom. These steps were written by a person who has been involved for several years in bringing microcomputers into classrooms on a statewide basis and are reproduced below in their entirety. They form an excellent summary for this chapter.

Planning for Computers in the Classroom

1 Plan instructional applications rather than technological applications. Begin by identifying a need, realizing that technology may or may not be the solution. Given the ever-increasing capabilities of technology and the lure of another ''new approach,'' we often purchase a solution and then begin looking for a suitable problem to solve. For small classes, a teacher doesn't need a computerized student management system. A mimeographed test or quiz may be more appropriate than a computer-based application. If the initial computer technology experience is not relevant or positive to the user, expensive gear may be relegated to limited use or to the closet.

2 Equipment cost is only part of a proposed application. Too often money appropriate for a computer application is spent solely for equipment, drastically reducing funds available for a successful application. Sad commentaries have been written about computers being left in their original packing cartons for a full school year because of lack of training in equipment operation or classroom application. Generally speaking, expect to spend about as much on planning time, courseware purchasing, in-service training, equipment maintenance, and follow-up support as on equipment.

3 Several factors must be considered in selecting equipment. A prime consideration in the purchase of equipment should be the availability of programs that meet identified needs. Although a particular computer may have many more features than another and cost less, instructional courseware for that computer may not be readily available. Local support and maintenance should also be major considerations. Discount-house purchases can turn out to be the most expensive alternative.

4 Be wary of exaggerated claims for computer courseware. The development of computer courseware for education is still in its infancy. It is best to preview a demonstration program (if available). As a minimum prerequisite to purchase, review evaluations of the program's technical and instructional qualities as well as its content. Because of the current state of the art of courseware production, be alert for errors in content and format.

5 Buy now; wait later. Except in rare circumstances, don't hesitate to buy ''state of the art'' equipment now because you think something better is coming tomorrow. The same decision will face you if you wait. Although technology will continue to advance, your unit will be a wise investment, providing you with three to five years or more of good service. It can take one to three years for design, development, and distribution of high-quality computer classroom programs for new, ''advanced'' microcomputers.

6 Change is a central concept in implementing computer applications successfully. *Implementing change* might be a more appropriate term than *implementing a computer application.* Human nature often implies a resistance to change unless the amount of gain is equal to or greater than the amount of effort required. You can greatly increase your chances for a successful computer application if you involve users in planning, proceed in manageable progressive steps, and provide adequate in-service training and follow-up activities.

7 Plan a broad-based approach to computer implementation. Historically, computers have been introduced into the school setting by an enthusiastic teacher with interest and expertise in computer science, programming, or both. Programs introduced through this approach will often flourish for the duration of the teacher's assignment but then be jeopardized when the teacher leaves or changes roles. For long-term success, it is crucial to integrate a computer application into the curriculum in a formal sense to prevent ''person-dependency.'' Planning in a formal sense should include allocation of resources, assignment of staff, scheduling, and in-service training of large segments of the total staff.

8 Purchase existing computer products rather than developing programs in-house. Many successful low-cost computer programs have been developed in-house by existing staffs. However, it takes one to two years of dedicated training to master a programming language, and two to three years of programming experience to produce a program comparable in quality to those produced by major commercial firms. These companies have a full range of staff, including instructional designers, content experts, systems analysts, and programmers, whose skills are difficult to duplicate locally. Estimates of programming time range from 20 to 200 hours to develop 1 hour of classroom instruction. For selected applications, authoring programs currently available may offer alternatives to existing products.

9 Computers do not replace teachers. Computers can serve as topics of study (computer science, computer literacy, programming) or as classroom tools to aid instruction (drill and practice, tutorials, simulation, testing, problem solving, student management). Combined with a teacher, the computer becomes a powerful instructional tool in the classroom.

10 Introduction of computers requires additional financial resources. As with implementation of any new approach or program, equipment costs, in-service training, supporting materials, and maintenance entail additional expense. These costs are offset, however, by reduced requirements for teachers' time to conduct drill and practice activities, increased numbers of students served by existing staff, improved quality of instructional programs, and expanded opportunities for students to acquire new skills for employment.[7]

NOTES

1   The National Center on Educational Statistics (NCES) of the U. S. Department of Education keeps track of the increase in computers in schools. The NCES report of Sept. 7, 1982, entitled "Instructional Use of Computers in Public Schools," indicated an increase of over 100 percent between the fall of 1980 and the spring of 1982 (from 53,000 to 120,000).

2   Watt, D. H. (1982). Education for citizenship in a computer-based society. In R. J. Seidel, R. E. Anderson, & B. Hunter (Eds.), *Computer literacy.* New York: Academic Press.

3   See: Auvenshine, C. D. E., & Mason, E. J. (1982). Needs assessment in planning rehabilitation services. *Journal of Rehabilitation Administration, 6,* 72–76.

4   For example: Thomas, D., McClain, D., cited in R. Nomeland. (1981). Some considerations in selecting a microcomputer. In J. L. Thomas (Ed.), *Microcomputers in the schools.* Phoenix, AZ: Oryx.

5   Lemos, R. S. (1981). Free computer too expensive. *Educational Computing Magazine, 1*(4), 31–32.

6   Joiner, L. M., Miller, S. R., & Silverstein, B. J. (1981). Potentials and limits of computers. In J. L. Thomas (Ed.), *Microcomputers in the schools.* Phoenix, AZ: Oryx. This position was supported by a field test of computer-based instruction in secondary schools in which students tended to work effectively for about 10 to 15 minutes on computerized learning activities. However, in this project it was possible for students to do this several times a day in different subjects. See: Mason, E. J., Smith, T. A., Gohs, F. X., & Cohen, D. W. (1982). *Final report: Evaluation of the IST Courses.* FY 1980–1981 Pilot Study. Lexington, KY: Prepared for the Alaska Department of Education by Educational Skills Development.

7   Obie, E. (1982, February). Planning for computers in the classroom. *ETA Newsletter* (a publication of the Office of Educational Technology and Telecommunications,

Alaska Department of Education). Reprinted by permission of the author; slight modifications have been made for the purposes of this text.

SUPPLEMENTARY READINGS

Ahl, D. H. (1983). Buying a printer. *Creative Computing,* 9(3), 12, 16, 18, 20, 23, 26, 29.

Anderson, J. J. (1983). Print about printers. *Creative Computing,* 9(3), 30, 32, 34, 36, 38, 42, 44, 48, 50-52, 55, 59-61.

Boe, T. (1982). Effective integration of computer methods in the science laboratory. *AEDS Monitor, 20*(7, 8, 9), 18-20.

Burke, L. M. (1982, May-June). Getting to know your computer: A practical approach — One byte at a time. *Classroom Computer News, 5*(2), 41-42.

Consumer Reports. (1983, September). The entire issue is devoted to small computers. Articles explain components and provide useful information for consumers.

Glatzer, H. (1981). *Introduction to word processing.* Berkeley, CA: SYBEX.

Houston, J. (1984). Don't bench me in. *BYTE, 9*(2), 160-162, 164.

Jones, B. L. (1982). Microcomputers and the administrator: Reviewing requests. *AEDS Monitor, 20*(7, 8, 9), 36-38.

Miastowski, S. (1982). Buyer's guide to low-cost computers. *Popular Computing,* 1(10), 71-95.

Miastkowski, S. (1982). Buyer's guide to small computer printers. *Popular Computing, 1*(8), 65-67.

Naiman, A. (1982). *Microcomputers in education: An introduction.* Chelmsford, MA: Northeast Regional Exchange.

Springer, D. M. (1982). School district computer use survey/results. *AEDS Monitor, 20*(7, 8, 9), 28-31.

Thomas, J. L. (Ed.). (1981). *Microcomputers in the schools.* Phoenix, AZ: Oryx.

CHAPTER 5

SETTING UP
THE CLASSROOM

CHAPTER CONTENTS

FACTORS TO CONSIDER IN PLANNING FOR CLASSROOM
COMPUTING

  The Role of Computers in the Classroom
  Requirements for Training of Staff
  Requirements for Training of Students
  Software and Hardware Requirements

INSTRUCTIONAL MANAGEMENT

  Monitoring Techniques
  Record Keeping
  Instructional Software and Materials
    Availability
    Rules and procedures
    Support and supervision
  Group and Individual Management Techniques
    Management of individualized learning
    Management of group learning

MANAGEMENT OF HARDWARE AND SOFTWARE

  Maintenance and Inventory
  Security

ORGANIZING RESOURCES

  Location of Computers in a School
    Computer laboratory
    Media center
    Computers in the classroom
  School Computer Committee

SUMMARY

NOTES

SUPPLEMENTARY READINGS

104

Microcomputers are such impressive machines that many people are tempted to buy one before they have given sufficient thought to how it will be used. The low price of hardware is probably a major reason why so many educators have been willing to give microcomputers a chance in the classroom. In Chapter 4, planning and purchasing of hardware were discussed. Since setting up a computer in the classroom involves a lot more than purchasing one, plugging it in, and turning it on, in this chapter we will focus on procedures for accommodating educational computers in the classroom.

In order to be able to use computers to improve education, teachers and other school personnel will have to consider how to train staff and students, what purposes computers can serve in the classroom, and how computers can fit into the overall curriculum. In addition, educators will have to look at the kinds of tasks computers can be expected to do. The position taken in this chapter is that for computer technology to fulfill its promise, it must be integrated into the overall plan of curricular offerings of the school.

FACTORS TO CONSIDER
IN PLANNING FOR CLASSROOM COMPUTING

Before an instructional computing program is set up, a number of factors should be considered:

- The role of the computer in the school curriculum
- Requirements for training of staff
- Requirements for training of students
- Software and hardware requirements

In the following sections, each of these is discussed.

The Role of Computers in the Classroom

The role computers can play in the classroom depends upon the curriculum and how that curriculum is put into practice. The following steps are useful in examining a curriculum to determine the best role for computers.

1 *Specify the goals and objectives of the curriculum.* The precision with which a curriculum is specified varies; but usually a curriculum plan includes statements of goals and objectives, the sequence of instruction, and definitions of some general approaches to instruction. This information is sometimes contained in a teachers' manual. The objectives may be stated in terms of behaviors that the students would be expected to exhibit after instruction and may include some indication of level of complexity (e.g., knowledge, comprehension, problem solving).[1]

2 *Examine the curriculum to determine where and how computers might be effectively used.* Unfortunately, there has been very little research on the

Cognitive level   Instructional computing activities

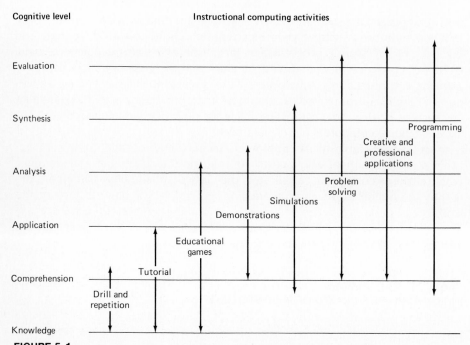

FIGURE 5.1
Cognitive levels of instructional computer activities. (*Adapted from P. Berg. Computers in rural Alaska. In D. Peterson*, Intelligent schoolhouse. *Reston, Va.: Reston, 1984.*)

unique capabilities of computers to support certain kinds of learning.[2] However, on the basis of logic and experience, some educated guesses about the match between what must be learned and computers can be proposed. Figure 5.1 shows one approach to this kind of analysis. In Figure 5.1 the cognitive levels of objectives from knowledge (simple) to evaluation (complex) form the horizontal rows.[3] (Levels of complexity and types of instructional activities are discussed in other chapters, e.g., 3 and 10.) Objectives at the simple end of the scale (knowledge and comprehension) are typically facilitated by such instructional computing activities as drill and practice, tutorials, and some educational games. Objectives that involve higher-level skills (application and analysis) can be supported by games, demonstrations, and simulations. Finally, objectives at the highest levels (synthesis and evaluation) can be addressed by rather sophisticated simulations, problem-solving situations, programming, and other creative applications.

Generally speaking, more complex instructional computing activities tend to be more costly. They can require greater skill from the software developers to produce and more sophistication on the part of teachers and students to use. These more costly and sophisticated techniques should be reserved for situations where they are really needed. For example, drill and practice would be an effective way to help students learn to recite the names of state capitals when given the name of a state; more sophisticated techniques would not be necessary. On the other hand, an objective that requires the student to interpret a set of population statistics for the United States would be at a higher level — comprehension, perhaps. Although drill and practice might be effective here, tutorials (with their greater emphasis on explanation) would seem to be a more promising approach. Educational games can be sometimes effective in increasing students' motivation;[4] however, in this particular case, devising an instructional game might be difficult, given the type of content involved.

3 *Evaluate the existing curriculum to determine where computers might be applied to increase the degree of attainment of goals and objectives.* In the classroom, a teacher can look through records of students' performance and add general impressions about which techniques have worked and where. For example, an individual teacher may feel that too much class time is being consumed by instruction on lower-level objectives and may want to have more available for higher-level objectives. In that case, the teacher might spend less time on simple kinds of learning that computers can teach well, and instead concentrate on facilitating social development, motivating further learning, or teaching more complex material. Analysis of the match between potential computer activities and instructional objectives may suggest areas in which instructional computers may help.

4 *Evaluate the existing curriculum in terms of how it might be changed or updated to utilize computers (and other technologies) more effectively.* In reviewing an existing curriculum, one may notice that instruction in programming techniques has been ignored except for an advanced computer mathematics course for juniors and seniors in high school, and that there is no instruction in computer literacy for the majority of students in the school system. To correct this problem, one can attempt to fill gaps in the present curriculum by adding to or modifying the program. Or on the other hand, one can seek a long-term solution by predicting future needs and revising the curriculum accordingly. The first procedure is probably easier for most school systems to implement, in that it does not require extensive redefinitions of the school's program. However, the second can lead to a better-integrated program.

5 *Plan the curriculum and its operation according to the information accumulated.* In this step, the curriculum is revised and restated on the basis of results of the previous steps. Goals, objectives, sequence, and course definitions are clarified. It should now be evident what is expected of computers in the school's curriculum.

Teachers need to be involved in the school's planning and to do their own planning for using computers in the curriculum. Since computers are better at some instructional tasks than others, teachers can bring their knowledge of instructional strategies and learning into good use during the planning stage.

Requirements for Training of Staff

As with any new technology, expertise on the part of the user is critical for success. As the microcomputer industry has moved toward more sophisticated machines, the demand for sophisticated users and maintainers of those machines has escalated. However, the training requirements must not be so demanding that they render use of the equipment impractical. Since technological innovation tends to increase efficiency, it is likely that technological change will continue to occur at a rapid pace. There is a continuing debate about how *gains* from use of the technology compare with *costs* of training.

One way to reduce the need for staff training is to use equipment and software that are very easy to operate. Such software and equipment are referred to as *user-friendly*. Following are four important characteristics of user-friendly software:

1 The user does not have to be concerned with the actual programming code. Rather, information is displayed for the user in a straightforward, non-technical manner, and the user can provide information to the computer in like manner.

2 The computer and the user communicate with each other in simple, understandable terms.

3 A variety of responses and errors by the user are anticipated and handled by the programming. Remedies are built into the programming to prevent the user from losing data or becoming stuck in an endlessly repeating procedure.

4 The procedures for getting started and for concluding a session are simple and as automated as possible.

Actually, user-friendly software also renders hardware user-friendly, since it simplifies machine operation.

Although careful selection of user-friendly software can go a long way toward minimizing training requirements, some training of teachers is going to be necessary. We shall now take a look at six skills that may be needed by a classroom teacher for implementing microcomputer instruction, and how these skills can be acquired.

1 *Operation and maintenance of hardware:* The teacher should be familiar with the operation of the computer system used in the classroom. This includes being able to use the computer and to explain its use and major components to students. Thus, a teacher needs to be familiar with the major components of the computer and the functions played by each. (For example, the keyboard is used for input, the CRT screen for visual display, and the disk drive for input of stored programs.) The teacher should also have a rudimentary knowledge of troubleshooting and minor repairs. The continuity of instruction may depend on each teacher's ability to remedy the obvious kinds of problems that often occur. (For instance, the computer cable may not be connected to the CRT; the power cord may not be connected; the disk drive may need repair.) In addition, it is desirable that at least one person in a school have a somewhat deeper familiarity with troubleshooting and repairs; this gives an additional measure of stability to the instructional program. (But even this would not be a professional level of expertise.) Teachers should also know of the basic rules for safe use of the computer, such as making sure the power is off before connecting or disconnecting any hardware or peripherals.

   2   *Identification and selection of software:* More and more instructional software is becoming available for microcomputers. However, the quality of this software may not always be consistent. Before making additional purchases, teachers should be aware of software that might already be available from the school, the school district, state education agencies, and other sources. Teachers should know how to distinguish good software from bad and how to determine any discrepancies between the actual and the stated purpose of a given program.

   3   *Integration of microcomputer instruction into the curriculum:* Since the computer opens up a number of instructional options (programming, problem solving, tutorials, creative computerized applications, etc.), the teacher should be familiar with these various options and their place in the curriculum. Being able to determine which instructional objectives are best served by the microcomputer and a particular software package is basic to successful instructional computing.

   4   *Techniques of instruction with computers:* Teachers must be familiar with classroom techniques for instruction with microcomputers. They need to know how to set up a classroom and how to provide proper instructional support to students who are learning with a microcomputer. Often this means performing a role much different from that in traditional large-group instruction. Specifically, the teacher tends to be more involved in managing, supporting, and assisting students when computers are being used for instruction. A teacher needs to know where various kinds of computer activities fit into the instructional sequence, what computers can do particularly well, and what types of assistance students will require for a given activity.

   5   *Knowledge of instructional support functions of computers:* Teachers should also be aware of how computers can assist with classroom instruction. For example, computers can be used in producing classroom materials, in managing instruction, in diagnostic and prescriptive teaching, in word processing, and so forth. When teachers become familiar with these sorts of applications, computerized classroom instruction can often be made more effective.

   6   *Awareness of new advances:* Teachers need to keep abreast of new products and developments in educational technology. Keeping one's knowledge current is ultimately the individual teacher's responsibility. However, periodic schoolwide or districtwide workshops can be very helpful in maintaining teachers' awareness of new developments. Familiarity with software and hardware catalogs and other printed resources published by commercial sources can help a teacher keep up with new software developments. Similarly, familiarity with journals and other periodicals that deal with instructional computing can also help a teacher keep abreast of new developments in the field. Users' groups can provide additional support and assistance.

These six items listed are only a brief sketch of the requirements for training of teachers in instructional uses of microcomputers. In fact, much of this book is directed toward meeting educators' needs for such training. Teachers will probably receive more training in the instructional uses of computers as part of their preservice work in the coming years. However, computer technology is changing so rapidly that in-service programs can be expected to continue as an important aspect of training in instructional computing.

Requirements for Training of Students

Teachers are not the only ones who require training in order to implement instructional computing programs successfully. Students must also be trained to use the equipment. Younger students do not seem to have the inhibitions common to adults when it comes to meeting a microcomputer for the first time; and often it is easier to prepare children to work with computers than it is to prepare adults. Four principal goals of a program to prepare students for educational computing are:

1 Familiarity with the necessary hardware and its operation
2 Ability to operate required software
3 Comprehension of operation and safety rules
4 Knowledge of what to do when problems arise

Students need not have a detailed understanding of the electronics of a computer, any more then they need to understand the workings of a typewriter in order to type on one. At the beginning stages of computer use, critical skills are ability to communicate with the computer through a keyboard, game controllers, or other devices; and ability to use tape drives, disk drives, and other peripherals as the need arises. Students should also have some understanding of how the computer communicates with them by presenting text or graphics on the CRT screen, or by driving some device such as a printer or sound synthesizer. As with training of teachers, the simpler and more natural communication between student and computer can be made, the easier it will be for students to become familiar with the technology.

Some of the better software currently available is constructed so that it requires little explanation or training. That is, it is user-friendly. Although instructions or training activities are often included as an integral part of the software package, in some cases a teacher may want to explain how to perform an activity or give special instructions. Further, the student should usually know ahead of time the purpose of the lesson, the objectives, and the criteria for success.

Students will routinely need training in how to use computers safely. Com-

TABLE 5.1
SAMPLE SET OF RULES FOR CLASSROOM MICROCOMPUTER USE
(Elementary School Level)

1 Do not touch plugs or wires.

2 Do not take the computer apart.

3 No food or drink next to the computer.

4 Do not hit or handle the computer roughly.

5 Do not move the computer equipment.

6 If you see others moving or mistreating the computer, ask them to stop or tell your teacher about it.

7 Be sure your hands are clean and dry when using the computer.

8 If you see smoke or hear a strange noise, do not touch the computer. Tell your teacher or another adult immediately.

9 Do not eat or drink near the computer.

10 Report any unusual sounds or other strange activity of the computer to the teacher.

puters are manufactured in accordance with product safety standards, but these standards may assume prudent behavior on the part of the user. The equipment may require proper grounding, wiring insulation, and circuit breakers. Also, computers and software are susceptible to damage. Thus, it is wise to develop rules for the use of microcomputers and associated instructional materials, to post these rules near the machines, and to ensure that every student is familiar with them. A sample set of rules for a classroom computing area is shown in Table 5.1. It covers such areas as students' safety, preventing damage to hardware, preventing damage to software, keeping the area neat and orderly, emergency procedures, security, and good manners.

Students should know what to do when problems arise. Problems can arise when there are interruptions in electric power, faulty recordings of software, or hardware malfunctions, or when students enter responses that were not anticipated in the programming. Problems such as these can interfere with the learning process and lead to a good deal of frustration. Anticipation and prevention of these problems will help reduce frustration. Having procedures for dealing with problems that may arise will also help.

Software and Hardware Requirements

Generally speaking, it is easier and cheaper to use software that has already been developed than to write new programs. However, this assumes that software is available which matches educational objectives and meets established standards for quality. If acceptable software is available, it should be used. Custom software development, or modification of existing software for specific purposes, should be attempted only when there are no acceptable alternatives available. Software development requires a good deal of expertise and time, as we have noted before. Usually classroom teachers do not have the resources for extensive software development. However, some teachers may be willing to make the investment in time to produce custom software for specialized needs. Awareness of the time and resources required will help to avoid the frustration of unfinished projects.

INSTRUCTIONAL MANAGEMENT

Success with classroom instruction using computers requires preparation. Some of the factors to be considered are:

- Monitoring techniques
- Record keeping
- Instructional software and materials
- Group and individual management techniques

Monitoring Techniques

Monitoring students' activities and performance is important with traditional instruction, and just as important with computerized instruction. The instructional objectives to be accomplished with computers should typically be a regular part of the student's instructional program. The major differences with instructional computing activities are that the computer may be doing a substantial part of the instruction and that the program tends to be oriented more toward individual and small-group activities. In this setting, the teacher becomes more of a manager, problem solver, motivator, and provider of encouragement and less a provider of information or instruction. In this role, however, the teacher must be aware of the intent, approach, and content of the instruction as well as of students' progress and performance. Although instruction with computers tends to emphasize individual and small-group instruction, the teacher should be familiar with the principles of large- and small-group behavior, since individual students are typically surrounded by the rest of the class.[5]

Teachers should be proficient in classroom management techniques whether or not they are using computers. Knowledge about how groups function, leadership styles, methods of communication, the importance of goals, and classroom climate are all important aspects of classroom management.[6] (For example, it has been shown that disciplining a child has a ''ripple effect'' on the whole class, even when the class has been divided into small groups and the child is in one of the groups or working alone.[7])

The teacher should be knowledgeable about the contents of the manuals and supporting documentation that accompany instructional computing packages, and familiar with supporting materials the students will be using. These may include textbooks, workbooks, suggested group activities, and additional references. It is a good idea for the teacher to try at least a sampling of the software ahead of time. If the software is intended primarily for use by the teacher (as classroom management packages and software for classroom demonstrations are), the teacher will of course need to acquire a much greater degree of skill with the software before classroom use.

Different kinds of instructional objectives require different approaches. With individualized computer activities such as drill and practice, tutorials, simulations, games, and problem solving, the teacher's monitoring tasks are fairly standard. First, the teacher should determine that a particular activity is occurring at the correct time in an instructional sequence, that the student has mastered the prerequisite skills, that the several computer activities which make up a given set are performed in the proper order, that progress is being made in completing activities, and whether special assistance will be needed to run the software. Also, the teacher will have to be more vigilant in monitoring students' performance when the computer does not automatically make a record of what a student has done.

The monitoring role assumed by the teacher is extremely important. A computer can be programmed to identify some of a student's problems and respond appropriately. However, most current software cannot provide for special cases, and no software can detect puzzled or bored looks on the faces of students. Nor does existing software have an extensive repertoire of remediation activities and alternative approaches and explanations. These are precisely the kinds of skills good teachers can bring to an instructional program. Thus, higher-level teaching behaviors promise to be the domain of the teacher for some time to come. They should constitute a good part of the teacher's monitoring effort during instructional computing sessions.

Record Keeping

In computerized instruction, records may or may not be kept by computer. When teachers and students are familiar enough with computers to use such systems, and the hardware and software are available, computerized record keeping is usually preferable. However, computerized record keeping is not always feasible.

Computerized record keeping can take several forms. Records can be kept using software specifically designed for that purpose. Sometimes these systems may be part of a computer-managed instruction (CMI) package.[8] While packages of this sort offer many advantages for keeping students' records, they tend to demand adherence to a particular strategy of instruction and may or may not be attractive to a given teacher. (Computer-managed instruction was described in Chapter 3.) Alternatively, computerized systems may be specifically designed for record keeping. Advantages of computerized record keeping include having a potentially complete and easily accessible set of records; having the ability to access individual records rapidly and to summarize them in several ways; having a compact and uncluttered method of record storage; and having a medium for record storage and retrieval that is consistent with the medium of instruction. Disadvantages include having to learn the techniques for storing, retrieving, and summarizing records; perhaps having to spend a considerable amount of time entering records on a regular basis; having to create backup records at regular intervals; and the danger of losing all or part of electronically stored records if no adequate backup procedures have been instituted.

Some instructional packages have their own built-in management systems. Automated management systems have the advantage of reducing the drudgery of data entry. However, these systems have some limitations. For example, with automatic data entry it may not be easy to relate status and performance in computerized activities to performance in other media (e.g., workbooks) or in different subjects. Further, if several computerized systems are in use simultaneously, the complexity of collating records from the different systems may be substantial. If the systems use floppy disks, and if multiple copies of each disk are used within a school or classroom, combining students' files from several diskettes may be a complex matter. Finally, some computerized instructional systems provide a standard sequence of activities for each student and therefore may not be able to accommodate alterations prescribed for individual students. Computerized record keeping has a great deal of potential for the classroom teacher, but its implementation requires considerable forethought and planning.

Record keeping can also be done by other means than computers. Some instructional computing packages come with supplemental materials in the form of student worksheets or workbooks. With such materials, students' records may be kept by the students themselves as they work on the supplements. Sometimes teachers use progress charts posted on the wall in the computer area. Such charts have the advantage of being readily available for students to view at any time. However, this is also a disadvantage, since the progress of each student is available for all classmates to see and may be a source of embarrassment for slower students. In a sense, manual recording of performance in computerized learning activities seems like something of an anachronism. However, the form of record keeping that is most appropriate in a particular situation should be used. It should be recognized that some kinds of information are easier to keep manually, and for these the gain from automation might not be sufficient to warrant a change.

Instructional Software and Materials

Generally, the procedures teachers should employ in the management of computer software and associated materials are the same as in any well-managed learning situation. The following are suggested for managing computerized learning programs.

Availability   Necessary materials, supplies, and equipment should be available when students need them. Nothing is more frustrating to a student than to find that materials needed for an activity are damaged, missing, or otherwise unavailable. This type of problem is not unique to computerized instruction.

The need for necessary instructional materials to be available close to the computers — so that students can concentrate on the instruction rather than on trying to find items they need — cannot be overemphasized. Diskettes can be replaced in plastic inserts that fit into loose-leaf binders, cardboard or plastic diskette boxes, special racks or shelves, or custom packages furnished by the software distributor. The diskettes should be stored away from electrical fields caused by other equipment and in such a way as to reduce the possibility of physical damage. When each item has a convenient and standard storage location, random piles of diskettes and lost diskettes can be avoided.

A teacher or some other staff member should have responsibility for keeping an inventory of materials so that items which are in short supply or become defective can be replaced or repaired. Where possible, a supply of extra materials and backup diskettes should be maintained as an added precaution. Part of good management of computerized learning is simply providing access to everything the student needs to complete the activities.

Following is a summary of techniques for ensuring the continued availability of materials, supplies, and equipment:

1   Store all software, manuals, and other references so that they are easily available when they are needed. (See Figure 5.2.)

2   Establish procedures for regularly taking inventory to determine whether any materials are missing or defective and whether any consumable materials must be replenished.

3   Design the instructional area so that required materials are within easy reach and each item is kept in a standard place.

4   Determine which, if any, software and materials should be kept separately and used on a checkout basis.

Rules and Procedures   Communicating procedures and rules for using computers to students and staff will make management less difficult. A preliminary session for reviewing rules for students before starting instruction is often a good idea. This should be followed by periodic monitoring to make sure that materials and computers are being handled properly. Further, posting the procedures for using computers and related materials in a prominent place near them can serve as an effective reminder.

Unexpected problems in running software can wreak havoc on a well-conceived management plan. Problems may occur at any time. Through training and practice, teachers and students can become skilled troubleshooters who are able to identify and correct many of the problems they may encounter. Computer users should be told to write down the nature of the problems in a log. (See Figure 5.3.) Often this information can help a technician to diagnose a prob-

FIGURE 5.2
Above: Methods of storing diskettes. *(Inmac.)*

FIGURE 5.3
Below: An example of a computer log.

COMPUTER LOG				
Computer _____				
Room_____				
User	Date	Type of activity	Time of day	Problem or difficulties

lem. (For example, knowing that the computer room is becoming very warm might suggest that there is a problem with ventilation — rather than with electronics — which is causing the computers to perform erratically.)

Following are suggestions for clarifying rules and procedures for students:

1 Establish rules for the use of materials, and be sure that students and staff are familiar with these rules.

2 Establish procedures for reporting and recording problems with software. Each problem should be recorded in sufficient detail so that recurrent problems can be recognized and their causes corrected.

3 Students should be taught how to use and care for software and materials.

Support and Supervision To ensure that educational computing activities operate smoothly, students must be supervised by someone who knows about instructional computing. Specifically:

1 Arrange for adequate supervision to ensure that the procedures are being followed and that corrective actions are taken when necessary.

2 Have someone knowledgeable about specific applications available to help students with problems that might occur.

Group and Individual Management Techniques

Instructional settings can vary in size, from individual instruction at one extreme to a whole classroom or several classrooms at the other. Further, the manner of using computers can vary. For example, short supplemental exercises might be used to augment regular instruction; or a whole course might be administered by computer, complete with achievement testing. In addition, teaching styles and preferences vary considerably, and what works well for one teacher may not work at all for another. Therefore, it is difficult to prescribe a single format or formula for management of computerized instruction. The size of the instructional units (individuals, small or large groups, or whole classes) will be determined by factors such as instructional goals, teaching style, and constraints imposed by the physical setting.

The teacher should recognize the strengths of the computer and be ready to take advantage of them. (For example, a computer can be programmed to give graphic demonstrations of what is happening inside a volcano during an eruption; and a teacher should be ready to use the computer for this kind of demonstration when the class is studying volcanoes, if the programming is available.) But teachers should also be aware of tasks that the computer or the software cannot do. Some of the tasks that teachers themselves should be prepared to deal with are listed below:

1 Take steps to reduce boredom or frustration among students.

2 Ensure that students are making appropriate use of instructional time.

3 Help students to understand material that they may find difficult.

4 Show the importance of what is being learned and its relationship to the remainder of the curriculum.

5 Monitor the overall and specific educational progress of each student and make adjustments where indicated.

6 Provide motivation, reinforcement, warmth, and encouragement to students.

7 Ensure that each student has access to the computer and that an equitable approach is taken in sharing this valuable learning resource.

8 Maintain discipline in group situations, and keep the group on task. Computers are not very effective in dealing with unanticipated stress in groups or with off-task behavior.

This list of general management considerations will be most useful for settings in which some group or individual computerized learning is taking place. We now turn to a classroom situation in which students are utilizing computerized courseware and proceeding at their own rates through the instructional material on a regular basis every day; following that, we will look at group learning.

Management of Individualized Learning Table 5.2 lists a number of techniques for individual computerized instruction. This list is not meant to be

TABLE 5.2
INDIVIDUAL MANAGEMENT TECHNIQUES

1 Define and make a record of a specific program of instruction for the student.

2 Determine a schedule for daily or weekly activities and for completion of program.

3 Adopt a system for monitoring progress and performance, and communicate this to the student.

4 Provide direction and assistance to ensure that the student understands all aspects of the instructional process.

5 Monitor an early session or two in detail and correct any problems which occur.

6 Once the student is off to a good start, monitor the records of progress and performance and regularly check on his or her progress during instruction. Give tutorial or other assistance, as necessary, when problems are encountered by the student.

7 Regularly offer encouragement and praise for good work. Explain why the instruction is important and how it relates to other aspects of the instructional program. Strive to make learning fun.

8 Review overall progress periodically. Suggest further or remedial activities as necessary. Adjust the program or time schedule if necessary.

9 Maintain a healthy climate for learning. Make sure that materials and equipment are available when needed, that opportunities for interaction or quiet study are available when needed, and that the physical environment is comfortable.

10 Provide regular feedback to the student regarding his or her progress. Upon completion of major instructional milestones or units, provide formal statements of progress. Be sure that credit is awarded where credit is due.

11 Upon completion of an entire activity or project, define the next steps for the student and review the process in your own mind to determine how it might be modified or improved for other students.

exhaustive, but it does include a number of techniques teachers have employed successfully in the classroom.[9] Some of the techniques amount to nothing more then simply being systematic and well organized. For instance, defining and recording a specific program of study, determining a schedule, adopting and implementing a system for monitoring progress and performance, and providing regular formal and informal feedback fall into this category. Some of the techniques have to do with identifying and solving individual students' problems. Other techniques have to do with maintaining a positive climate for learning. The reader should review these techniques and relate them to instruction with other kinds of media. Such analysis would suggest that techniques useful in any form of individualized instruction (projects, essays, workbook exercises, etc.) are also appropriate for computerized individual instruction.

Management of Group Learning   Group dynamics and principles of effective instruction are elements of effective group management. Techniques for the management of effective group instruction are listed in Table 5.3 (page 120). Some of the techniques in Table 5.3 parallel those suggested for individual instruction in Table 5.2.

MANAGEMENT OF HARDWARE AND SOFTWARE

Maintenance and Inventory

Computer hardware and software can be a major investment for a school. In order to maintain the computer resources, it is necessary to designate someone who will be responsible for the computers and software. If all computers are kept in a central facility, such as a media laboratory, the director of that facility could be given this responsibility. On the other hand, if the school's computers have been distributed to the classrooms, then the teachers should be responsible, reporting to someone who is designated the computer coordinator.

Responsibility for the hardware implies keeping an inventory of the current location and status of every piece of equipment. It includes periodic light maintenance, such as cleaning disk drive heads and operationally testing each machine. It also involves reviewing equipment logs and investigating problems or malfunctions noted by users. In addition, the person responsible for the equipment oversees its repair. Being responsible for the school's computer equipment and supplies is time-consuming. This task should not be underestimated. It could easily overburden a staff member who already has a number of other major responsibilities.

Many schools have arranged for the staff member who is in charge of equipment to receive specialized training in equipment maintenance. The ability to perform light maintenance locally reduces expenses for the school and avoids the delays and inconvenience of taking a computer into a repair facility.

Software resources should be catalogued and made available to users on a

TABLE 5.3
GROUP MANAGEMENT TECHNIQUES

1 Identify students who work well together and provide or assist in the development of group tasks and projects. Utilize group activities when appropriate to the educational tasks.

2 Explain the relevance of the tasks and projects to the group.

3 Set aside adequate time for group work. Communicate time limits to students.

4 Provide encouragement to students and seek to sustain their motivation.

5 Monitor individual and group progress and performance.

6 Identify core and supplemental resources and make them available.

7 Maintain focus and order. Keep the groups on target and on schedule. Allow groups to work on their own or under supervision when necessary. Designate student group leaders or monitors, if possible.

8 Seek participation by all group members. Reformulate the group if necessary to prevent its domination by a single individual or subgroup.

9 Develop (or help students develop) tasks for groups. Make records of these tasks and who will be responsible for completing them.

10 Provide assistance in resolving problems related to group functions.

11 Maintain and review records of progress and performance. Provide feedback to groups regularly.

12 Ensure that materials, hardware, and software are available when needed.

13 Point out capabilities and weaknesses of hardware and software, and be ready to suggest ways to utilize alternative approaches.

14 Maintain continuity of group activities by reminding the group of previous tasks that have been completed and new tasks that are scheduled. Make a record of any problems, for future reference.

15 Promote interest and enthusiasm. Maintain a healthy climate for learning.

16 Provide closure for activities and give credit for good performance. Initiate new activities and projects.

loan basis. One approach is to make the school librarian responsible for lending the software, so that software can be borrowed from the library by teachers or students just as other educational materials are.

Although arrangements may vary from one school to another, one person is generally responsible for computers. If responsibility is shared among a group of people, involvement is certainly broadened; but unless someone is clearly in charge in this arrangement, no one feels responsible for the overall operation.

Security

The possibility of vandalism and theft makes security an important topic for consideration. However, the need for maintaining security of computers often conflicts with the desire to give greater access to them. Following are suggestions for establishing security:

1 Computer laboratories and rooms containing computer equipment should be more secure than regular classrooms. Double locks on doors and reinforced windows or screens are common security measures.

2 Equipment should be stored in a locked area during extended vacations. If the computers are located in the classrooms during the school year, they should be collected for storage over the summer months.

3 Keys should be necessary in order to gain access to computer areas at times when there is no one in the room to supervise. Keys sometimes find their way into the wrong hands. Locks should be changed when all known keys to the computer areas cannot be located.

4 Equipment should be made secure where it is used. For example, cases can be purchased that fit over particular brands of computers and then are bolted or locked to the table. Some computers can be locked to the table with D-rings and bicycle locks; and many computers come with locks mounted in their cases to prevent access to the electronics inside.

5 Fostering a sense of pride and shared responsibility among the students will probably reduce unnecessary damage to the equipment.

ORGANIZING RESOURCES

Integration of resources into the instructional program is probably the most important single factor to consider in maximizing the effectiveness of educational computing. Instructional computing must be integrated into the school program to effectively meet the goals and objectives of the curriculum.

Location of Computers in a School

The location of the computers in the school can have important implications for the way instructional computing is integrated into the curriculum. Further, the degree to which students and faculty members are willing to use computers can be significantly affected by the location of the computers in the school.

There are three major alternatives for locating computers in a school: (1) When large groups of students must use computers on a regular basis, a school may choose to concentrate resources in a computer laboratory. (2) Another school may choose to have computers in the classrooms so that students can use them to complete class activities that include computerized assignments. (3) A third school might make computers available through a media center, to meet whatever needs the students, the teaching staff, and parents may have for them. We will next consider each of the three schemes for locating computers in more detail.

Computer Laboratory When large groups of students must work with computers at the same time, a computer laboratory may be desirable. Such a facility provides a centralized location for hardware and software. A laboratory may consist of 10 to 12 computers (usually enough to permit a class to work in groups of two or three) or as many as 25 or 30 computers (enough for each student in a class to work alone at a machine).

Computer laboratories in schools tend to have several characteristics in common:

1 A computer lab requires a large room with adequate ventilation and sufficient electrical outlets. It should be large enough to house all the necessary hardware and software that will be used by the students. Further, the room should be capable of being locked when it is not in use.

2 A lab usually requires additional staffing commitments. The lab may be staffed by a qualified teacher or by a combination of teachers and aides.

3 Laboratories are efficient for large-scale, multiuse instructional settings. Large-scale staff training and adult education evening classes are also possible with such a facility.

4 Computer labs allow concentration of computer hardware and software to achieve the maximum impact. (With this approach, for example, a school that can purchase only one or two units of a particular peripheral device can still make the device available to all students and teachers.)

The optimum number of computers for a laboratory is an important consideration. One computer for each student is not necessarily the ideal ratio. Many educational computing activities are more effective in small-group settings. For example, some problem-solving tasks might involve judgments, estimates, or perspectives for which there are no correct answers; and having a group present to discuss the alternatives is an important part of the learning task. On the other hand, one student per computer would be a more desirable ratio for drill and practice in mathematics. Generally, a ratio of one computer to two or three students is acceptable and desirable for many kinds of instruction (e.g., programming, computer literacy, simulations of scientific experiments, and educational games).

It is advisable to plan for additional work space in the lab or a nearby classroom. This work space can increase efficiency in a lab with only a small number of computers. For example, a typical programming student spends less than one-third of the class time actually working on a computer. The work space provides a place for students to work on flowcharts, written assignments, and other activities. For this reason, it is recommended that a school computer laboratory be organized into centers or specialized areas for computing, for individual and group work, and for small-group discussion.[10]

A computer laboratory should emphasize primarily one kind of computer. This will ensure that the same software will run on several machines. Mixing several different kinds of computers in a lab complicates staff training, maintenance, and software requirements. For a lab composed of several makes and models, standardizing individual instruction and comprehensive group instruction is also difficult. However, in a lab in which most of the computers are alike, one or two different kinds should be included, to give students experience with other types of machines, hardware, and operating systems.

A well-equipped computer laboratory in a school will have at least one printer for each eight computers. Usually, dot-matrix printers are preferable because of their speed, flexibility, and durability when compared with other kinds of printers. (Printers are discussed in Chapter 2.) An overhead projector, a projection screen, and a computer set up on a table or desk with castor wheels so that it can be moved about the room are also desirable. Since chalk dust can cause maintenance problems with computer equipment, white smooth-surface wallboards on which one can write with erasable felt-tipped pens are preferable to chalkboards. A video projector with a large screen is an asset. Two physical features found in many labs are a folding curtain to divide the room when different kinds of activities are going on at the same time, and a carpet or floor covering that does not produce much static.

A sample layout of a computer lab is shown in Figure 5.4 (page 124). Other layouts are, of course, possible. However, the storage areas, workplaces that do not have computers, and folding curtains are features that tend to be found in a large number of school computer labs.

Media Center In many schools the media center is a service center where teachers and students can borrow or use educational aids such as tape recorders, videotape players, and projectors. Most media centers can also help teachers to produce educational materials by providing duplicating facilities, special lettering machines, and occasionally even videotaping or photographic equipment. The media center may not exist as a separate entity in a school. Rather, it might be part of the library or resource room. Some larger schools may have a media center director; but in most schools that function is assumed by a staff member who also has other duties.

Placing computers in a media center tends to foster better integration in the school's curriculum than the other approaches to locating computers in a school. It can be an economical choice in that it uses existing facilities and staff. One way to set up a media center is to locate the majority of the school's computers and software in the library under the supervision of the librarian or media specialist.[11]

A media center is a less costly, smaller-scale approach than a computer laboratory. A media center avoids the expense of additional space and staff associated with a computer lab. Further, this approach can be more effective at integrating computer learning activities with other educational technologies. Software and computers can be used by individuals and groups in the center, and they can also be checked out to teachers for use in classrooms.

However, there are shortcomings to the media center approach. For example, large-scale group activities are more limited in the media center than in a computer laboratory. Further, librarians and media specialists can be overtaxed

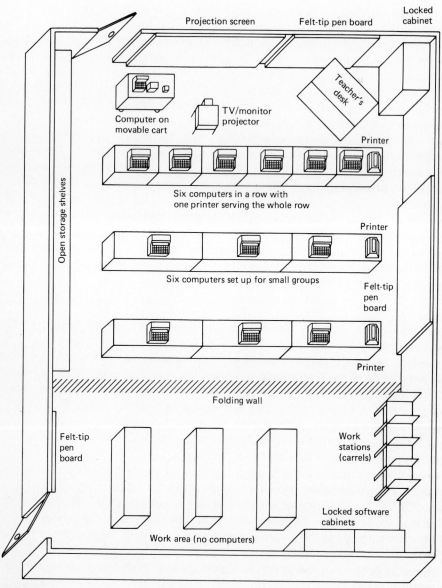

Projection screen   Felt-tip pen board   Locked cabinet

Computer on movable cart

TV/monitor projector

Teacher's desk

Printer

Open storage shelves

Six computers in a row with one printer serving the whole row

Printer

Six computers set up for small groups

Felt-tip pen board

Printer

Folding wall

Felt-tip pen board

Work stations (carrels)

Work area (no computers)

Locked software cabinets

FIGURE 5.4
A typical layout for a computer laboratory.

by the additional duties and responsibilities entailed by an instructional computing program superimposed on a media center.

Computers in the Classroom   Having computers in the classroom gives the advantage of immediate access to computers throughout the school day. It may be especially appropriate for small schools and elementary schools. But in large schools, and particularly high schools, this can be the most expensive option. It may also be the most inefficient, depending on the level of utilization in the classroom. Many computers in classrooms are not used for more than two or three hours per day. The remainder of the time, the class takes part in large-group instruction, physical education, music instruction, and other group-oriented activities. Further, one computer in a class of 20 to 30 students may not provide the level of stimulation possible in a consolidated laboratory in which many students are simultaneously engaged in problem solving on computers. However, moving students to and from a computer lab on a regular basis may be disruptive and time-consuming. Further, teachers who are accustomed to self-contained classrooms may be better able to integrate instructional computing into the curriculum when they have a computer in their classroom.

The classroom computer should be located so that it will not be a distraction to the class. Sometimes a small portable screen or curtain is used to separate the computer from the main activities of the classroom (see Figure 5.5, page 126). Sufficient chairs and space for small groups should be included in the computer work area. A sign-up sheet can be used to avoid crowding and conflicts (see Figure 5.6, page 127).

The type of organization that is best will vary from school to school. Such considerations as space, building design, educational goals, experience of staff, and funding are important factors in determining the best approach. Table 5.4 (page 128) summarizes several of the advantages and disadvantages of each approach. The relative advantages of each approach may not be readily apparent in a given situation, however. A school computer committee can weigh the merits of one approach against another; such committees are discussed next.

School Computer Committee

A school computer committee helps to ensure broad-based participation in the educational computing program. The ideas and suggestions generated by the committee will help make the computer program sensitive to the needs of all departments and programs in the school.

When the school computer committee addresses the problem of where to locate computers in the school, it might consider questions like the following:

1   *What are the goals and objectives of the curriculum?* Every educational program should be based on an organized structure that includes a set of well-defined goals and objectives.

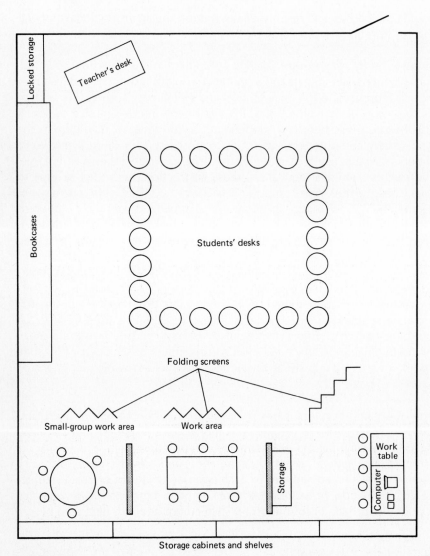

FIGURE 5.5
A classroom with a computer resource center.

2 *How can computer resources be organized to achieve the objectives?* An educational computing program may begin with modest goals for the first year. A certain amount of trial and error may be necessary before the committee is able to determine the best way to organize. The committee may choose to field-test an approach for one semester and evaluate the results before making a final decision. There may be some merit in modifying one of the three standard

COMPUTER SIGN-UP SHEET

Week of: _____

	Monday	Tuesday	Wednesday	Thursday	Friday
9:00	John J.				
9:30	↓				
10:00			Jane R.		Programming Group A.
10:30			↓		
11:00			Bill S., John J.		
11:30			and Phill M.		
12:00	Mary K.			Computer Club	
12:30					
1:00					
1:30		Bill S.			Robert W.
2:00					Jane A.
2:30			Peter	Alice	Programming Group B
3:00		Fred	↓		↓
3:30		John			
4:00					

FIGURE 5.6
Computer sign-up sheet.

approaches to locating the computer (laboratory, media center, or classroom) to meet unique local requirements. For example, a computer lab might be set up, but teachers will be permitted to check out two of the machines for short periods of time; or one computer might be permanently assigned to three teachers for sharing in their classrooms on a schedule to be arranged by them.

3 *How is the effectiveness of a program determined?* The school computer committee can establish criteria for determining whether the computer program is effective in the school. This will entail designing an evaluation and procedures for obtaining feedback from students, teachers, and other members of the school community.

SUMMARY

In this chapter a variety of factors associated with setting up the classroom for instruction using microcomputers were covered.

First, a number of decisions the classroom teacher must make concerning the integration of computerized instruction into the curriculum were explored. These decisions included such basic considerations as the role of the computer

TABLE 5.4
ORGANIZATION OF COMPUTER RESOURCES

Feature	Computer laboratory	Media center	Classroom
Large-group activities	Labs are designed for large-scale activities.	This depends on the media center. Some can accommodate classes.	Large-group activities are limited.
Integration with other media	Computer labs emphasize computers at the expense of integration.	Media centers tend to integrate media.	Computers in classrooms are integrated with other activities.
Efficiency in terms of cost and computer utilization	Labs can be most efficient in medium to large schools.	Use of computers can be spread to all staff members and students at moderate cost.	Classroom computers tend to be used less than two hours per day.
Immediate availability to teachers	Computer utilization must be coordinated with other staff needs.	Computer must be scheduled through media center coordinator.	Computer is always available.
Amount of technical support available to user	Labs are usually run by a trained specialist.	Media center personnel usually have technical training.	Teachers may be on their own.
Flexibility of computer utilization	Lab resources can be used flexibly, and can be checked out to classrooms.	Depending on arrangement, can be very flexible.	Usually limited to individuals and small groups.
Encouragement of cooperative staff effort to achieve identical curriculum objectives	Computer labs can focus staff energies on specific computer application.	Media center approach may focus staff attention on identified priorities in education computing.	Teachers tend to pursue their own objectives.
Cost	Large schools can achieve economy of scale with a lab.	Media center approach uses existing facility and staff.	Placing computers in a classroom is usually the most expensive option.

in the curriculum, requirements for training of staff and students, identification or development of software, and selection of hardware.

Second, management of instruction was discussed. Traditional instructional strategies (such as lectures, demonstrations, tutorials, and individual and group problem solving) were considered in terms of methods of using computers in the classroom. Further, matching objectives, content, and instructional strategies with computers was described. Management techniques (including techniques for dealing with monitoring, record keeping, materials, and individual and group learning) were considered.

Third, management of hardware and software was discussed.

Finally, three alternatives for organizing instructional computing in a school — the computer laboratory, the media center, and placement of computers in classrooms — were compared.

Careful attention to planning of classroom organization and location of computers can pay large dividends by making programs more effective. Taking a systematic approach to setting up an instructional computer program in a school is imperative.

NOTES

1 Gagné, R. M., & Briggs, L. J. (1974). *Principles of instructional design* (2nd ed.). New York: Holt, Rinehart & Winston.

2 Barnes, B. J., & Hill, S. (1983). Should young children work with microcomputers — Logo before Lego? *The Computing Teacher, 10*(9), 11–14.

3 Bloom, B. S. (Ed.). (1956). *Taxonomy of educational objectives. Handbook I: Cognitive domain.* New York: McKay.

4 Malone, T. W. (1981). Toward a theory of intrinsically motivating instruction. *Cognitive Science, 4*, 333–369.

5 Raney, M. A., & Johnson, L. V. (1975). *Educational social psychology.* New York: Macmillan.

6 Schmuck, R. A., & Schmuck, P. A. (1983). *Group processes in the classroom.* Dubuque, IA: Brown.

7 Kounin, J. S. (1970). *Discipline and group management in classrooms.* New York: Holt, Rinehart & Winston.

8 Baker, F. B. (1978). *Computer managed instruction: Theory and practice.* Englewood Cliffs, NJ: Educational Technology.

9 Boyd, R. (1983). A sample of teaching with a microcomputer. *The Computing Teacher, 10*(9), 60–61.

10 Poirot, J. L. (1980). *Computers and education.* Manchaca, TX: Sterling Swift.

11 Skapura, B. (1983). Start small and be very very good. *The Computing Teacher, 10*(8), 57–58.

SUPPLEMENTARY READINGS

Burghes, D. (1982). In-service micro courses for the teaching profession. In C. Smith (Ed.), *Microcomputers in education.* New York: Wiley.

Burke, L. M. (1982). Getting to know your computer. *Classroom Computer News, 2*(5), 41–42.

Cauchon, P. A. (1983). Computers at Canterbury School. *The Computing Teacher, 10*(9), 71–74.11.

Coburn, P., Kelman, P., Roberts, N., Snyder, T., Watt, D., & Weiner, C. (1982). How to set up a computer environment. *Classroom Computer News,* 29–31, 48.

Gummersheimer, V. H. (1982). When do I get to use the computer? *The Computer Teacher, 10*(4), 24–25.

Lathrope, A. (1982). Micro in the media center. Upcoming library conference, new publications announced. *Educational Computer Magazine, 2*(3), 22–23.

Maxim, G. W. (1977). *Learning centers for young children.* New York: Hart.

Naiman, A. (1982). *Microcomputers in education: An introduction.* Chelmsford, MA: Northeast Exchange.

Phillips, W. P. (1983). How to manage effectively with twenty-five students and one computer. *The Computer Teacher, 10*(7), 32.

Temkin, K. (1981). In search of administrative software. *Classroom Computing News, 2*(1), 34–35.

Trost, S. R. (1982). Videotext for learning: How and when? *Creative Computing, 8*(5), 50–54, 56, 58, 60.

CHAPTER 6

KEEPING THE COMPUTER BUSY WHEN IT IS NOT INSTRUCTING STUDENTS

CHAPTER CONTENTS

Previous chapters have gone into considerable detail about instructional uses of computers. In this chapter, data processing in general is discussed, and then several noninstructional applications are described: word processing, database management, spreadsheets, and networking. In addition, noninstructional applications that relate to the work of teachers, students, administrators, support staff, and special educators are covered.

Various kinds of software for the applications discussed in this chapter are available for many of the microcomputers commonly found in educational settings. If at all possible, readers should try to obtain samples of software and try running them on a computer to see how they work. Some of the details of the present discussion might apply more to one brand of microcomputer or software package than another. Therefore, readers are cautioned to review particular software packages before assuming that they will work precisely as described here.

The criteria for choosing the applications discussed in this chapter are as follows:

- The application should be one for which microcomputers are well suited.
- Software for this application should be commercially available for the microcomputers most often found in schools and other educational settings.[1]

DATA PROCESSING

What Is Data Processing?

Data processing has been defined as the "converting of facts into usable form."[2] While that definition may sound both reasonable and simple, one might ask what it means in practical terms and, further, how data that are processed differ from the unprocessed variety.

To answer these questions, we turn to a simple illustration involving a school administrator who is responsible for maintaining the records for a moderate-sized school district of about 4500 students. (See Figure 6.1.) A medical inspector from the Department of Public Health has been sent to the school district as part of a regional effort to prevent an outbreak of flu, and asks whether any of the students in the district have not been vaccinated against the disease. The administrator knows that several students have not had their shots, but to find their names will require going over the medical records of the whole district. If a record-keeping system were available on computer, it would be far faster to "process" the data by computer than by hand. That is, the students' medical records are the unprocessed data; a list of names of the students who have not been vaccinated would be the processed data.

Adding, subtracting, multiplying, and dividing numbers or scores are a kind of data processing known as *calculating*. For an illustration of calculating, let us return to our school administrator. The president of the school board has requested that the average standardized achievement test scores for each class

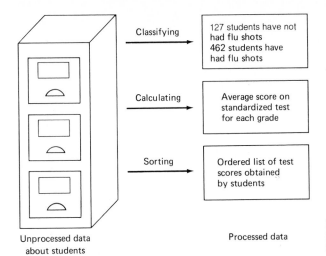

Classifying → 127 students have not had flu shots
462 students have had flu shots

Calculating → Average score on standardized test for each grade

Sorting → Ordered list of test scores obtained by students

Unprocessed data about students

Processed data

FIGURE 6.1
Data processing makes information usable.

in the district be presented at the school board meeting that evening. If the data had been prepared for computer analysis, a computer could do all that calculating very rapidly. However, it would be an impossible task to do so much arithmetic by hand in such a short time. Whether the processing is done by computer or by hand, the processed data will consist of a table of the average scores by class and school. One might say that the original data are summarized in the report. Or one might say that the individual test scores are the unprocessed data whereas the report contains the processed data.

Now suppose that our administrator is asked to furnish the guidance department of the high school with an ordered list of scores and the names of the students who obtained them, so that special plans can be made for instruction of those students who scored extremely well and those who did very poorly. Without a computer, this would be another time-consuming chore. Each score would have to be compared with every other score until all the scores were arranged from lowest to highest. The unprocessed data here would be the unsorted list of scores and names; the processed information is the sorted list.

Data Processing Operations

The following are operations used in data processing. When they are applied to data, the data are considered *processed*. Any of these eight operations may be used alone or with one or more of the others.

1 Recording
2 Coding
3 Sorting
4 Calculating

5 Summarizing
6 Communicating
7 Storing
8 Retrieving

Each of these operations is explained below.

1 *Recording:* Recording has to do with the transfer of data from one medium to another. For example, it includes writing or typing information onto a sheet of paper and typing data into machine memory. Records are formed by recording data. An important aspect of recording is verification, or double checking, to ensure that the data are accurately recorded. Verification should be part of any recording operation.

2 *Coding:* The process of assigning codes to classes of information is called *coding.* For example, job classifications might be identified by a number, so that ''plumber'' is represented by 1, ''electrician'' by 2, and ''clerk'' by 3. Letters can also be used as codes. Sometimes cash register receipts from stores show letter codes for items purchased (e.g., ''TY'' for toy department and ''MDS'' for merchandise). Codes save space on a printed page or in a computer's memory, and they may be recorded more rapidly than whole words.

3 *Sorting:* Arranging data in order or in groups according to some plan is known as *sorting.* For example, on a school's roster, all the students in a particular grade are placed together; the list then can be said to be sorted on the basis of grade. If applications to a college are listed in order of date of application, the list is sorted by date. Sorting can also be a method of selection. Consider the illustration given earlier, the need to identify students who have had flu shots: here, students can be sorted into two groups — those who have had shots and those who have not.

4 *Calculating:* Computers can add, subtract, multiply and divide. Application of these processes to data is known as *calculating.*

5 *Summarizing:* The process of taking a large amount of data and presenting it in usable form after other data processing procedures have been applied to it is called *summarizing.* For example, to compute an average from a long list of scores, we first do some calculating. Then the average can be used as a summary of the list. Summaries can be given in tabular form, as lists of statements, in pictorial form (such as a graph), or in other modes.

6 *Communicating:* Data may exist in one place (e.g., in a file cabinet, a computer's memory, or a bookkeeper's ledger), but it may be needed elsewhere. Transmitting data to (and receiving data from) another location is what is meant by *communicating.* Computers can communicate with one another using modem systems and telephone lines. Computers can also communicate with disk storage systems. Further, people can communicate with computers using keyboards and monitors.

7 *Storing:* Placing data in some orderly form for later use is known as *storing.* Data may be stored in a variety of ways. For example, for short-term storage during data processing, data may be stored in the random-access memory of the computer. For longer periods, data can be stored on hard disks, floppy disks, punched cards, magnetic tape, microfilm, printed paper, or some other medium. New methods of storage are constantly being explored.

8 *Retrieving:* Once information is stored, it is of no use if it cannot be retrieved. Retrieval of information stored by electronic means depends upon proper coding and formatting. That is, the data must be placed on the disk or tape in such a way that they can be located and read when needed.

These eight operations (recording, sorting, coding, classifying, calculating, communicating, storing, and retrieving) are combined in programs that convert computer systems into data processing machines. Some of the useful functions a computer can perform with these programs are noted in later sections of this chapter.

Speed and Accuracy in Data Processing

If you were processing data by hand, you might think you were doing well if you managed to perform about 20 to 30 operations (such as addition) a minute. At this rate, if you worked without stopping, you could complete 1000 additions in about 45 minutes to 1 hour. That number of additions could be performed by most microcomputers in 1 second or less. For example, retrieving 1000 scores from the files, calculating the averages, and typing a table of the results might require more than a day to do by hand. A computer will read the data from files existing in a suitable form (e.g., on floppy or hard disks) in perhaps 1 minute or less, take 1 or 2 seconds to do the calculations, and print the summary table in 1 or 2 minutes. The practical meaning of *speed* in computerized data processing is that a computer will require only minutes to complete a task that would take a single worker a day or two.

Differences in speed between computer systems may not be observable in a particular application and therefore may not be of great concern to users of that application.[3] A user whose primary application involves typing data into a computer from a keyboard at the rate of 6 characters per second will probably not be aware that one computer can process 1 million characters per second and another 2 million per second.

Computers are not only fast but also extremely accurate data processors. Their accuracy can be better understood in terms of the functions they perform. For example, if a person were asked to locate files with certain specific entries by going through a full file cabinet, it would not be surprising if his or her error rate were as high as 10 or 15 percent. However, it would be surprising to see a computer make any errors at all on this task if it were working properly.

The most common source of error in computer-processed data is error by the user, such as the wrong data typed at the keyboard. In addition, programming problems (called *bugs*) sometimes arise which can produce processing errors. (Perhaps one of the most notorious bugs in the short history of micro-computer software was in the software for the BASIC programming language when a particular microcomputer was first introduced on the market. When 0.1 was divided by 10, the result was 0.001 rather than 0.01, the correct answer.[4]) Besides user error and programming bugs, other sources of error are heat accu-mulation in the equipment, problems with electrical current, and equipment that requires repair or maintenance.

On a practical level, then, computers can process data much more quickly and accurately than people doing the same thing by hand. Some computers are faster than others, and there are even programming techniques and equipment that can make computers process more quickly than they ordinarily do. But even the slowest computers are able to process large amounts of information more rapidly and accurately than people can. We now turn to the kinds of chores usually given to computers.

WORD PROCESSING

When computers are used to perform data processing operations on words and text, the procedure is called *word processing*. Creating, editing, viewing, stor-ing, retrieving, and printing text are all greatly facilitated when computers are used for word processing. Word processing permits extraordinary flexibility, far beyond anything that is possible with an ordinary typewriter. When a computer is used as a word processor, words are input through a keyboard, much as they would be typed on a typewriter. The letters and words then appear on a CRT screen. Since they are not permanently etched on the screen, these letters and words can be easily edited. Whole paragraphs can be moved between docu-ments, or within a document. This flexibility allows an author to do complete editing before anything is placed on paper. When a document is finished, it may be saved on a disk and then transferred to paper using a printer.

An Illustration of Word Processing

A simple illustration of the editing capabilities of word processing should suffice to show the potential of the procedure.[5] Let us say that we have a microcom-puter programmed to do word processing. The following is typed into the com-puter and is presently displayed on the CRT:

THE EFFECTS OF WORDPORCESSING ON LANGUAGE ARE
TO NEW TO RECOINGNIZE.

The reader will immediately notice several problems with this sentence. First, words are misspelled. Second, we might want to change the wording or word order to improve clarity.

We will repair the spelling errors first. Typically, there is a *cursor* — a symbol the size of a single character (it may be a box, a line, a dash, etc.) — on the screen. The cursor is an indicator that tells the user where the next character typed on the keyboard will appear in the text. We place the cursor in the next position after the incorrect letters in the first misspelled word, using special cursor-movement keys on the keyboard (keys for moving the cursor up, down, right, or left). Then we hit the DELETE key on the keyboard to "erase" the inappropriate letters. Next we type in the correct letters. Finally, we move the cursor out of the sentence. The space in the sentence made by the cursor closes automatically. The other misspellings are corrected in the same way. In a few seconds, the sentence looks like this:

THE EFFECTS OF WORD PROCESSING ON LANGUAGE ARE
TOO NEW TO RECOGNIZE.

Now suppose that we want to edit the sentence to improve clarity. Using the same cursor-movement and DELETE keys, we can erase the words ARE TOO NEW TO RECOGNIZE. We then type IT IS STILL TOO EARLY TO JUDGE in front of THE EFFECTS . . . at the beginning of the sentence. On the CRT screen, the old parts of the sentence appear to have moved over to make room for the new. The improved sentence now reads:

IT IS STILL TOO EARLY TO JUDGE THE EFFECTS OF WORD
PROCESSING ON LANGUAGE.

In the same way that words can be moved and replaced, whole paragraphs and sections can be relocated or altered. Further, uppercase and lowercase, margins, tabs, and other useful features are usually available in word processing programs.

Writing on a CRT screen suggests some new ways of thinking about written materials. The screen of the CRT monitor shows a highly changeable image of the text. This image is analogous to the clay used by a sculptor or model maker. Key words or phrases (e.g., words from a spelling or vocabulary list) may be quickly located in the text and moved, altered, or deleted. The value of teaching language arts, particularly writing, with a word processing program has been recognized.[6]

Word processing programs become even more powerful writing aids when they are paired with thesaurus and dictionary programs. These programs can automatically check spelling and provide alternative words to avoid repetition. Word processing makes writing and document preparation an entirely new experience.

Uses of Word Processing

Word processing programs can be very useful to school administrators, clerical staffs, guidance personnel, and anyone else who must prepare texts or correspondence. With a word processor, for example, one can produce numerous identical letters — with only the address and salutation changed, so that each recipient of the letter will have the impression that it was written to him or her alone. Similarly, memoranda and other correspondence can be addressed to selected teachers or a whole school. Documents that must be newly prepared every academic year can be quickly constructed using the version from the past year, by simply changing dates, names, and other entries as necessary.

A *template* of a frequently used document can be saved on a disk. When a new version of the document is needed, the template is retrieved from the disk and the new information is added. The new document in turn can be saved on a disk for long-term storage; and as many copies as are required may be printed. An example would be an annual list of room assignments, indicating the teachers and classes assigned to each room in a school. First, the template is prepared. This contains only the title and the room numbers. This template is then saved on a disk. At the start of each semester, the new list is prepared by retrieving the form from the disk, displaying it on the CRT, and filling in the teachers' names and class numbers. Finally, the completed list is printed for distribution and saved on a disk. It can easily be retrieved and changed during the semester if necessary.

This discussion of word processing has only scratched the surface. It is safe to say that word processing is at present one of the primary uses of microcomputers. There are many programs available that are quite reasonable in price, considering what they can do. Some have special features to make letter writing easier. Others are designed to support preparation of large documents and contain such features as page numbering, automatic transfer of large files to disks, and commands to assist in preparing tables. Many word processing programs can be operated with dictionary and thesaurus programs, as we noted earlier. Some even include mathematical functions and operations. As with other software, one should do some shopping before purchasing a word processing program, to ensure that all the desired features are included.

DATABASE MANAGEMENT SYSTEMS

A database management system (DBMS) primarily utilizes recording, coding, sorting, summarizing, storing, and retrieving operations. With a DBMS one can form files, store and retrieve them, update the information in the files, and print summaries. One might think of these files in terms of the contents of a conventional file cabinet. Some DBMS programs are meant to handle a large number of small files, such as index-card files. Others are designed to manage very large files; these require hard-disk systems with large off-line storage capabilities. Many database management systems are designed to handle such large amounts of data that they can be run only on large computer systems with huge internal and external storage capacity. The kind of system used in the example given later (see page 142) would probably require a microcomputer with at least 128K to 256K of random-access memory, two or more disk drives, and a high-speed printer.

Structuring Data

Designing a structured database is a task for someone sophisticated in the field of data management. However, educators should know something about how DBMS programs structure data in order to be able to choose a system suitable for their needs. How data are structured in a database will have important implications for how the DBMS works.

Four approaches to data structure are generally used in designing database management systems: (1) list, (2) hierarchical, (3) network, and (4) relational. Each of these is explained below:

List structure: This is a relatively simple approach to data structure in which information is stored sequentially. (See Figure 6.2.) The assumption underlying this structure is that data will be accessed sequentially.

Hierarchical structure: Information is stored in ordered fashion so that subordinate elements are stored under superordinate ones. For example, street address may be stored under student's name, and entries under street address would be city, state, and zip code. Thus, a hierarchical structure might resemble an inverted tree. (See Figure 6.3.)

Network structure: The network structure provides more than one avenue to access a single piece of information, as shown in Figure 6.4. The process of accessing information may begin with any data unit; this provides greater flexibility in searching.

FIGURE 6.2
Sequential-list data structure.

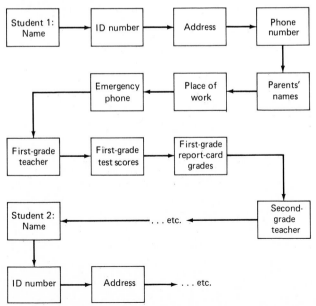

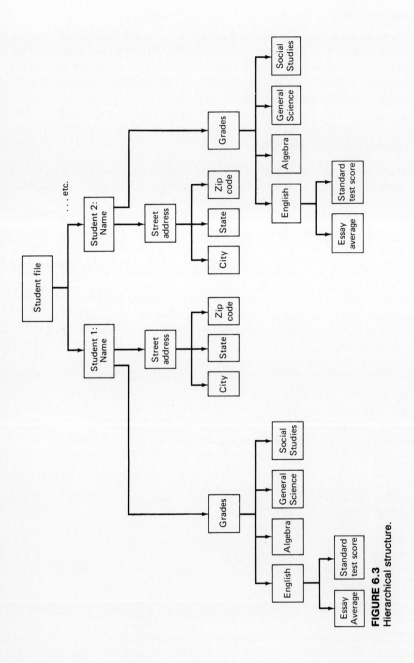

FIGURE 6.3
Hierarchical structure.

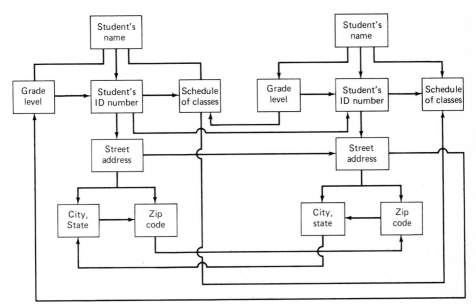

FIGURE 6.4
Network structure.

Relational structure: Information is stored in tables which contain data in the form of relations. Figure 6.5 shows students' names stored with zip codes in one table, with grade level in another. Such tables could be created to contain all the records kept on students in a school. Relational structure can greatly increase the flexibility of a DBMS; however, it requires a considerable amount of computer memory. At present, microcomputers do not have sufficient memory to make full implementation of relational databases an easy matter.

Among the desirable features of a DBMS software package, the educator should consider the flexibility of the database and the ability to update all files with new entries. Changing situations or hindsight will eventually reveal new needs. A flexible database management system that permits expanding or

FIGURE 6.5
Structure of relational database.

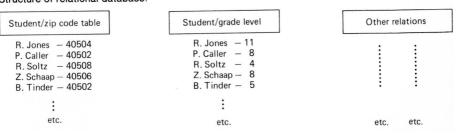

changing the database is preferable to one that requires reentry of all the data every time a new need is recognized. Further, a DBMS that requires entry of each piece of data only once, even though it will be used in several different files, is desirable. In addition, the ability to automatically update every file with each new entry can save valuable time.

An Example of a DBMS Application

To illustrate the use of a database management system, consider a high school guidance counselor who is required to maintain confidential records of test scores, disciplinary actions, and notes from counseling sessions with students. The school administration does not want these data to be in the school's mainframe computer-based record system, because of the sensitive nature of the material. (Even with security codes and various other precautions, the data could possibly be accessed by someone who had no proper use for them.) Therefore, it has been decided that the confidential guidance records will be kept separately, using a microcomputer system in the guidance office. A hierarchical DBMS has been chosen by the guidance counselor, because it is easy to learn and use and because it presents certain features for security not found on other systems.

To understand how this system works, we must review DBMS vocabulary. First, the database is made up of files. A *file* is simply a collection of related data. The guidance counselor in our example may keep a separate file for each grade. Second, the data in each file are organized into records. A *record* is a set of related information that can be identified by a *keyword* (or label). Each first-year student has a record in the first file, each second-year student has a record in the second file, and so on. The keyword for each student's record is the student's name. Third, the information in a record is stored in a series of *fields*. Each field has a name, a length, and a position. Figure 6.6 shows the relationship

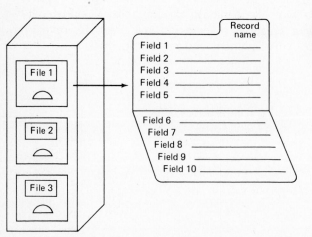

FIGURE 6.6
Files are made up of records which contain fields.

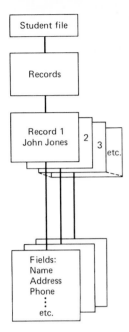

FIGURE 6.7
File structure showing relationship of files, records, and fields in a database containing information about students.

between files, records, and fields, compared with a conventional file cabinet. Figure 6.7 shows the structure of the guidance counselor's database.

In this example, the software consists of a series of programs stored on disks that are designed to create and manage files. The first thing that happens when the program is placed into the computer is that all the functions which have been designed into the program are summarized on the screen, providing a *menu* of program options. For example, the program might permit setting up new files, entering data to existing files, printing reports from information gathered from the data, etc. The *main menu* might appear on the screen as follows:

```
MAIN MENU


CHOOSE NUMBER FROM BELOW:


    (1)   SETUP

    (2)   ENTER

    (3)   SELECT

    (4)   UPDATE

    (5)   SORT

    (6)   PRINT

    (7)   QUIT
```

The user is requested to choose a function. Since the first thing that must be done is to set up the files, the guidance counselor must initially run the SETUP program. After SETUP is loaded from the disk into the microcomputer's RAM, the following is displayed on the CRT screen:

```
    SET-UP FILES
************************
1.   CREATE NEW FILE
2.   DELETE EXISTING FILE
3.   CHANGE EXISTING FILE
4.   GO TO MAIN MENU

     SELECT NUMBER:

************************
```

This display is called the *program menu.*

If creation of a new file is desired, 1 is typed, and the CREATE NEW FILE display appears on the CRT:

```
    CREATE FILE
***********************
FILE NAME: TEST SCORES
           _____

   FILE DEFINITION (TO END HIT 'RETURN')

FIELD    FIELD NAME    SIZE   TYPE-CODE

1.       STUDENT NAME   25       A
2.       BIRTH DATE      8       A
3.       TELEPHONE       8       A
4.       GENDER          1       A
5.       STUDENT NO.     7       N
6.       TEST1 NAME     20       A
7.       TEST1-DATE      8       A
8.       SCORES-TEST1    4       N
9.       TEST2 NAME     20       A
10.      TEST2-DATE      8       A
11.      SCORES-TEST2    4       N
12.
```

The purpose of this display is *file definition,* that is, specification of the characteristics of the data to be included in the file. First the file name is requested, and then the fields in each record are defined. The cursor appears at the start of the next field to be defined. As information is filled in, the RETURN key is hit, and the cursor moves to the next blank line.

This example shows some of the characteristics of file definition. First, the file is named TEST SCORES. The guidance counselor will use this name to retrieve the file from the disk when it has been stored. Second, each field is named. Third, each field is assigned a certain size, which is the number of characters that can fit into the field. For example, dates have been allocated 8 characters. This is done so that each day, month, and year can be represented by two digits, and a separator can be placed between the day and the month and between the month and the year. Thus, December 11, 1983, becomes 12/11/83 and occupies the 8 spaces. Finally, each field is identified as a numerical (N) or an alphabetic (A) field. This is important because computers are usually programmed to treat numbers differently from chains of characters (called *strings*), which may be alphabetic, symbolic, and numeric.

When the data definitions have been completed, the data can be entered. To do this in our example, one must return to the main menu and run the ENTER program. This program begins by requesting the name of the file. It then gets the file definition from the disk, and a data entry display is shown on the screen with the various field names. Field length is indicated by a number of dashes, and the cursor appears in the first position on the first line:

```
        DATA ENTRY

*******************************

STUDENT NAME:
             _____
BIRTH DATE:
             _____
TELEPHONE:
             _____
GENDER:
             _
STUDENT NO:
             _____
TEST1 NAME:
             _____
TEST1-DATE:
             _____
SCORES-TEST1:
             ____
        :
        :
        :
      etc.
```

Since the CRT will typically be capable of showing only about 20 to 24 lines at a time, only that many lines will appear on the screen. As new data are added, the display moves (or *scrolls*) upward to reveal more of the display at the bottom of the screen while the topmost text disappears off the top. The screen is like a window through which only part of a record can be seen at any given time.

Once a record is entered, it may automatically be stored on disk and the blank display shown again so that the next record can be added. When all the data have been entered and stored on the disk, the guidance counselor can return to the main menu, where various possibilities exist for retrieving and printing selected information.

Referring to the main menu shown earlier, we have already seen what the SETUP and ENTER subprograms do. The SELECT program allows the user to choose particular records. For example, suppose that the guidance counselor wants to send out a notice to the parents of all the third-year students who have scored below 65 in test 1. This group could be selected from among the students on the disk, and a temporary file of these students could be created. Then, using the print program, mailing labels could be printed from this temporary file.

The UPDATE program allows the addition of information to individual records. For example, when new report cards are issued, the counselor may want to add the new grades to the files.

The SORT program makes it possible to order records according to given specifications. To illustrate, let us say that the guidance counselor wants to order the students' overall performance on the most recently administered standardized test, so that those who performed extremely well can be identified for enrichment activities beyond the regular program and those whose scores were lowest can be given the appropriate assistance. The sorted list of students that is developed using SORT can be printed with the PRINT program.

The PRINT program in our example has a number of options. For example, the user can print mailing labels after retrieving addresses from the files. Also, there is an option to print complete records, including field names, or parts of records. In this way, information from a record that is not required for a report can be omitted. In addition, there is a summary option that can be used when the guidance counselor does not want to know information about individual students, as in completing a monthly report on the number of students who came in for guidance counseling.

By use of the SELECT and PRINT subprograms, the report can summarize the numbers of boys and girls at each grade level who appeared for counseling.

The QUIT option terminates the program.

This summary of a hierarchical database management system was deliberately simplified; and it was not meant to describe any particular program actually on the market. Rather, it was meant to give the reader a sense of how such a program operates.

Using Database Management Systems in Schools

Database management systems are used in many noninstructional school activities. Some specific applications are briefly described below. However, this list is not meant to be comprehensive or to endorse certain uses. Each of the uses described depends on "off-the-shelf" software that can be purchased in computer stores and through mail-order outlets. None is an expensive custom-made program.

• *School library:* A DBMS is used as a card catalog and indexing system in a junior high school library. The program permits retrieval of the usual card catalog information using author, title, Library of Congress number, or subject. The files are stored on a hard-disk system. Complete instructions for using the machine are on a page on the table next to the equipment. The system is connected to a printer. Teachers, students, and the librarian are able to print selected reading lists, titles by a particular author, or a catalog of holdings by subject area.[7]

- *Records for the school cafeteria:* All the records and recipes are kept with a database management system. The food-on-hand file is posted daily. The other files include information about equipment maintenance, menus, and supplies; these are updated only as necessary. The system is used to print daily recipes and menus, and monthly summaries of food used and number of meals produced. An annual inventory of equipment is printed for the school administration.

- *Athletic department:* A high school athletic department uses a database management system to do several things. First, it keeps track of the skill levels attained by students in their athletic courses. It also maintains a register of students with special skills who might be recruited to help with class demonstrations. Finally, equipment inventories and maintenance records are maintained with the DBMS.

- *Special education resource pool:* A moderately large school district uses a DBMS to catalog materials, resources, expertise, and programs that are available within the district for handicapped children. The system is capable of locating entries in the database with an identification number, or by codes that indicate type of handicap, age, grade level, or range of test scores. The data are updated monthly by the district office as new information is received. Once a month the district office sends updated information to the schools.

- *Test development:* In a junior high school the language arts department maintains a file of test items. For each item, the question itself, a topic descriptor, the source, the difficulty level (determined from previous administration), the intended grade level, the correct answer, and the years during which the item was used in the schoolwide achievement testing program are on file. This information can be used by teachers to help prepare language arts tests.

- *School administration:* A small school district is able to keep its personnel files with DBMS on a microcomputer and a floppy-disk system. The disks are kept locked in a file cabinet so that only people with authorization have access to them. The information on the disk is printed whenever a change is made. Since these records are important, a duplicate disk is maintained for backup. The system was designed so that personnel records can be sorted by category of employee (e.g., teacher, principal, clerk, bus driver), address of employee (zip code), name, and category of certification. For example, if the superintendent is looking for a teacher who has a food handler's permit to assist with refreshments at a school dance, the computer could find that person quickly. The district can also keep its building maintenance files with the same DBMS. For this application, sorting can be done by the month in which required maintenance is scheduled. Thus, if, according to the regulations of the local fire department, the furnace requires cleaning in April, June, September, and December, the computer can keep track of this. With this system, maintenance of school equipment and facilities has become more efficient and effective.

• *Services for students:* In addition to the applications discussed earlier for the guidance department, there are many uses for a database management system in various services for students. The complete system of students' records can be kept with a DBMS. Files can be created for specific purposes. For example, students' medical records can be stored in one file, their academic records in another, and their attendance records in a third. Storing all these data on one system permits certain flexibility in combining files. For example, from the medical records one can determine which students have chronic illnesses or disabling conditions. This information can be paired with data on attendance and achievement to identify students who are having difficulty keeping up with their work because of their health. One well-developed application using DBMS is college and vocational counseling and advising.[8]

These applications do not represent an exhaustive list. Most database management systems are highly flexible and useful.[9] In fact the variety of applications is probably endless. Further, there is considerable variation in features between programs. For example, some permit arithmetic operations within the program; some have many word processing features; some can do complicated sorting very quickly. Some handle only short files; others permit very long detailed entries. The versatility of these programs can render them useful for many functions within a single educational setting. Therefore, selection of a DBMS should be done carefully, with a view toward meeting various needs. In addition, consideration should be given to file compatibility, since files created with some programs may not be accessible with other programs.[10] Proper choice of a database management system can result in more efficiency and capability for a number of noninstructional school functions.

SPREADSHEET PROGRAMS

What Is a Spreadsheet?

A spreadsheet is a long multicolumned ledger that is used in business to keep records of expenditures, receipts, profits, etc. (See Figure 6.8.) Such a sheet enables one to sum across columns and rows, calculate expenses, and project profits and losses. Even though some sheets are very large, with as many as fifty columns and rows, there may not be sufficient space on a page to keep track of a single account or activity. Sometimes several pages will be required to include all the needed entries.

A person who has to keep financial records might dream of the perfect

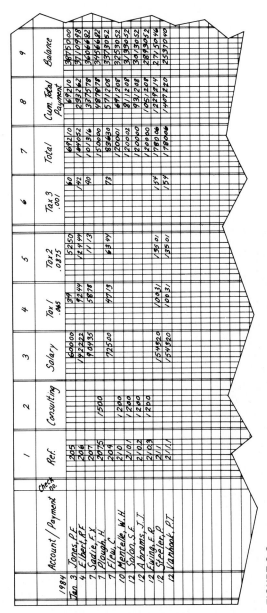

FIGURE 6.8
An accounting spreadsheet.

spreadsheet. First, such a sheet would have as many columns and rows as are needed for any application. This would eliminate the need for continuation pages. Second, many different values would be computed automatically from simple entries. For example, if every employee is to be paid a certain basic monthly salary, the spreadsheet could be set up so that entering this amount will result in the automatic computation of deductions, including those for taxes, benefits, insurance, etc.

The ability to design extremely large spreadsheets and the ability to perform a number of calculations automatically are major attractions of computerized spreadsheets. Another advantage of these programs is that they permit calculations on a conditional basis. For example, an employer may have to pay insurance for any employee who earns more than $600 in one month. Because overtime and sales commissions may differ from one month to the next, the payment will not be required for every employee every month. Using a spreadsheet program, the computer can be instructed to make the deduction only if an employee's salary exceeds $600. The ability to use conditional statements gives a flexibility to spreadsheet programs that makes them practical for a variety of situations which occur in keeping books and records. In addition, a computerized spreadsheet program might permit testing of mathematical or statistical models; printing of tables; and application of a variety of arithmetic, statistical, trigonometric, algebraic, and logical functions.

It has been said that the first spreadsheet program designed for small computers, VisiCalc, did more to expand use of microcomputers when it first was introduced in 1979 than any other product at the time.[11] This happened partly because spreadsheet programs were quickly found to be useful for a variety of applications not originally envisioned for them, such as project planning, record keeping, and problem solving.[12]

Spreadsheet programs can be utilized in schools in many ways. In addition to their obvious suitability for maintaining school financial records, spreadsheets can be used to determine final grades and grade-point averages. They are also useful for planning and decision making. For example, with a computer and spreadsheet software at a school board meeting it is possible to explore costs of various options and plans during the meeting itself.

An Example of a Spreadsheet Application

We now take a look at how a typical spreadsheet program works. As with other applications in this chapter, this discussion is not designed to represent any specific commercial product; rather, it is meant to give a picture of how spreadsheet programs operate.

We begin by looking at the layout of a spreadsheet on the CRT screen. Initially, the top of the screen contains a horizontal line of letters and a vertical line of numbers at the left; the rest of the screen is blank.

The screen appears as follows:

```
COMMAND:

          A         B         C         D
       ---------------------------------------
   1
   2
   3
   4
   5
   6
   7
   8
   9
  10
```

The cursor is in the leftmost top location on the spreadsheet. This location is identified as A1, since it is the point where column A crosses row 1. The cursor can be moved, using keyboard commands, to any location on the sheet. Notice that the heading on the top line indicates columns A, B, C, and D. Rows are identified by the numbers 1 to 10 on the left of the screen.

The screen of the CRT may be thought of as a "window" view of the spreadsheet. That is, the CRT displays only a small part of the spreadsheet at a time. The spreadsheet can be "scrolled" by moving the cursor. This means that, if we want to see columns E through H, we need only move the cursor to the extreme right until these letters appear (A to D will move off the screen to the left). Similarly, we make lines 11 and beyond appear by moving the cursor to the bottom of the screen. This is like moving the CRT window to a new location from which to view the spreadsheet. If the cursor is moved to reveal lines 20 to 29 and rows E to H, the screen appears as follows:

```
COMMAND:

          E         F         G         H
       ---------------------------------------
  20
  21
  22
  23
  24
  25
  26
  27
  28
  29
```

The word COMMAND appears at the top of the spreadsheet window. In this location we can indicate the commands we want the spreadsheet to follow, such as reading files from a disk, saving files on a disk, and treating the entry in a particular row or column as a label or a numerical value. The following illustration, in which the costs of different computer systems are compared, will serve as an example.

We begin by labeling the A column COMPONENT and listing the components and features we want to include in our system. We then label the columns with the names of the systems we are considering and fill in the prices. The command LABEL A1 TO D1 tells the machine that entries in columns A to D in the first row will be labels.

```
COMMAND:   LABEL A1 TO D1
     A          B           C           D
1 COMPONENT  SYSTEM 1    SYSTEM 2    SYSTEM 3
2 64K RAM      1,110        595         895
3 DISK DR       299         350         450
4 COLOR CRT     450         399        INCL
5 PRINTER       299         359         399
6 BASIC        INCL         100          99
7 MODEM         119         250         119
8 SOFTWARE      729        1234         678
```

When all the prices are entered, we can use the features of the spreadsheet program to study them. Suppose that we are interested, initially, in two figures: the cost of the hardware and the cost of the software for each system. We obtain these figures by placing in the COMMAND line the instructions: B9: B2+ ... B5+B7:FOR C9 to D9. These commands tell the computer that the sum of the entries in B2 through B5 plus the cost of the modem is to be placed at B9. The last part of the command instructs the computer to perform similarly in columns C and D. We get the software costs in a similar manner, adding the entries for SOFTWARE and the BASIC language. If the costs are included in the price, the entry INCL will automatically be treated as zero. The results of the commands to add hardware and software costs are shown below:

```
COMMAND: B9:B2...B5+B7:FOR C9 TO D9
     A          B           C           D
1 COMPONENT  SYSTEM 1    SYSTEM 2    SYSTEM 3
2 48K RAM      1,110        595         895
3 DISK DR       299         350         450
4 COLOR CRT     450         399        INCL
5 PRINTER       299         359         399
6 BASIC        INCL         100          99
7 MODEM         119         250         119
8 SOFTWARE      729        1234         678
9              2277        1594        1863
10              729        1334         777
```

Clearly, the hardware for one computer system costs most; but the software package for that computer costs least. It might therefore be helpful to know the total cost of each system. Further, the ratio of hardware to software costs for the present applications might be used as an indication of relative software costs in general for each system. First we indicate that lines 11 and 12 in column A should contain the labels TOTAL and RATIO, respectively. Then, we place the proper equations on the COMMAND line, and the total cost of each system (line 9 + line 10) and the ratio of hardware to software costs (line 9/line 10) are computed and placed in lines 11 and 12:

```
COMMAND:
        A              B           C           D

1 COMPONENT    SYSTEM 1      SYSTEM 2    SYSTEM 3

2 48K RAM        1,110         595         895
3 DISK DR          299         350         450
4 COLOR CRT        450         399        INCL
5 PRINTER          299         359         399
6 BASIC           INCL         100          99
7 MODEM            119         250         119
8 SOFTWARE         729        1234         678
9 HARD. TOT       2277        1594        1863
10 SOF. TOT        729        1334         777
11 TOTAL          3006        2928        2640
12 RATIO          3.12        1.19        2.40
```

Since we have added two lines, the top line is now off the CRT screen. This is shown above by the dotted lines; on a real computer system, line 1 would not now be visible.

We can now see from lines 11 and 12 that system 1 is most expensive in terms of hardware and total cost. However, the software costs least for this machine, and the ratio of hardware costs to software costs is most favorable (that is, software costs least relative to hardware). If additional tasks will be assigned to the computer after a time, this is an indication that the software will be less expensive for the first system.

Now suppose that the local computer dealer is prepared to give the school a special sale price for system 1. She will provide the modem and disk drive for a total of $250 if the district will buy the full system from her. This changes all the figures we have computed in the spreadsheet for system 1. However, with the spreadsheet program, the change is easy to accommodate. Either we can make a new column showing the new prices, or we can change the entries for the disk drive and modem, and the last four lines will be changed automatically by the computer. This is illustrated below:

```
COMMAND:
        A              B           C           D

1 COMPONENT    SYSTEM 1      SYSTEM 2    SYSTEM 3

2 48K RAM        1,110         595         895
3 DISK DR          125         350         450
4 COLOR CRT        450         399        INCL
5 PRINTER          299         359         399
6 BASIC           INCL         100          99
7 MODEM            125         250         119
8 SOFTWARE         729        1234         678
9 HARD TOT        2109        1594        1863
10 SOF. TOT        729        1334         777
11 TOTAL          2838        2928        2640
12 RATIO          2.89        1.19        2.40
```

By dividing the $250 evenly between the disk drive and modem, we automatically adjust all the figures for system 1 below line 8. This illustration is, admittedly, oversimplified. However, with more complicated tables and problems, this feature can be extremely useful.

Purchasing Spreadsheet Software

A number of spreadsheet software packages are on the market for microcomputers. Some can use files created by other programs (e.g., database management programs); this provides additional capability and flexibility of operation. If such joint usage of programs is planned, one should be certain that the files of all program packages will be compatible. One way to ensure this would be to get a demonstration from the vendor.

Another consideration in purchasing software is memory requirements. The random-access memory available on many microcomputer systems does not normally exceed 64K without additional hardware. Once the spreadsheet program is loaded into memory, there might be only 15 or 20K remaining for data; this is often not sufficient to handle enough data for processing a whole problem. Various approaches have been used to get around this difficulty, involving disk storage or continuation tables. However, small microcomputers do not offer enough memory to efficiently process the data in many larger spreadsheet applications (such as the payroll and financial records of a medium-sized school system with 100 to 150 employees).

NETWORKS

Networking is one of the most recent applications of microcomputers, and one of the most promising. It requires special hardware and software. In this section we will discuss different kinds of networks, the necessary software and hardware for each, and some examples.

A *network* may be defined as a system of elements that are combined to work together. For example, a radio network consists of a number of stations in different locations that transmit cooperatively to enable a broader dispersion of the signal than would be possible by any one station transmitting alone. Similarly, computers operating in networks can expand their capabilities beyond what they are capable of achieving alone.

Types of Networks

Three kinds of computer networks are: (1) resource-sharing networks, (2) communications networks, and (3) distributed processing networks. (See Figure 6.9.) A single computer system might be involved in more than one kind of network. The three types of networks are discussed below.

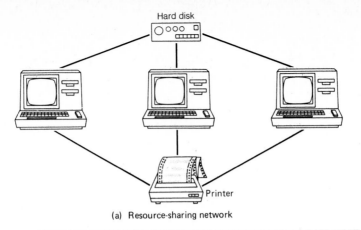

(a) Resource-sharing network

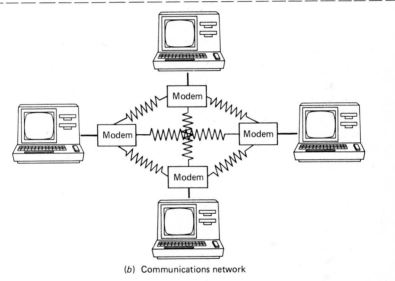

(b) Communications network

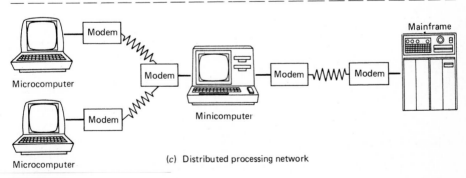

(c) Distributed processing network

FIGURE 6.9
Three kinds of computer networks.

1   *Resource-sharing networks:* These networks are designed to allow several computer installations to share peripheral devices. For example, purchasing an expensive hard-disk system for each computer in a school district might not be an effective way to use funds, but several computers can form a network to share a hard-disk system. Expensive high-quality printers and plotters may also be shared in networks. For example, a high school physics department may require a graph plotter for about three hours a week, a chemistry department may require it for only five hours a week, and an electronics shop may require it for about three hours a week during the second half of the semester. For the remainder of the time, it can be used by the school's maintenance staff to keep track of deviations in the air conditioning and heating systems, an application that results in reduced labor demands and better maintenance. The academic programs have important needs for the plotter, but these needs are too limited to justify the purchase of one. By networking the microcomputer systems in the classrooms with the school's central minicomputer system, both the academic departments and the maintenance staff can take advantage of this expensive plotter.

2   *Communications networks:* These networks are designed to facilitate transfer of information from one location to another. Sometimes communication networks operate as mail systems or bulletin boards. For example, if you want to ask the library at another elementary school in the network about borrowing a book, you can type a message into your computer and then send it to the computer in the other school, where it is printed. The hard copy of the message is then placed in the librarian's mailbox. Or it might be recorded on a disk. Periodically, the librarian can query the computer to see if there are any new messages. If there are, they might be displayed on the CRT or printed. A microcomputer in a school can also be used to transfer data or records to and from the central district office. For example, a teacher might want a copy of the school board's policy regarding class trips. The policy can be obtained quickly and easily by accessing the policy database maintained by the district's central computer.

3   *Distributed processing networks:* Microcomputers can be used to process data in many situations; but when there are very many data or when too many operations are required to be handled efficiently by a microcomputer, processing can be passed on to a more capable computer over telephone lines. This is called *uploading*. The processed data can be returned to the microcomputer (*downloaded*). Software can also be uploaded and downloaded. For example, some national networks download programs from their large central computer to subscribers' computers. With such networks there is an initial fee and then a connection charge each time the system is used. In addition to software, these networks can provide a number of the benefits of communications and distributed processing, such as access to financial databases, airline schedules, consumer information, and news services. These networks are sometimes called *videotext systems.* Two of the better-known companies offering these kinds of services are The Source and CompuServe Information Services.[13]

Making Connections in a Network

You will recall from Chapter 2 that a *modem* translates between a computer's digital signal and the kind of signal carried by a telephone line (see Figure 6.10). Modems are required for each computer in a network. Some of the modems are rather sophisticated and allow more than one computer to be connected. There are a few standard modem connections, among them the RS232 series. One must make sure the modem required for a particular network is compatible with the machines, the telephone lines, and the computer systems involved. One must also be sure that the cable used with a modem is of the proper type, and that the lines in the cable are connected to the proper connectors. Sometimes the intricacies of connecting modems to computers require considerable expertise.

The speed at which a modem can transmit is an important consideration. This speed, measured in bits per second, is called the *baud rate.* A typical speed for many modems is 300 bits per second. However, modems that are used with microcomputers may have transmission rates of 9600 bits per second or more.

FIGURE 6.10
Modems enable computers to communicate using telephone lines. *(Novation, Inc.)*

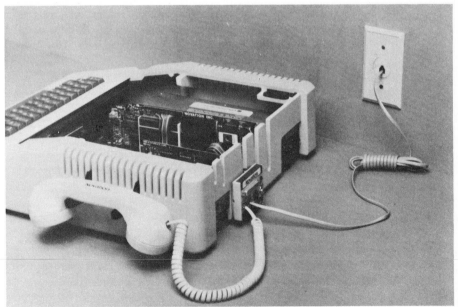

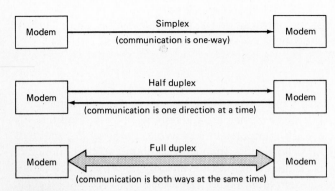

FIGURE 6.11
Three kinds of transmission circuits used with modems.

Faster baud rates help keep telephone costs down, particularly when long distance telephone lines are involved. They are also useful for reducing the time required to pass information back and forth between systems in the network.

The type of carrier of the signal between modems is also a concern. In addition to telephone lines, signals may be carried by coaxial cable and microwaves beamed to satellites. It is wise to seek expert assistance regarding these matters when planning a network.

Modems use three different kinds of transmission circuits (see Figure 6.11). Some modems have all three, others only one or two. The three kinds of circuits are:

1 *Simplex:* Communications are possible in only one direction. In effect, one computer system assumes the role of receiving station and the other the role of sending station.

2 *Half-duplex:* Communications are possible in only one direction at a time. There must be some way to reverse the signal. (This situation is similar to a citizens' band — CB — radio conversation, in which each person uses the word *over* to signal that the transmission is complete and a reply is awaited.)

3 *Full-duplex:* Communications can occur in two directions at the same time. (This is similar to an ordinary telephone conversation, in which both parties can talk at the same time and the messages are carried by the wire simultaneously.)

Network Software

Some network software is sold in packages for use with particular computer systems and for particular purposes. For example, in a network designed to share a hard-disk storage system, the software to enable different computers to access the disks may be provided by the disk manufacturer or may be part of a database management package. Modem producers are another source of network software. Network software might also be obtained by subscribing to large communications network services.

OTHER NONINSTRUCTIONAL APPLICATIONS

To this point we have discussed four of the most widely used applications of microcomputers in schools: word processing, databases, spreadsheets, and networks. Yet we have hardly scratched the surface. A large number of applications have been developed for more specific needs. In this section, we will look briefly at some of these applications. It is impossible to be comprehensive in this discussion; the microcomputer can do so many things that its applicability is almost limitless.

Applications for Teachers

A number of programs are available to take over some of the time-consuming tasks teachers have to do. These programs permit the computer to perform specific functions such as maintaining classroom records, analyzing readability of test passages, and helping teachers manage the individual learning experiences of their students.

- *Computerized grade book:* A typical grade-book program will allow teachers to enter the grades for a class of 50 students or more.[14] The entries may be test scores or grades for homework assignments and other activities. The teacher first sets up a file for the class which includes the names of all the students in the class. Then the grades are entered as they become available. Some of these programs allow weighting systems, and some allow performance criteria to be established. A program may automatically produce average scores of the whole list or subsets of scores in weighted or unweighted form. Additional features often include deletion of students or particular scores, changing scores, and printing lists of names and scores or averages. Most of these functions could also be done with a spreadsheet program; however, programs that are specifically designed for keeping grades may be easier to use in the classroom.
- *Readability programs:* Readability programs can save a great deal of time by helping teachers to determine the reading level of text material. They are particularly useful when reading material must be simplified for students with lower-than-average reading skills. Such programs are also useful in determining whether reading passages are appropriate for the students for whom they are intended. These programs will usually require the teacher to type in a sample paragraph. The readability of the material is then analyzed.[15]
- *Generation of tests and activities:* "Generation" programs usually require the teacher to enter a collection of test items and answers or a collection of

activities. The teacher can form and print a master copy of the test or exercise and from this produce enough copies for the class. A separate answer sheet may be printed for scoring the test.[16]

• *Classroom management systems:* Management systems are somewhat more ambitious than the other programs in this list.[17] In general they represent a computer-managed instruction or CMI approach (see the discussion of CMI in Chapters 3 and 5). They permit the teacher to keep track of what each student has completed in a program, what still remains to be completed, and how well the student is doing. They may go so far as to recommend supplemental or practice activities. The teacher must keep the system up to date by typing in the status of students' progress. Some of these systems enable the teacher to print some or all of a student's individualized learning activities on a daily or weekly basis. Programs of this kind may ultimately contribute to a change in the role of teacher from instructor to classroom manager.[18]

This has been only a brief listing of noninstructional applications for the teacher. Other applications are being announced all the time. Some applications are created by teachers to meet very specific classroom needs. These programs may not be available through commercial channels, because the market would be too small. By cooperating, teachers can help each other to take advantage of local developments in software.

Applications for Students

Many student-oriented applications are, of course, instructional; these will not be covered here. However, students may use computers for performing library searches, for writing reports with a word processing program, and for keeping records of their own progress (for example, following the development of their physical skills in a team training program). Such noninstructional applications often originate with the students themselves. Sometimes students will take standard programs (such as spreadsheet and database programs) and use them creatively for their own needs or interests. They may also write their own programs. (For example, a student might create a cryptographic program for sending secret messages to friends.) Students can also utilize communication networks to get messages about district events or to communicate between home and school. Although such applications are not yet widespread, the technology and software are available.

Applications for Administrators

The general applications covered earlier — word processing, database management, spreadsheets, and networks — have all proved highly valuable to school administrators. However, some programs may be more specific in their appeal to school administrators. In each case, there are many software packages on the market from which to choose. Following are some examples.

- *Resource scheduling:* Scheduling resources — including classrooms, classes, teachers, equipment, and transportation — ranks among the major tasks of school administrators. Computerized scheduling can reduce errors and increase efficiency. Further, a computer-based scheduling system will usually permit greater flexibility in changing schedules than would ordinarily be possible with a system done by hand.[19]
- *Planning and decision making:* Although most spreadsheet programs are useful for planning and problem solving, some software packages have been designed specifically for the kinds of planning school administrators have to do. Among these are programs for simulations, linear programming, PERT charting, queuing techniques, salaries, and enrollment and revenue projection.[20]
- *Attendance:* In keeping attendance records, it is necessary to distinguish between excused and unexcused absence and tardiness. Most attendance programs will permit such entries after a file for each grade or class has been prepared. This kind of application can save time and effort in the production of weekly, monthly, and annual attendance reports, and in locating the attendance record of a single student.[21]
- *Personnel and financial records:* Although personnel and financial software has been prepared for use in schools, many of the commercially available programs for small businesses are also suitable for this purpose. The amount of data can expand rapidly with these applications, even in a small school system. Thus, a microcomputer may be too small or slow for full-scale use of such applications.

School administrators can find many additional uses for microcomputers. Other widely recognized applications include controlling inventory, storing and retrieving information, monitoring energy usage in a school building, and designing forms. Networking can afford administrators immediate access to central databases and information resources. Further, communications within a school system can be facilitated with a computer-based electronic mail system.[22] It is expected that as the role of microcomputers in educational settings develops further, school administrators will make increased use of them.

Applications for Support Staff

Guidance counselors, school nurses, school psychologists, reading therapists, school social workers, and other professionals in the schools can also make use of microcomputers. Applications for two such professionals — the guidance counselor and the school psychologist — are reviewed briefly below.

Guidance Counselor   The four general types of applications software discussed earlier in this chapter can be very useful to a guidance counselor. Word processing can be used to prepare messages in memos, reports, and records. Spreadsheets might be valuable for preparing reports about performance on various tests. As we saw earlier, many of the guidance counselor's records can be kept efficiently on a microcomputer. In fact, there are advantages to keeping records on a microcomputer rather than a large computer, the major one being that the guidance counselor has more direct control over the system and can ensure better security of records.

School Psychologist   School psychologists are employed by school districts to perform a variety of services, which include developing instructional programs tailored to individual students' needs, giving educational and psychological tests, writing reports outlining their interpretations of results of psychoeducational tests, and consulting with teachers and parents. School psychologists are very often involved in small-scale research or evaluation projects in schools. We will now examine what the microcomputer can do for the school psychologist.

• *Testing:* Software has been developed that enables a computer to administer certain psychological tests and to interpret performance on these tests. In addition, microcomputers whose only purpose is to give tests and analyze test results have been built; these computers have the programming installed in ROM.[23] These innovations have the potential of assisting the school district to utilize the services of the school psychologist in a more cost-effective manner. However, such applications do not always mean better services to students. For example, since the school psychologist does not spend as much time with the student in testing, he or she is less familiar with the student when recommendations are made. Further, with some tests the behavior exhibited during testing is more important for the interpretation than the score that the student obtains. Finally, there are a number of tests that use open-ended answering procedures or involve tasks which cannot be readily reduced to forms which are easily scored or interpreted by a computer. On the other hand, when the relatively routine parts of a psychoeducational examination can be handled by a computer, the psychologist is freed to do more important things. The computer is particularly useful for testing response time and for studying levels of knowledge and certain kinds of problem solving. It is not so well equipped to examine feelings, emotions, and abstract concepts.

• *Report writing:* A school psychologist can use a word processing package to write psychoeducational reports. In some school districts there is a prescribed format for these reports; an outline of the format can be created using the word processing program and then saved on a disk. Each time a new report is written, the outline can be retrieved from the disk and completed on the CRT screen. Another approach is to let the computer prepare the report.[24] This is usually done by designing the software to contain parts of completed sentences; the remainder of each sentence is filled in by the computer on the basis of test scores. For example, the computer program may contain the following statement: "This student's ability to handle simple multiplication facts is _____." Then, depending on how the student scored on items of this type, the computer will add to the stem when it is printed "below average" or "about average" or "above average." Since interpretation of psychological data is a complex task involving many skills and a great deal of knowledge, reports prepared by a computer should be treated with extreme caution.

• *Consultation and case management:* School psychologists must follow the educational progress of a large number of students. Many school psychologists have found database management systems to be very satisfactory for this purpose. The data that must ordinarily be maintained include: (1) the unique reason why each student has been referred for psychological services; (2) each student's test scores and interpretations made from them; (3) narratives describing observations, interviews, and background information; (4) recommendations made for the educational program for each student; (5) the period of time before the student's evaluation must be followed up by an assessment of progress; (6) records of progress or follow-up activities. Add to these the variables of grade, school, class, pertinent data from the cumulative folder, medical records, and other related data, and it is easy to see that a fairly substantial database is formed. Although general DBMS software will usually be sufficient, some psychologists prefer systems that have been designed specifically for school psychologists.[25]

• *Research:* Microcomputers can be used to administer experimental treatments.[26] For example, let us say that a school psychologist would like to test the effectiveness of two different kinds of drill in number facts. The microcomputer can be used to present the drills and to test the students' learning afterward. The computer can also perform statistical analysis of the data.[27]

While some elements of school psychologists' functioning can be enhanced by computerization, the expert judgment of psychologists and other professionals cannot be replaced by current technology. There is a danger that the efficiency and complexity of a computer operating with sophisticated software can mislead people into thinking that the computer is capable of doing things it cannot do; when this happens, the quality of service suffers.

Applications for Special Education

The use of microcomputers with the handicapped is rapidly expanding. In instructional and noninstructional applications, microcomputers are proving extremely useful to special educators. Among the standard applications already discussed, networking software can be combined with a database program to create a management system for the instruction of students who are homebound or institutionalized. This permits instruction of these students at any time of day when they are ready. The instruction can be presented by the micro-computer, and performance can be monitored by a central computer which keeps track of progress and activities.

Microcomputers are helping handicapped people to perform all sorts of functions that were previously impossible for them. For example, talking computers are being used with blind students;[28] and handicapped people are being helped to communicate, maneuver, and manipulate objects in their surroundings.[29] This is beginning to result in improved access to education by students with extreme educational difficulties or handicaps — students who would once have been considered at best minimally capable of benefiting from instruction.

Another development in special education that is gaining impetus is resource sharing. Networking has allowed teachers of handicapped students to communicate with each other more efficiently and effectively. One such project, the Handicapped Educational Exchange (HEX), was developed as a computerized bulletin board. The HEX system permits communication between microcomputer systems using modems and telephone lines. It allows users across the country to post messages or ask for information. One unique aspect of HEX is that it can speak to the deaf with devices that were designed to enable deaf people to use telephones.[30]

SUMMARY

Computers are data processing machines. They process data by applying operations to them. Eight data processing operations — recording, sorting, coding, classifying, calculating, communicating, storing, and retrieving — are combined into sequences of instructions to the computer; these sequences form applications programs.

Table 6.1 indicates which data processing operations are major components of four common noninstructional computer applications: word processing, database management, spreadsheets, and networks. In Table 6.1, some broad generalizations are made. For example, it does not show summarization as an operation common to word processing programs; but some of these programs are capable of automatically forming a table of contents page from the headings and subheadings within a document, and this would be a kind of summary.

Word processing involves the use of computers to assist in creating, editing, storing, retrieving, and printing text. *Database management systems* are software packages that make a computer function as a highly efficient file cabinet capable of rapidly and accurately storing, retrieving, adding, deleting, and sorting the data it contains. *Spreadsheet programs* convert the CRT into a window through which to view highly flexible ledger sheets capable of automatically calculating and performing logical operations. Spreadsheet programs are useful for maintaining financial records and for planning and problem solving. *Network software* enables a computer to communicate with other computers. A modem

TABLE 6.1
DATA PROCESSING OPERATIONS TYPICALLY USED BY VARIOUS APPLICATIONS PROGRAMS

	Programs			
Operations	**Word processing**	**Database management**	**Spreadsheets**	**Networking**
Recording	X	X	X	
Coding	X	X	X	X
Sorting	X	X	X	
Calculating			X	
Summarizing		X	X	
Storing	X	X	X	X
Communicating				X
Retrieving	X	X	X	X

is required for each computer in a network. Networks may be established to permit resource sharing, distributed processing, or communications within a school district.

Microcomputers have been shown to be extremely useful devices in and out of the classroom. They are being used increasingly by administrators and support personnel, such as the guidance counselor and the school psychologist, for problem solving and decision making, record keeping, testing, and report writing. They are also beginning to be used in education of the handicapped, for sharing resources and to facilitate communications and movement. As computer applications continue to develop, their use will become even more widespread.

NOTES

1   Inclusion in the following discussion does not represent an endorsement by the authors of either the application as described or any particular software package.
2   Wanous, S. J., Wagner, G. E., & Lambrecht, J. J. (1981). *Fundamentals of data processing* (2nd ed.). Cincinnati, OH: South-Western.
3   There is a lot more to computer speed, including the speed of the microprocessor (usually expressed in millions of operations per second), the speed of disk storage and retrieval (usually expressed in hundreds of thousands of bytes per second), and the speed of other components. For the average user, however, most of these are so fast that differences seem imaginary. When the computer system does not require long waiting times for the user while it functions, most users will not think about processing speed.
4   Fastie, W. (1982). Images. *Creative Computing, 8*(8), 228.
5   This discussion of word processing was not based on any particular program or piece of equipment; rather, it was written to convey some basic concepts common to most word processing programs. Arthur Naiman gives a method for evaluating word processing programs in: *BYTE.* (1984). *9*(2), 243–246.

6 Watt, D. (1982). Word processors and writing. *Popular Computing, 1*(8), 124–126.

7 A system like this could be set up using the program by: J. M. Hellman. (1983, March). *Creative Computing, 9*(3), 216, 218, 220, 222, 225, 226, 228, 230, 232, 234, 236, 238, 240, 242, 244, 246, 248, 250, 252.

8 The *MC/CVIS Occupation Selection Program* and the *MC/CVIS College Selection and Performance Program* are examples. They were designed to assist students in gathering information about occupations and colleges, and they work on a microcomputer. Information about these programs may be obtained from CVIS Distribution Center, Carrol Hall, Western Maryland College, Westminster, MD 21152.

9 Gagle, M., & Koehler, G. J. (1981). Data-base management systems: Powerful newcomers to microcomputers. *BYTE, 6*(11), 97, 98, 100, 102, 104, 106, 108, 110, 112, 114, 116, 118, 120, 122.

10 Kalish, C., & Mayer, M. (1981). DIF: A format for data exchange between applications programs. *BYTE, 6*(11), 174, 176, 178, 180, 182, 186, 188, 190, 192, 194, 196, 198, 200, 202, 204, 206.

11 Stein, D. (1982, September). The CalcWars. *Business Computer Systems,* 68–70, 72–76.

12 For example, in early 1982 Joe Shelton began writing a column in *SOFTALK,* a magazine which emphasizes the products of Apple Computer Company and is published by Softalk Publishing Company, North Hollywood, CA. The column has explored novel applications and creative solutions using VisiCalc, a spreadsheet program produced by VisiCorp, San Jose, CA (previously Software Arts, Inc.), and other spreadsheet programs.

13 The Source is a subsidiary of Readers Digest. Information about The Source can be obtained by writing to Source Telecomputing Corporation, 1616 Anderson Road, McLean, VA 22102. The address for CompuServe is 5000 Arlington Center Boulevard, Columbus, OH 43220.

14 A number of these programs are available from software publishers or are in the public domain. Examples of commercially available software for microcomputer systems are: (1) Electric Grade Book (Charles Mann and Associates); (2) Teacher's Aid (Dr. Daley's Software); (3) Class Mark Tracking (Sheridan College, Centre for Instructional Development). As with other purchases of software, the subtle differences between various products can be important; it is worth the effort to shop around before deciding which to buy. Many computer magazines publish programs written in BASIC or other high-level computer languages that can be keyed into the computer and saved on a disk or tape for later use. An example of such a grade-management program, written by W. Teoh, can be found in the October 1981 issue of *Creative Computing,* pages 166, 168, 170, 172–177.

15 The School Utilities – Volume 2 software package from Minnesota Educational Computing Consortium (MECC) allows consideration of text using six readability tests. *Creative Computing* magazine printed a listing of a program by Larry Noonan in March 1981 (pages 166–168, 170, 172, 173) that computes readability level.

16 Examples of programs that develop tests include Teachers' Utilities – Volume 1 from MECC, and T.E.S.T. from TYC Software of Geneseo, NY.

17 The Comprehensive Achievement Monitoring (CAM) system of the Minnesota Educational Computing Consortium (MECC) is a program that can be useful to a teacher in a classroom where each student's educational program is individually monitored. CAM is designed to provide teachers, students, administrators, and parents with information for decision making regarding curriculum. It stores information about objectives, students' performance, and test forms; and it can provide reports about the performance of groups or individual students. Science Research Associates (SRA) offers another program, Classroom Management System. This system facilitates keeping individual records of students' performance, and can provide the appropriate tests to students at the right time. The package contains a master list of materials and tests. It can furnish reports for classes, groups, and individual students.

18 This is suggested in one independent review of SRA's Classroom Management System. See: Zausmer, R. (1981). Classroom management system. *Creative Computing, 7*(10), 62, 65–66.

19 Bolton, B. A. (1982). Solving administrative problems: Student scheduling and tracking for the microcomputer. *Educational Computer Magazine, 2*(2), 24–26.

20 Judd, D. H. (1981). Administrative decision tools: A microcomputer reality available now. *Educational Computer Magazine, 1*(2), 6–7. An example is the diskette School Utilities – Volume 1, from the Minnesota Educational Computing Consortium, which is based on the Minnesota tax tables.

21 An example of this kind of program is the ATTENDANCE software package from Charles Mann and Associates, Yucca Valley, CA.

22 One of the first statewide electronic mail systems for schools was developed as part of the Educational Technology for Alaska (ETA) Project in 1979 for communication between school districts and the Alaska Department of Education. This project is described in: *Informational Technology and its Impact on American Education.* (1982). Office of Technology Assessment, Congress of the United States.

23 Examples of computerized psychological testing systems are: (1) the Psychometer 3000 of CompuPsych, Liberty, MO, a complete microcomputer-based testing system that includes a special touch-sensitive panel instead of the usual keyboard, a color CRT, and many of the features of other microcomputer systems; and (2) FAST-TEST, a product of Psych Systems of Baltimore, MD (this is a software package that is compatible with the hardware of the Digital Equipment Company).

24 Examples of software that will produce psychological reports are (1) the NEURO-PSYCH-MONITOR, produced by *Clinician's Digest,* Casper, WY, which can be used with the Halstead-Reitan Neuropsychology Battery; and (2) WISC-R Computer Report, from Southern Micro Systems for Educators, Burlington, NC (this software prepares reports of performance on the Wechsler Intelligence Scale for Children – Revised Form).

25 Psychologists Data Management System (PDMS), developed by J. Grimes (Iowa Department of Public Instruction, Des Moines, IA), and G. Ross-Reynolds (Nicholl State University, Thibodeaux, LA), is one example of a database management system designed specifically for the school psychologist.

26 One example of a software and hardware package that allows design and control of experiments is the COGNITIVE TESTING STATION by Digitry (Edgecomb, ME). This package not only simplifies design of the experiment and presentation of stimuli but also facilitates storage of the data as it is collected.

27 Several statistical analysis packages are available for running on microcomputers. Examples are: (1) the KEYSTAT system, available from Brooks/Cole; and (2) a hardware-software combination package offered by MPX Systems of Berkeley, CA, which includes a microcomputer, peripheral equipment and software in a single package. However, the size and processing speed of microcomputers limits their use for statistical analysis to relatively small data sets.

28 Maryland Computer Services, Inc., for example, offers a number of computer prod-

ucts expressly designed for the blind. Systems include microcomputers and terminals that produce synthesized voice output; software packages for the blind for functions such as word processing; Braille translation; and database management systems.

29   *Creative Computing* magazine devoted much of its March 1982 issue to computers and the handicapped. Articles discuss such devices as a talking wheelchair for a severely disabled person, and how computers can help people to work at home. See also: Barnes, L. (1982, November). A dream of walking. *SOFTTALK,* 82–84, 86, 88, 90. And see also: Computers for the handicapped: Panacea or pie in the sky? (1982, May–June). *Programs for the Handicapped,* No. 3. Washington, D.C.: U.S. Department of Education, Office of Special Education and Rehabilitation Services. Artificial limbs have been proposed that operate on signals originating in the brain and transferred to circuitry in the limb, enabling the wearer to control the prosthesis. Such promising applications are being explored at Drexel University and Moss Rehabilitation Hospital in Philadelphia, PA (personal communication, G. D. Moskowitz, Professor of Mechanical Engineering, Drexel University).

30   Barth, R. (1982). The Handicapped Educational Exchange. *Educational Computer Magazine, 2*(2), 48–49.

SUPPLEMENTARY READINGS

Archibald, D. A. (1983, January). Apple on the phone: What is and what's to come in telecommunications. *SOFTALK,* 184–188, 190.

Barley, K. S., & Driscoll, J. M. (1981). A survey of data-base management systems for microcomputers. *BYTE, 6*(11), 208, 210, 212, 214, 218–220, 222, 224, 226, 228, 230, 232, 234.

Crouse, D. B. (1981). The computerized gradebook as a component of a computer-managed curriculum. *Educational Technology, 21*(5), 16–20.

DeLong, D. (1983). Demystifying data-base management. *Business Computer Systems, 2*(2), 48–54.

Glatzer, H. (1982). *Introduction to wordprocessing.* Berkeley, CA: SYBEX.

Lewis, A. (1984). The word-processing maze. *BYTE, 9*(2), 235–236, 238.

McCulloch, C. S. (1982). Computer applications in school psychology: Survey report. National Association of School Psychologists.

Naiman, A. (1982). *WordStar.* Berkeley, CA: SYBEX.

Naiman, A. (1982). A WordStar primer: How the program works. *Business Computer Systems, 1*(2), 53, 53, 57, 58, 60.

Nichols, E. A., Nichols, J. C., & Musson, K. R. (1982). *Data communications for microcomputers: With practical applications and experiments.* New York: McGraw-Hill.

Solnetseff, N. (1981). What do we tell administrators? *Creative Computing, 7*(2), 100, 102.

Stein, D. The CalcWars. (1982). *Business Computer Systems. 1*(1), 68–70, 72–76.

CHAPTER 7

EVALUATING
INSTRUCTIONAL SOFTWARE

CHAPTER CONTENTS

Commercial vendors of software usually extol the virtues of their products. On the other hand, many educators say that there is very little good-quality software available for use in classroom instruction. This disparity of views about the quality of software can leave a teacher in a quandary. Teachers need to know how to decide whether or not software has merit, so that they can choose instructional computing materials effectively. This chapter focuses on how to determine the quality and effectiveness of instructional software.

The information provided in this chapter should assist teachers in the selection and evaluation of educational software. The topics covered include recognizing quality in software and prescreening software; sources of information about quality; and procedures for in-depth screening and evaluation of software. In addition, field testing of software is discussed.

WHY EVALUATION IS IMPORTANT

Poor Software Selection Is Not Uncommon

A fourth-grade teacher wanted to use a microcomputer to support mathematics instruction for his students. The teacher had access to a microcomputer laboratory in his school building for several hours per week. He obtained a drill and practice software package for elementary mathematics instruction that appeared to have some potential for giving his students practice with mathematics facts.

When the software arrived, the teacher led several of his students to the computer laboratory for some mathematics practice. For a few minutes, everything went well. However, it soon became apparent that the software was not well matched to the students' needs. Most of the drill items were for skills and concepts the students had already mastered. Thus, the level of instruction was too low, and the students found the activities boring. Further, the instructions were vague. Therefore, students often provided correct answers in a form that was not recognizable by the computer (e.g., *four* instead of *4*). When this kind of thing happened, the computer could not continue to execute the program. Each time the computer halted, the entire program had to be restarted to allow the students to proceed. This frustrated the students, since they had to repeat several minutes of drill before they came to new material. There were other problems as well. It was clear that this software package was not useful.

This example may seem exaggerated, but it is not. Episodes like this are all too familiar to many teachers who have tried to use computers for educational purposes. The implication is clear. Teachers should be able to determine *beforehand* whether instructional software will be useful. The need to do this is one reason why evaluation of software is so important.

Software Is Important as an Instructional Tool

A portrait painted with a house painter's brush would not show the fine detail of which the artist's hand is capable. An automobile mechanic must have a large variety of rather specialized tools, many of which are adapted to unique parts used by automobile manufacturers. In any profession, the quality of the worker's tools in part determines the quality of the work done. In teaching, as in any other field, selection of the right tool is critical to performance.

Instructional software is a tool of the educator. Just as a plumber will do a better job with the right wrench, a teacher will do a better job with the right software. Teachers know this, as they select tools to fit instructional needs daily. These tools include materials such as textbooks, worksheets, films, and laboratory kits, and also techniques such as remediation. As a result of their training and experience, teachers generally know what to look for in selecting materials and techniques for use in the classroom. However, when dealing with new or unfamiliar technologies such as instructional computers, teachers may be less well equipped to differentiate between materials on the basis of quality.

Computers are not necessarily or automatically effective as instructional aids. When they are used in random and unplanned ways, they can be ineffective. As we have noted elsewhere, what is to be accomplished in a curriculum should be considered first; only after needs have been identified should software be chosen or developed. Obtaining what looks like attractive software and then trying to figure out what to do with it does not work very well. But following the right sequence provides a framework for evaluation of software. Computers can make a lot of sense when their application has been integrated into an instructional program.

GUIDELINES FOR EVALUATION OF SOFTWARE

What to Look For in Software

The developers of the MicroSIFT Evaluation Guide[1] suggest that education software can be judged on the basis of three important characteristics:

1 *Content:* For software to be effective in a learning situation, its content should have educational value. Further, the software should be consistent in content and objectives with the needs of the curriculum. Content should of course be accurate and free of errors. It should also be free of racial, sex, or ethnic biases.

2 *Instruction:* The purpose of an instructional package should be well defined, and the package should be capable of achieving its purpose. The presentation of content should be clear and logical. Valid principles of instructional design should be followed in presentation of content. The level of difficulty should be appropriate to the audience. Graphics, color, and sound should be used appropriately. The package should be motivational and should stimulate students' creativity. The student should be able to control the rate of presentation and should get information from the program about his or her performance. Instruction should be integrated with previous learning and should be generalizable to other relevant situations.

3 *Technology:* Support materials should be available, comprehensive, and effective. Information displayed on the CRT screen and printed materials that come with the package should be clear and effective. The intended users — teachers and students — should be able to use the software easily and independently. The design should employ computer capabilities that are relevant to the instruction. (For example, color graphics are useful for art instruction; sound synthesis is useful for teaching music; and large character sets are useful for children with vision problems.)

These elements will be discussed in greater detail later in the chapter. However, a checklist for screening software is presented first. *Screening* is a form of rapid preview. Its purpose is to eliminate from consideration any program that clearly will not be suitable for the intended use. Screening is preferable to spending a lot of time on detailed analyses of every program.

How to Identify the Worst Software Quickly

Educators can save time by using checklists that allow them to identify the worst instructional materials quickly. Such screening allows them to spend more time evaluating the better materials. Useful criteria for screening have been provided by Ann Lathrop.[2] These have been arranged as a checklist in Table 7.1. In screening, software with any of the characteristics on the list can be rejected.

Software developers should make special efforts to avoid the types of problems listed in Table 7.1. As software designers and developers become more skilled and the quality of software improves, problems like these should become less common. Meanwhile, when educators use screening devices like Table 7.1 to identify poor-quality software quickly, they avoid the problems such software causes and at the same time send a message to software developers that educators will use only high-quality products.

How to Screen Software When a Sample Copy Is Not Available

Screening software with checklists like Table 7.1 is useful only if a copy of the program is available for review. However, if a teacher does not have access to a particular software package or would have to go to some trouble or expense to obtain a copy for screening, there are other ways to evaluate the material.

First, as with any instructional product, a teacher may ask questions of persons who can be expected to provide accurate and useful advice. Persons whom teachers ask for advice should have expertise in instructional computing. (A computer teacher might be such a person.) When seeking advice from others, one should be able to describe exactly what the software is supposed to accomplish — including the instructional goals and objectives and how the computer will fit into the curriculum. An expert in instructional computing may be able to give some hints about strategies for effective use of a particular software package.

TABLE 7.1

CHECKLIST FOR ELIMINATING POOR SOFTWARE

Characteristic	Check if present
1 *Audible response to students' errors:* When the student makes an error, the computer should not announce it to the whole class by emitting a sound.	_____
2 *Rewarding failure:* Students should not find it more fun to make a mistake than to provide a correct answer. This often happens in hangman-type programs, where the computer gives more colorful responses to errors than to correct answers.	_____
3 *Any sound that cannot be controlled:* While sound can be effective for motivation or reward, it can also be distracting. Constant repetition of a sound can also become annoying.	_____
4 *Technical problems:* Programs must run smoothly and without errors.	_____
5 *Uncontrolled screen advance:* The user should be able to control the rate of screen advance in accordance with his or her needs and rate of progress.	_____
6 *Inadequate instructions:* Instructions should be clear and appropriate for a student's reading level. Students should not have to guess or determine by trial and error how to operate a program.	_____
7 *Errors of any kind:* Mistakes in factual content, spelling, grammar, etc., are not acceptable.	_____
8 *Insults, sarcasm, and derogatory remarks:* Students must not be attacked or belittled by comments made by the program. For example, the program should not call the student a derogatory name whenever an error is made.	_____
9 *Poor documentation:* Instructional objectives, suggested activities for students, modification of the program or instructional sequence by the teacher, and other classroom information should be included.	_____
10 *Refusal to supply a backup copy:* If the publisher has placed special codes in the software to prevent its being copied, at least one free backup copy should be provided for emergency use. There should also be a policy for replacement of damaged or worn disks.	_____

Source: Adapted from: Lathrop, Ann. (1982, September–October). The terrible ten in educational programming (My top ten reasons for automatically rejecting a program). *Educational Computer Magazine.* Copyright © 1982 by *Educational Computer,* 3199 Dela Cruz Boulevard, Santa Clara, CA 95050. Sample issue, $3; 10-issue subscription, $25.

Second, evaluations made by others can provide an excellent opportunity to avoid costly duplication of effort. Software evaluations can be found in magazines and journals on educational computing. They can also be obtained directly from agencies which evaluate software. Such agencies range from school districts to universities and research and development agencies. Evaluations based on research projects are also available in journals and technical reports.

Third, information provided by vendors can be useful for screening software. This information can often be found in materials developed for advertising and marketing. However, it must be remembered that if a vendor makes an investment in a product and goes to the trouble and expense of marketing it, the intention is to sell the product and make a profit. Therefore, the advertising will tend to portray the product in the most positive light; the strengths of the product will be stressed, and its limitations and weaknesses minimized. Nevertheless, the vendor is obliged by law to provide accurate information, and that information should help to identify characteristics of the product which might eliminate it from further consideration. (For example, a product may have been designed to reinforce development of basic concepts in a given content area, whereas the teacher may be searching for software that develops problem-solving skills through simulations and other techniques.) Other relevant information to be found in advertising includes hardware requirements, availability of backup diskettes, the type of student for whom the software was designed, and availability of evaluation data. Some vendors are willing to send software on a trial basis or to demonstrate their products. All this can give very useful information before a purchase is made.

Fourth, and finally, the value of common sense in choosing software should not be minimized. For example, if a school district has recently purchased many computers of a particular brand, buying software that can be run only on computers of a different brand would not make sense. In addition, if the cost of a particular type of software and the hardware required to run it exceed what an institution can realistically be expected to spend, an alternative product should be considered. Also, if the use of a particular product would require a teacher or school to restructure a curriculum or instructional program in ways that are not desirable or feasible, that product, no matter what its strengths are, should not be chosen. (For example, if a curriculum has been structured so that language arts are integrated with a reading curriculum, and a particular software series treats reading as a separate subject, use of the software would require changing the language arts program. If the existing curriculum has been successful, and other software packages are available that would not require the change, then the change probably should not be made.)

Thus, there are a number of ways to obtain information about the capabilities and qualities of software without investing a great deal of time and energy in actual field testing. To summarize briefly, the following may be useful initial sources of information about software:

1 Colleagues and others who know about software

2 Evaluations made by others
3 Information provided by software vendors
4 Common sense

Having screened out inappropriate or poor-quality software, the teacher is in a position to make decisions about selection and acquisition of software. Teachers may want to make evaluations themselves or to study evaluations made by others. The next sections of this chapter discuss these options. We take up evaluations by others first, and then approaches to making one's own evaluations.

SOURCES OF EVALUATIONS

Before an item of software is used with students, some firsthand experience with the package is desirable. However, time and effort can be saved by reviewing software evaluations made by others. Fortunately, there are several convenient sources of evaluations. But in the changing field of instructional computing, today's good source may not be available tomorrow; and teachers need to be alert for new sources as they emerge. Two well-established sources of software evaluation are EPIE and MicroSIFT; other sources include computer magazines and state, regional, and local agencies.

EPIE—Consumers Union

In October 1982, Consumers Union (publisher of *Consumer Reports*) and Educational Products Information Exchange (EPIE) announced a service designed to provide schools and parents' groups with in-depth, unbiased evaluations of educational computing products. The service is designed not only to provide educators with the means to make informed choices about hardware and software, but also to provide a voice for consumers so that manufacturers can recognize and respond to suggestions for improvements and changes in design. The service provides subscribers with detailed reports on computer hardware and software (the report is called *PRO/FILE and Evaluation*), and a monthly newsletter for school consumers *(MICROgram)*. The service uses Consumers Union's expertise in testing products and EPIE's ability to provide evaluations of educational materials. The price for EPIE's services is intended to be affordable to schools, school districts, and libraries and is available from EPIE — Consumers Union.[3]

Samples of *MICROgram* and *PRO/FILE and Evaluation* have appeared in issues of *The Computing Teacher* after January 1983.[4] *PRO/FILE* includes information such as product title and publisher, the hardware configuration needed to run the package, the components of the package, the group for whom the software was intended, content of the package, use of the package in the curriculum, copyright date, and authors. Each evaluation includes overall ratings of instructional design and software design, a summary, recommendations to the producer (a somewhat unusual feature), sample frames from the software, a listing of other reviews of the package, observations of student users, descriptions of general program structure and how teachers and students use the software, and an assessment of the educational value of the package. Overall, the EPIE — Consumers Union service is a very good one, which can save teachers an enormous amount of time and effort through its reviews and by pointing out other reviews of instructional packages for microcomputers. The evaluations are comprehensive and well packaged.

MicroSIFT

In 1979 the Computer Technology Program of the Northwest Regional Educational Laboratory (NWREL) was awarded a multiyear grant from the National Institute of Education for a project to develop software evaluation procedures and to disseminate information about software evaluations. The result was a clearinghouse, MicroSIFT (the name is an acronym for *Micro*computer *S*oftware and *I*nformation *for* *T*eachers). This landmark project was directed by Dr. Judith Edwards of NWREL. Its results are being used successfully by educators across the country. Important outcomes of the project were:

A comprehensive instrument for evaluating instructional software for microcomputers
Evaluation of a large quantity of existing software
Dissemination of information about software evaluations

The evaluation instrument developed by MicroSIFT provides for a detailed description of the software, an evaluation of its content, and consideration of instructional and technical characteristics. The evaluation process is based on expert judgments by experienced professionals. The process is well designed and yields consistent results. The complete evaluation process was to include a stage of field study and testing. However, this aspect of the process has not been implemented by MicroSIFT to date. Educators have tended to find evaluations performed according to the MicroSIFT technique very useful in selection of software.

The MicroSIFT Network (SIFTnet), consisting of over 25 organizations, was formed during the school year 1980–1981. The participants are those who provide elementary and secondary schools with computer services (e.g., state departments of education, regional educational service agencies, and consortia). SIFTnet participants reviewed the evaluation procedures and contributed evaluations they had made of specific courseware using the MicroSIFT technique. These evaluations were then compiled and summarized in report form.

MicroSIFT has made a major effort to disseminate the results of these evaluations. The results are distributed in reports from the project and published in major magazines and journals; they are also distributed through another unique service developed by MicroSIFT — a computerized information network,

Resources in Computer Education (RICE). RICE includes descriptive and evaluative information about computer courseware and can be searched using procedures and descriptors of the Educational Resources Information Center (ERIC). ERIC is the primary library database of information relating to education in the United States. Educators can request information from RICE about software for specific subjects and grade levels. The database can be accessed by computers in most major libraries and at research or training institutions. Information about RICE can also be obtained directly from the Northwest Regional Educational Laboratory and other regional educational laboratories. However, access to the actual RICE database must be obtained through the Northwest Regional Educational Laboratory.

It remains to be seen whether computerized databases will be utilized successfully by teachers for locating information about instructional software. Such databases can provide a powerful tool for obtaining bibliographic and evaluative information.

Major Computer Magazines

Even a cursory examination of magazines such as *Popular Computing, Classroom Computer News, Electronic Learning, Educational Computer Magazine, The Computing Teacher,* and *Educational Technology* will reveal that all of them regularly carry reviews of educational software. Chapter 8 of this text includes a comprehensive list of periodicals that regularly contain evaluations. Some of these evaluations utilize formal procedures such as those followed by MicroSIFT; others have less structured formats. These reviews can provide rich sources of up-to-date information about microcomputer software.

There are two basic ways to make use of these evaluations. First, by subscribing to these publications (or gaining regular access to them in some other way), teachers can review items as they appear and in this way stay abreast of new releases in instructional software. Second, when a teacher needs information about the quality of a particular educational package under consideration, these evaluations can be useful aids. One problem is that it is not always easy to find reviews of a specific product. Sometimes a review can be located simply by searching among periodicals that were published about the time the product was introduced. However, using indexes and computerized databases available through libraries and other resource centers would result in more systematic and dependable searches.

Teachers may be familiar with bibliographic indexes that can be used to locate educational publications; *Education Index* and *Readers' Guide to Periodical Literature* are examples. They may be less familiar with bibliographic databases that may be of help in locating evaluations of software. Bibliographic Retrieval Services (BRS) and the DIALOG Information Retrieval Service from Lockheed Information Systems have databases specific to microcomputer software. The library of a university or research institution can usually provide information about how to access these resources.

State, Regional, and Local Agencies

As using computers for instruction becomes more commonplace, the number of agencies providing support to teachers interested in using these techniques is increasing. State departments of education have become increasingly aware of the prevalence of microcomputers in schools and the need for state-level support of school personnel in implementing computers for instruction. As a result, many state departments of education have started offices of educational computing services. In addition, many have entered into cooperative projects with various public and private agencies to offer services.

Project BEST is one example of these cooperative ventures. In 1982 the U.S. Department of Education granted funds to the Association for Educational Communications and Technology (AECT) to begin what came to be known as Project BEST (Basic Educational Skills through Technology). Forty-two state agencies participated. Project BEST[5] was designed to increase the capacity of state departments of education to support local school districts in the use of microcomputers. Because of Project BEST and other efforts, awareness of microcomputers as instructional tools is growing, and state departments of education have been placing a greater emphasis on educational computing. They have begun to provide information about software evaluation and even to conduct or sponsor evaluation activities. Departments of education are becoming useful resources to teachers who seek information about software evaluations.

Many regional educational organizations have been formed by local and state educational agencies to provide support services to local school districts in a variety of areas, including instruction. Some of these agencies are known as *instructional materials centers, regional resource centers,* or *educational services centers.* Since school personnel have begun to show interest in instructional computing, many of the regional agencies have begun to offer assistance. As a result, some of the most knowledgeable professionals in instructional computing in a local area may work in these agencies and can help teachers locate software and courseware evaluations.

There may be people who are knowledgeable about software evaluation working in a school district. A teacher may find assistance from the members of a school district's instructional computing committee, from a district's curriculum coordinator, or from personnel who work in instructional or media services at the district office. It is generally a good idea to look for assistance as close to home as possible. Persons who work close by are likely to be able to give timely assistance and can understand local contexts and conditions.

Some institutions of higher learning have been rather slow to develop programs that relate to instructional computing. However, in response to demands from educators in the field, colleges and universities are developing capacity in this area. As faculties at colleges and universities develop expertise in instructional uses of microcomputers, they also become valuable resources to teachers who need information about software evaluation.

We have described sources of information about the quality of instructional software. However, it is possible that at times no information about a particular package will be found. The teacher will then have to do the evaluation. How teachers may go about evaluating software on their own is discussed next.

APPROACHES TO EVALUATION

Not all teachers (or other educators) will actually have to perform software evaluations. But even those who do not have to make their own evaluations might participate in evaluation projects sponsored by colleges, school districts, or other agencies; and many more will read and use evaluations made by others as they select software for their classrooms. Thus, some knowledge about software evaluation is a necessary for all teachers who will actually use educational software.

MicroSIFT: A Practical Approach

The MicroSIFT evaluation technique, one of several techniques available for evaluating software, is a practical approach that does not require a great deal of specialized knowledge or research skill. The MicroSIFT approach is designed to provide information about the quality of instructional software. A grasp of the procedures described here will help a teacher to make better use of information from software reviews. Readers who are interested in learning more about the procedure are referred to the *Evaluator's Guide for Microcomputer-Based Instructional Packages,* developed by MicroSIFT.[6]

The MicroSIFT evaluation process has four phases:

Phase 1 — Sifting: In this phase, software is sifted (that is, screened) for general appropriateness. If software clearly does not meet instructional needs or is designed to use hardware that is not available, it is not considered further.

Phase 2 — Description: In this phase, a brief description of the package is written; it includes program format, instructional purpose and techniques, available documentation, and the hardware necessary to run the package.

Phase 3 — Review: In this phase, the content and instructional and technical characteristics of the software package are evaluated. A software evaluation form has been developed for this purpose. To use it, one must be experienced in the subject and grade level and familiar with the evaluation techniques.

Phase 4 — In-depth evaluation: In this phase, field tests or intensive evaluations by students (or both) are done to determine the usefulness of the materials. However, this part of the evaluation process was not extensively addressed in the MicroSIFT project.

MicroSIFT uses the terms *content, courseware, materials, package,* and *program* in its software evaluations. These terms are defined in Table 7.2; knowl-

TABLE 7.2
DEFINITIONS FOR MicroSIFT EVALUATION PROCESS

Term	Definition
Content	Facts, terms, ideas, concepts, principles, theories, and constructs which make up the subject matter of an instructional package.
Courseware	Software and printed materials that support instruction in a complete course of study or a definable subset of a course.
Materials	Books, folders, envelopes, worksheets, and similar items. *User support materials* are items which assist a person to use the computing program.
Package	One or more computer programs with related materials. A package represents a microcomputer application.
Program	A computer program, written in BASIC, Pascal, machine code or some other computer programming language.

Source: Computer Technology Program, Northwest Regional Educational Laboratory. (1983). *Evaluator's guide for microcomputer-based instructional packages.* Eugene, OR: International Council for Computers in Education.

edge of the definitions is necessary for understanding the MicroSIFT evaluation procedures.

Figure 7.1 shows the MicroSIFT courseware description form. This is a form on which the evaluator can record ratings and comments; it is completed during phase 2, the description phase. When it is completed properly, the courseware description form presents basic information about courseware in a systematic way.

A second form, the MicroSIFT courseware evaluation form (Figure 7.2), is used after the description form has been filled in and an investigation of the program and support materials in the package has been completed. The evaluation form contains sections pertaining to the content and instructional and technical characteristics of the software package. Where the term *package* is used, all components should be taken into account in making the indicated evaluation. On this form, quality is rated on 21 items having to do with characteristics of the software. Comments concerning the ratings can be made on the back of the form. If the teacher has an opportunity to observe students using the package, this can be helpful in making ratings on the form. When observations cannot be made, professional judgment may be used. The *MicroSIFT Courseware Evaluator's Guide* provides descriptions of the criteria to be used in making ratings. Provision for making an overall recommendation is also included on the form.

Other Approaches

The MicroSIFT technique for evaluating instructional software is valuable because it provides a standard method. It represents the culmination of years

COURSEWARE DESCRIPTION

Title _____ Version Evaluated _____

Producer _____ Cost _____

Subject/Topics _____

Grade Level(s) (circle)   pre-1   1   2   3   4   5   6   7   8   9   10   11   12   post-secondary

Required Hardware _____

Available for Hard Disk?   ☐ Yes   ☐ No   ☐ Unknown

Required Software _____

Software protected?   ☐ Yes   ☐ No   Medium of Transfer: ☐ Tape Cassette   ☐ ROM Cartridge   ☐ 5" Flexible Disk   ☐ 8" Flexible Disk

Back Up Policy _____

Producer's field test data is available   ☐ On Request   ☐ With Package   ☐ Not Available

INSTRUCTIONAL PURPOSES & TECHNIQUES	DOCUMENTATION AVAILABLE:
(Please check all applicable):	Circle P-(Program) or S-(Supplementary Material)

INSTRUCTIONAL PURPOSES & TECHNIQUES
(Please check all applicable):

☐ Remediation   ☐ Drill and Practice
☐ Standard Instruction ☐ Tutorial
☐ Enrichment   ☐ Information Retrieval
☐ Assessment   ☐ Game
☐ Instructional   ☐ Simulation
  Management   ☐ Problem Solving
☐ Authoring
☐ Other _____

DOCUMENTATION AVAILABLE:
Circle P-(Program) or S-(Supplementary Material)

P S   Suggested grade/ability level(s)   P S   Teacher's information
P S   Instructional objectives   P S   Resource/reference information
P S   Prerequisite skills or activities   P S   Student's instructions
P S   Sample program output   P S   Student worksheets
P S   Program operating instructions   P S   Textbook correlation
P S   Pre-test   P S   Follow-up activities
P S   Post-test   P S   Other

OBJECTIVES: ☐ Stated   ☐ Inferred

PREREQUISITES: ☐ Stated   ☐ Inferred

Describe package **CONTENT AND STRUCTURE,** including record keeping and reporting functions:

FIGURE 7.1
MicroSIFT software description form. *(Reprinted with permission of Northwest Regional Educational Laboratory.)*

COURSEWARE EVALUATION 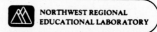 NORTHWEST REGIONAL EDUCATIONAL LABORATORY

Package Title _____ Producer _____

Evaluator Name _____ Organization _____

Date _____ ☐ Check this box if this evaluation is based partly on your observation of student use of this package.

SA-Strongly Agree   A-Agree   D-Disagree   SD-Strongly Disagree   NA-Not Applicable

Please include comments on individual items on the reverse page.

CONTENT CHARACTERISTICS

1. SA A D SD   NA   The content is accurate. (p. 16)
2. SA A D SD   NA   The content has educational value. (p. 16)
3. SA A D SD   NA   The content is free of race, ethnic, sex and other stereotypes. (p. 16)

INSTRUCTIONAL CHARACTERISTICS

4. SA A D SD   NA   The purpose of the package is well defined. (p. 17)
5. SA A D SD   NA   The package achieves its defined purpose. (p. 17)
6. SA A D SD   NA   Presentation of content is clear and logical. (p. 17)
7. SA A D SD   NA   The level of difficulty is appropriate for the target audience. (p. 18)
8. SA A D SD   NA   Graphics/color/sound are used for appropriate instructional reasons. (p. 18)
9. SA A D SD   NA   Use of the package is motivational. (p. 19)
10. SA A D SD   NA   The package effectively stimulates student creativity. (p. 19)
11. SA A D SD   NA   Feedback on student responses is effectively employed. (p. 20)
12. SA A D SD   NA   The learner controls the rate and sequence of presentation and review. (p. 20)
13. SA A D SD   NA   Instruction is integrated with previous student experience. (p. 29)
14. SA A D SD   NA   Learning can be generalized to an appropriate range of situations. (p. 29)

TECHNICAL CHARACTERISTICS

15. SA A D SD   NA   The user support materials are comprehensive. (p. 30)
16. SA A D SD   NA   The user support materials are effective. (p. 31)
17. SA A D SD   NA   Information displays are effective. (p. 31)
18. SA A D SD   NA   Intended users can easily and independently operate the program. (p. 32)
19. SA A D SD   NA   Teachers can easily employ the package. (p. 34)
20. SA A D SD   NA   The program appropriately uses relevant computer capabilities. (p. 34)
21. SA A D SD   NA   The program is reliable in normal use. (p. 35)

QUALITY

Write a number from 1 (low) to 5 (high) which represents your judgment of the quality of the package in each division:

_____ Content Characteristics

_____ Instructional Characteristics

_____ Technical Characteristics

RECOMMENDATIONS

☐ I highly recommend this package.

☐ I would use or recommend use of this package with little or no change. (Note suggestions for effective use below.)

☐ I would use or recommend use of this package only if certain changes were made. (Note changes under Weaknesses or Other Comments.)

☐ I would not use or recommend this package. (Note reasons under Weaknesses.)

Describe the potential use of the package in classroom settings:

FIGURE 7.2

MicroSIFT software evaluation form. *(Reprinted with permission of Northwest Regional Educational Laboratory.)*

Estimate the amount of time a student would need to work with the package in order to achieve the objectives:
(Can be total time, time per day, time range or other indicator.)

Strengths:

Weaknesses:

Other Comments:

of effort aimed at developing a practical and effective way to judge the quality of software. However, there are alternative perspectives on software evaluation, some of which are presented in this section. An understanding of these alternative techniques and some of the thinking behind them can lead to a more thorough appreciation of the issues involved in software evaluation.

The alternative approaches differ from MicroSIFT's in several ways. First, some of these techniques are intended to allow more depth in evaluating certain types of software (e.g., games, simulations, demonstrations) that cannot be dealt with specifically enough by a procedure like MicroSIFT's (which was designed to be broad enough to cover a great variety of software). Second, some techniques focus more attention on the quality of software from the viewpoint of instructional design. (This perspective is neglected in the design and development of a great deal of instructional software.) Third, since educational evaluation is a complex specialty requiring considerable training and skill, some techniques emphasize more formal research approaches. Let us now look at some alternative types of evaluation.

Evaluation of Specific Types of Software   There are several approaches to developing instruction for microcomputers, among them drill and practice, simulations, demonstrations, and tutorials. Each approach has features that make it unique. A single evaluation scheme cannot do justice to all types of software.

Consider, for example, simulations. While simulations and many other types of instruction can be presented with computers, specific features of instruction in simulations are quite different from those stressed in other kinds of instruction, such as drill and practice or tutorials. Neil C. Rowe has proposed a set of rules for good simulations based on the unique features of this kind of instruction.[7] Some of the rules concern specific elements of simulations that are often not part of software evaluation instruments. These rules were not designed as an evaluation instrument, but they could be used as a basis for developing one. The rules are grouped into five categories which specify the variables of the simulation, ensure that questions and directions to the users are clearly presented, ensure that results are clearly displayed, ensure that the simulation functions as intended, and cover other matters of overall organization. These rules focus on the design aspects of instructional simulations in much more detail than the MicroSIFT evaluation procedures. (Those interested in evaluating simulations might wish to consult Rowe's article for greater detail.)

Evaluation procedures can be designed in a similar way for other kinds of instructional approaches. For example, a tutorial can be evaluated in terms of content; and a drill and practice activity can be evaluated in terms of reinforcement of correct responses.

Instructional Design and Instructional Theory   Some educators believe that good-quality software is sparse because software developers often do not follow adequate instructional design procedures.

In an article on software development, M. D. Roblyer discussed some principles of effective learning and instructional design and their importance in software development.[8] In writing this article, Roblyer drew heavily upon the systematic instructional design methods of Gagné and Briggs[9] (to be discussed in Chapter 10). She stressed four major points of difference between much current instructional development and the systematic approach. Systematic instructional design has four aspects:

1 Use of a model
2 Emphasis on a written design
3 Use of a team approach to development
4 Provision for formative review and evaluation

Systematic procedures like Roblyer's are based on instructional and learning research and tend to support development of effective educational materials. Adherence to these procedures requires effort on the part of the developer. One can evaluate the quality of microcomputer courseware by considering the degree to which quality emerges from the design and development process.

A related approach to computer courseware evaluation has been suggested by Timothy Jay.[10] Jay's approach uses concepts about how humans process information, developed from research in cognitive psychology. The information-processing approach considers human thinking and learning as analogous to computer operations; for example, there are storage functions, information input and output, and so on. Recommendations for development and evaluation are based on theory. The approach focuses on five aspects of human information processing and describes their implications for evaluation of courseware:

1 Memory and attention
2 Characteristics of language and text
3 Graphics and visual processing
4 Cognitive characteristics of users
5 Feedback to users

When considering the fourth category (cognitive characteristics of users), for example, teachers make assumptions about the characteristics of the learners. Since younger (elementary school) students cannot be expected to think, solve problems, or learn in the same ways as older students, instructional courseware should require kinds of thinking and other cognitive skills appropriate for the intended grade level. This approach differs from others we have discussed in its strong adherence to principles of learning. To apply this approach effectively and interpret its results, a higher level of expertise is needed than for more practical methods such as MicroSIFT's. More evaluation techniques that assess software in terms of the psychology of learning and principles of instructional design are needed.

Research-Based Approaches   The success of courseware when it is in actual use is what really counts. Therefore, a strong argument can be made for evaluating computer courseware by testing it with the target audience under actual conditions of use. Expert judgment and comparisons with principles of instructional design do not guarantee that a courseware package really works with students. While the evaluation techniques already presented are extremely useful, and may be good predictors of successful learning, they are not really evidence that the software can be used successfully. (On the other hand, they are often less expensive than actual field tests.)

Designing a field test of educational techniques or materials may sound easier than it actually is. It might seem that if one could simply try a software product in the field, its effectiveness or ineffectiveness would quickly become apparent. However, this is not the case. In fact, a field test may not tell us very much at all. For example, it would not tell us whether the program tested was better than another program or no program at all. On the other hand, a field study will indicate whether students can use the software and whether it operates in the manner intended.

Evaluation studies must be designed with particular questions that need to be answered in mind. A teacher or another educator might design a field test to answer specific questions about courseware; there are numerous approaches and methods. The formative-summative approach, discussed below, has had considerable influence in the field. Because of the complexity of educational evaluation, a complete treatment is beyond the scope of this book; but readers interested in exploring the topic further are encouraged to review some of the references and supplementary readings listed at the end of this chapter.

Formative and Summative Approaches   Michael Scriven has proposed a distinction between the kind of evaluation one might do while an educational program is being developed and the kind done in a classroom when the finished product is tested.[11] Scriven called the former *formative evaluation;* the latter, *summative evaluation.*

Formative evaluation is an extremely useful concept for a developer of courseware. As an educational program is being constructed, completed units or lessons might be tested with a small group of students or a class. Examples of the kinds of questions that might be addressed in a formative evaluation of software are:

Can students run the program in the manner intended?

Are there serious bugs in the program that lead to frustration on the part of the students or create a need for additional supervision by the teacher?

Are the learning activities appropriate for the intended grade level?

Do the students see the connection between the software and the other activities (readings, workbook exercises, etc.) they are doing?

Are special facilities or equipment required to use the software effectively?

Does the software provide enough help or support for the student to complete the computer exercises?

Can students work in groups effectively with the software?

Does the software contain effective routines for handling errors?

Numerous other questions can be answered with a formative evaluation. This approach provides the developer of courseware with the opportunity to try out programs and techniques so that they can be improved before being completed.

The purpose of summative evaluation is to determine the overall effectiveness and worth of a program. Thus, a summative evaluation might be used at the end of a semester to see whether an educational program has been effective with students. Examples of the kinds of questions a summative evaluation might address are:

Did the students learn more as a result of having completed a computerized portion of the instructional program?

Have there been any changes in students' attitudes or behavior?

Have instructional goals and objectives been met?

Do teachers feel that the computerized portion of the program has enabled them to work more closely with individual students, or has it required more of their time for supervision and planning?

Other questions are possible, of course. The exact nature of questions to be asked would depend on the nature of the program and the information required.

Data that would be used in a formative or summative evaluation are varied. The selection of data would be based on the situation being evaluated and the questions being asked. For example, if the questions concern students' learning, then achievement tests, computer test records, and teacher-made classroom tests might be used. On the other hand, if the questions concern whether the computerized learning materials help teachers to work more with students on an individual basis, then teachers might be asked to estimate the amount of time spent with individual students when the computer-based activities were in use and when no computer activities were used. Or observers might be sent into the classrooms to record how teachers spend their time with students during different kinds of activities.

Just as data can be tailored to a specific situation and specific questions being addressed, an evaluation design can be chosen for specific purposes. For example, formative evaluation is used in developmental situations to give ongoing information to the developer that would be useful for improving the product or program. Summative evaluation deals with worth or effectiveness after an innovation has been tried. Alternative evaluation designs focus on such aspects of a program as effectiveness of management, appropriateness of procedures for accomplishing tasks, and effects on studies in other subject areas. Choosing the right evaluation design for a specific setting requires some knowledge of the

The Pennsylvania State University
College of Education
Curriculum Materials Center
University Park, Pennsylvania

various methods. Educators who want to perform extensive evaluations of educational programs and software might need some assistance from an expert in educational evaluation. People with training in educational evaluation are often found in universities, research agencies, state departments of education, regional educational laboratories, and curriculum development centers.

SUMMARY

Good-quality software is needed if students are to benefit significantly from instructional applications of computers. In this chapter, ways to determine the quality of educational software and courseware were discussed. Teachers were cautioned to think very carefully about how computer-based instruction fits into a curriculum or instructional plan. An instrument designed to screen courseware was presented.

Methods were suggested for obtaining information about software evaluations. Sources of information include colleagues and software experts, evaluations performed by others, information provided by software vendors, and common sense. Printed and other sources of courseware evaluations — including the services of EPIE and MicroSIFT, journals, magazines, and computerized databases — were discussed.

A practical method for courseware evaluation (MicroSIFT's) was described, along with several alternative approaches: evaluation of specific types of courseware, instructional theory and design, research-based procedures, and formative and summative evaluation.

Educators who are knowledgeable about how to select software for classroom use are likely to be successful using computers in instructing students. A knowledge of software evaluation is important for the modern classroom teacher. Over the next few years, more and more teachers will probably become skilled in educational software evaluation.

NOTES

1 MicroSIFT, Computer Technology Program, Northwest Regional Educational Laboratory (NWREL). (1983). *Evaluator's guide for microcomputer-based instructional packages* (rev. ed.). Eugene, OR: International Council for Computers in Education (ICCE).

2 Lathrop, A. (1982, September–October). The terrible ten in educational programming (My top ten reasons for automatically rejecting a program). *Educational Computer Magazine.*

3 For information, write to EPIE — Consumer's Union, P.O. Box 620, Stony Brook, NY 11790.

4 For example, see: *The Computing Teacher.* (1983). *10*(8), 33–42.

5 Ingle, H. T. (1983). Project BEST: What is it? . . . Who is involved? . . . And how are the states benefitting? *AEDS Monitor, 21*(9, 10), 31–34.

6 Northwest Regional Educational Laboratory (NWREL). (1983). *Evaluator's guide for*

microcomputer-based instructional packages (rev. ed.). Eugene, OR: International Council for Computers in Education.

7   Rowe, N. C. (1981). Some rules for good simulations. *Educational Computer Magazine, 1*(4), 37–40.

8   Roblyer, M. D. (1981). Instructional design versus authoring of courseware: Some crucial differences. *AEDS Journal, 14*(4), 173–181.

9   Gagné, R. M., & Briggs, L. J. (1974). *Principles of instructional design.* New York: Holt, Rinehart & Winston.

10 Jay, T. B. (1983). A cognitive approach to computer courseware design and evaluation. *Educational Technology, 23*(1), 22–26.

11 Scriven, M. (1967). The methodology of evaluation. In R. E. Stake (Ed.), *Curriculum Evaluation.* American Educational Research Association, No. 1. Chicago, IL: Rand McNally.

SUPPLEMENTARY READINGS

Anderson, R. E., Klassen, D. L., Hansen, T. P., & Johnson, D. C. (1980–1981). The affective and cognitive effects of microcomputer based science instruction. *Journal of Educational Technology Systems, 9*(4), 329–355.

Bloom, B. S., Hastings, J. T., & Madaus, G. F. (1971). *Handbook on formative and summative evaluation of student learning.* New York: McGraw-Hill.

Boruch, R. F., & Corday, D. S. (1980). *An appraisal of educational program evaluations: Federal, state, and local agencies.* Report of Contract Number 300-79-0467. Washington, D.C.: U.S. Department of Education.

Burns, P. K., & Bozeman, W. C. (1981). Computer assisted instruction and mathematics achievement: Is there a relationship? *Educational Technology, 21*(10), 32–39.

Cohen, V. B. (1983). Criteria for the evaluation of microcomputer courseware. *Educational Technology, 23*(1), 9–14.

Cook, T. D., & Campbell, D. T. (1979). *Quasi-experimentation: Design and analysis issues for field settings.* Chicago, IL: Rand McNally.

Edwards, J., Norton, S., Taylor, S., Weiss, M., & Dusseldorp, R. (1975). How effective is CAI? A review of the research. *Educational Leadership,* 147–153.

Edwards, J. B. (1980). MicroSIFT: Clearing the way. *The Computing Teacher, 7*(5), 10–11.

Eisner, E. W. (1982). *Cognition and curriculum: A basis for deciding what to teach.* New York: Longman.

Gagné, R. M., Wager, W. & Rojas, A. (1981). Planning and authoring computer-assisted instruction lessons. *Educational Technology, 21*(9), 17–26.

Golas, K. C. (1983). The formative evaluation of computer-assisted instruction. *Educational Technology, 23*(1), 26–28.

Gold, A. P. (1981). A technology of instruction based on developmental psychology. *Educational Technology, 21*(7), 6–13.

Hirschbuhl, J. J. (1980–1981). The design of computer programs for use in elementary and secondary schools. *Journal of Educational Technology Systems, 9*(3), 193–206.

Kaufman, R., & Thomas, S. (1980). *Evaluation without fear.* New York: New Viewpoints.

Merrill, M. D., Reigeluth, C. M., & Faust, G. W. (1979). The instructional quality profile: A curriculum evaluation and design tool. In H. F. O'Neil, Jr. (Ed.), *Procedures for instructional systems development.* New York: Academic Press.

MicroSIFT, Computer Technology Program, Northwest Regional Educational Laboratory (NWREL). (1983). *Evaluator's guide for microcomputer-based instructional packages* (rev. ed.). Eurgene, OR: International Council for Computers in Education (ICCE).

National Council of Teachers of Mathematics. (1981). *Guidelines for evaluating computerized instructional materials.* Prepared by the Instructional Affairs Committee of NCTM.

Research on School Effectiveness Project, Audit and Evaluation Program, Northwest Regional Educational Laboratory. (1980, December). *Computer Assisted Instruction.* Portland, OR: NWREL.

Riordon, T. (1983, March). How to select software you can trust. *Classroom Computer News,* 56–61.

Roblyer, M. D. (1981). Instructional design versus authoring of courseware: Some crucial differences. *AEDS Journal, 14*(4), 173–181.

Roblyer, M. D. (1982). Developing computer courseware must be easier than some things. *Educational Technology, 22*(1), 33–35.

Rowe, N. C. (1981). Some rules for good simulations. *Educational Computer Magazine, 1*(4), 37–40.

Steffin, S. A. (1983). A suggested model for establishing the validity of computer-assisted instructional materials. *Educational Technology, 23*(1), 20–22.

Steinberg, E. R. (1983). Reviewing the instructional effectiveness of computer courseware. *Educational Technology, 23*(1), 17–19.

Tennyson, R. D. (1981–1982). Interactive effect of cognitive learning theory with computer attributes in the design of computer-assisted instruction. *Journal of Educational Technology Systems, 10*(2), 175–186.

Worthen, B. R., & Sanders, J. R. (1973). *Educational evaluation: Theory and practice.* Worthington, OH: Carles Jones.

CHAPTER 8

YOU ARE NOT ALONE IN THIS

CHAPTER CONTENTS

LOCAL RESOURCES FOR EDUCATIONAL COMPUTING ACTIVITIES
  Users' Clubs
    Hardware-oriented users' clubs
    Software-oriented users' clubs
    Where to find out about users' clubs
    What to do when a suitable users' group cannot be found
  Cooperating Groups of Teachers
  Local Dealers
  Local School Districts
RESOURCES BEYOND THE SCHOOL DISTRICT AND LOCAL AREA
  Regional and National Conferences
  Publications
    Periodicals
    Books
  Consortia and Institutions Supporting Educational Computing
    Minnesota Educational Computing Consortium
    CONDUIT
    Alaska's Office of Educational Technology and Telecommunications
    Resources for evaluating software: MicroSIFT and EPIE
    Northeast Regional Exchange
  Professional Groups Interested in Educational Computing
FINDING OPPORTUNITIES FOR TRAINING
FINDING FUNDS TO SUPPORT EDUCATIONAL COMPUTING
SUMMARY
NOTES
APPENDIX: SOURCES OF INFORMATION ABOUT EDUCATIONAL
COMPUTER APPLICATIONS

191

Educators who do not have a technical background might understandably approach their first computer with caution. Teachers who are given responsibility for supervising instructional computing without having received proper training will feel similarly cautious. But trepidation can be considerably reduced when the teacher becomes aware of all the various kinds of assistance that are available. The present chapter was prepared to help readers realize that educators need not feel alone and isolated when they become involved in using computers in the schools.

An enormous amount of money and time might be required to develop a particular computer application. Fortunately, many different groups have been developing and refining educational computer applications over the last few years. All this developmental activity has resulted in considerable reductions in both costs and time necessary to effectively utilize computers. (For example, in the past a classroom teacher who wanted to keep students' records on a microcomputer would have had to develop the software or include the cost of the required programming in the equipment purchase request, because custom software is expensive. However, several companies now provide software suitable for such purposes.[1]) Some developmental resources are the result of cooperative efforts of teachers and school districts or of computer users' groups; some are funded by state departments of education. A number of commercial and nonprofit resources are also available.

As is noted in other chapters (Chapters 4, 9, and 10), the development of instructional and noninstructional applications of computers in schools can be costly and demanding, requiring knowledge of particular applications, expertise in computer programming and instructional design, and considerable time and effort. Resources that can reduce these demands by providing information, ready-made programs, assistance in problem solving, or other services can greatly contribute to a school's ability to utilize computers effectively. We will look first at the kinds of support that can be obtained from local profit and nonprofit groups, and then at resources available beyond the local area, including conferences, published resources — books, magazines, guides, etc. — consortia and other institutions, and professional groups. Finally, we will discuss ways that one might go about obtaining training and funds. An appendix to the chapter lists sources of information on educational applications.

LOCAL RESOURCES FOR EDUCATIONAL COMPUTING ACTIVITIES

Numerous resources to assist the microcomputer user exist on the local level, and many of them are free or available at a reasonable cost. Some exist within the educational establishment (schools, colleges, universities, state departments of education); others are found outside education. Convenience and low cost make these sources of assistance among the most important for the successful implementation of a program of educational microcomputing.

Users' Clubs

In many communities, users of microcomputers have formed clubs focusing on some central interest (Figure 8.1). For example, some clubs have been formed by users of particular kinds of hardware (such as specific computers, hard disks, and graphics devices). Other clubs are more interested in software. Among the services one can obtain from a users' group are these:

Help with problem solving from people who may have faced the same or similar problems

Information about products, peripherals, and software

Discounts through group purchase of diskettes, hardware, and supplies by the club

Classes or talks given by members on specific topics

Group cooperation on projects

Opportunity to interact with other people who have similar interests

Many local users' clubs are affiliated with national groups. Some make software or hardware available to members at special prices. Other membership benefits may include publications, newsletters, assistance with problem solving and programming, and periodic meetings with discussions about topics of interest to the members. Two broad categories of users' clubs are those oriented toward hardware and those oriented toward software and applications.

FIGURE 8.1
At a users' club meeting, topics of interest to members are discussed.

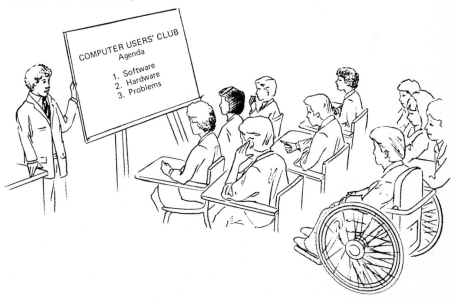

Hardware-Oriented Users' Clubs   The earliest users' clubs were hardware-oriented. People in these groups tended to have an engineering or technical background and enjoyed tinkering. Many ideas that have found their way into the marketplace originated from ideas and experiments of members of users' groups. It is well known that the microcomputer industry owes many of the developments of the 1970s in microcomputer hardware to the activities of early users' groups. In fact, some of the first successful hardware, including the Apple II computer, was developed by members of such groups.[2] However, today few clubs focus solely on hardware.[3]

At present, hardware-oriented users' groups tend to be interested in a single brand of computer or a particular kind of peripheral device rather than in development of innovations in hardware. For example, users' groups have been formed for such popular computers as the Apple and IBM microcomputers. This kind of users' group is sometimes sponsored by a manufacturer or vendor of hardware.

Users' groups exist in some communities for owners of portable computers — machines that can fit into a shirt pocket or a carrying enclosure no larger than a small valise or attaché case. Portable computers are whole systems in a single cabinet (including at least a computer, a keyboard, a monitor or another display, a mass storage device such as a disk drive, and sometimes a printer); they are designed to be moved easily from one location to another and often are sold with a package of business-oriented software. Owners of portable computers often form users' groups to help them expand their computers' capabilities. For example, a speech teacher or school psychologist might use a portable computer to keep records of work with students in each of several schools in a district. Special software might be needed for this application, and a users' group collectively might have the expertise to help write the programs.

Some users' groups have focused on applications of hard disks, modems, plotters, and other relatively unusual devices. Many of these users' groups flourish to provide support for those who develop unusual or special computer applications. For example, such clubs exist for people who design microcomputer-based devices for the handicapped. Since these applications are often custom-tailored to one person's handicap, there may have been little written about a particular application that would be of help to the designer. Users' groups can provide a way to get help with implementation of a custom-designed application.

Software-Oriented Users' Clubs   Many of the users' groups that focus on software emphasize the operating system — the software that manages a computer's operation, allows it to run programs, and controls peripheral devices. CP/M is one of the most widely used operating systems for computers, and a large number of computer clubs have been formed to bring together people who use it.

Software-oriented users' clubs often form around specific applications. For example, some users' clubs focus on games, others on business applications such as word processing and spreadsheets. Amateur programmers can benefit from users' groups dedicated to a particular programming language. Users' clubs for assembly language or Pascal programmers are not uncommon. Members can discuss their programming problems or demonstrate their new applications at club meetings.

Where to Find Out about Users' Clubs   Sometimes users' clubs are difficult to find. They usually do not advertise for members, nor do they operate on a regular basis from an established location.

Usually the best place to get information about local clubs is from a local computer dealer or a club member. Many dealers sponsor clubs as one of the ways they support their products. They may publish a newsletter for the club, provide a place to meet, or give discount prices to club members on certain items. Sometimes dealers will post on a bulletin board in the store a listing of users' group activities or even maintain an electronic bulletin board accessible with computers outfitted with modems and connected to the telephone.

Many users' clubs can be found in national listings. For example, *Computer Shopper,*[4] a monthly publication that primarily serves those interested in buying and selling computer equipment, lists names and addresses of local users' groups all over the world. To be listed, a club need only send the necessary information.

Producers of hardware and software also provide information about users' groups for their products. For example, purchasers of the Kaypro line of computers are given information about how to join Kaypro Users' Group (KUG); this information is in the documentation that comes with the computer. Numerous other microcomputer companies and publications furnish information about how to contact users' clubs. In the appendix to this chapter, several sources of information about national users' groups are listed.

What to Do When a Suitable Users' Group Cannot Be Found   Users' clubs tend to be composed of small groups of people with a common interest. If no users' group can be found for a particular interest, then starting one might be considered. An advertisement in a local newspaper and announcements on bulletin boards in schools, computer stores, and other public places will often bring sufficient response to begin a users' group.

School computer clubs may be thought of as users' clubs. These clubs give students the opportunity to organize the group, plan activities, keep club records, and pursue their interests in computers. Many schools provide this kind of activity for students as an extracurricular program utilizing the school's computer facilities after hours. Often the club members have sufficient knowledge to develop software, study the feasibility of certain applications, or provide consulting services for the school. (However, large computer-based applications should generally be left to a more experienced professional computing staff.)

Cooperating Groups of Teachers

Users' clubs need not be formal organizations with constitutions, bylaws, expensive dues, initiation fees, and strict membership requirements. Many effective clubs may not really be clubs in the formal sense at all. For example, a group of teachers interested in using computers for a particular topic — such as education of the handicapped, maintenance of records, and enrichment of learning in the classroom — might cooperate to help each other. A group of teachers can share such tasks as researching a topic of instruction, programming, putting material into the computer with PILOT (or another course authoring system), and preparing software documentation. Cooperative arrangements among teachers can lead to faster and more effective development of applications, and to more effective utilization of resources within a school.

Local Dealers

A local computer dealer can be a valuable resource. Although lower prices may be obtained by purchasing through mail order, or directly from a manufacturer on large orders, the high-quality consulting and maintenance services provided by a local dealer can more than offset such savings. However, not all dealers are willing or able to provide this kind of service. In choosing a dealer, one should consider reputation for service and support.

Some of the things a good service-oriented dealer can do are:

Assist in identifying software and hardware available for specific needs
Provide a demonstration of a system performing required tasks before any purchase is made
Offer training for users
Assist with installation
Provide maintenance and repair services

A dealer who is willing to go beyond exchanging money for equipment and offer services like these can save customers considerable time, money, and frustration. Such a dealer deserves some loyalty. However, one should not expect a dealer to decide what needs are or how they should be met. A good dealer can be expected to know something about the software and hardware that he or she sells and services; but other products may be better choices for some needs, and the dealer may simply not know about them or may be reluctant to recommend a competitor's products.

Local School Districts

The amount of support available from local school districts for educational microcomputing varies. In some districts, there may be very little help for a teacher who implements a program of instructional computing. In other districts, there may be volunteer committees or a person who is assigned to be responsible for aiding teachers with instructional computing. Even though resources in a local school district may be modest, they are nearby and should not be overlooked. A school district's committment to educational applications of computers can be increased when it has a users' club.

In some school districts, support has been so great that these districts are now able to offer services to others. Some school districts produce software for general use. For example, the Comprehensive Achievement Monitoring (CAM) software package available from the Minnesota Educational Computing Consortium (MECC) was developed by the Hopkins school district in Minnesota. Another product available from MECC, Mastery Management, was produced by the Hopkins district in cooperation with the Minneapolis and St. Paul school districts.[5]

An additional example of how some districts can offer services to others is provided by the Microcomputer Resource Center of the San Mateo County (California) Office of Education. The center keeps a number of hardware and software products available for educators to examine and evaluate; and although the center was established to serve educators in San Mateo County, others may use it. The center also operates SOFTSWAP, an exchange project for public-domain software. Several computer equipment companies provide hardware and maintenance support to the center, which is a joint project of the San Mateo County Office of Education and Computer-Using Educators (CUE), a national users' organization based in San Jose, California.

Santa Clara County Office of Education in California offers publications on topics in educational microcomputing. Among the products available from this district are a directory of microcomputing software in guidance and counseling and a teaching module for developing technology literacy.[6]

RESOURCES BEYOND THE SCHOOL DISTRICT AND LOCAL AREA

Many useful resources in educational computing exist outside of the local area. These include national users' clubs, publications of various sorts, and consortia or other cooperative arrangements dedicated to providing some kind of support to microcomputer users. In this section we look at some of these resources. The appendix to this chapter lists many of the sources. However, new groups come into being almost daily. If a particular kind of information is required, and the reader cannot find an appropriate source listed, making a search of publications or contacting some of the listed groups will probably uncover ways of obtaining the required assistance, if it exists.

Regional and National Conferences

Attending regional or national conferences is an excellent way to find out about microcomputer equipment. Many of these conferences are sponsored by associations of computer users and producers. They provide an opportunity for hardware and software producers to display their products, and for users to try those products and ask questions. In addition, conferences are held regularly which focus specifically on educational applications of microcomputers.

It would be difficult to make a list of these meetings and conferences, because many of them are not held on a regular basis. To find out about conferences being held in your region, consult some of the newsletters and periodicals listed in this chapter. Another source of information about meetings might be a users' group. Many universities have schools of education that sponsor instructional computer conferences from time to time; often the faculty or staff will be able to provide information about such meetings.

Among the larger meetings that are held every year are the West Coast Computer Faire, an industrywide microcomputer meeting at which new products are often displayed or announced.[7] Another major meeting held for similar purposes is COMDEX.[8] The annual meetings of the National Educational Computing Conference (NECC), and Ed.Com (National Computer Conference for Educators) focus on educational computing. Several meetings are held specifically for those interested in educational applications. For example, Lesley College in Massachusetts and the Computer Education Resource Coalition (CERC) sponsor an annual conference in the spring. At this meeting there are usually sessions on using computers and other technology in classrooms, and hands-on sessions in programming or using software. The annual meetings of organizations such as the Association for Educational Data Systems (AEDS) and the Association for Educational Communications and Technology (AECT) also tend to focus on information about using computers in education. Information about the meetings can be obtained directly from the associations or their publications. In addition, these conferences are often advertised or announced in many of the popular computer magazines.

Publications

A large number of books and periodicals about microcomputers have become available since the first microcomputers began to appear on the educational scene. Some of these tend to be rather technical in their orientation, but others are specifically written for people who do not have a vast background in computers. Several publications are dedicated to educational computing; others are oriented toward microcomputers in general but often have educational columns or features.

Periodicals   Magazines, newsletters, and other periodicals perform an important function. In the world of technology, new advances are made almost daily. The need to disseminate information about innovations in hardware, software, and applications is served by publications that can be issued weekly, monthly, or on some other frequent basis. A number of publications, particularly those with educational interests, are mentioned at the end of this chapter; but a complete list is certainly beyond the scope of this book.

Books Books about computers probably represented the fastest-growing segment of the publishing industry during the early 1980s. Publishers have formed sizable divisions dedicated to producing and marketing computer-related books. A major segment of that market includes books for people teaching about computers and books for people who want to learn about them. Books written for children are common, as are books designed to increase adults' knowledge about computers and computing. Many books cover programming for the novice and for people who are more experienced. Others review classroom applications, list programs, and review novel ways to use existing programs (such as spreadsheet and word processing programs). In addition, there are consumer guides to hardware and software and software anthologies. (Several anthologies are listed at the end of this chapter.) Many periodicals and magazines have book review columns as standard features. Such reviews are often good ways to determine whether a book about some aspect of computing will be useful to a potential reader.

Consortia and Institutions Supporting Educational Computing

Various cooperative ventures, nonprofit organizations, and educational institutions furnish useful services, products, and information concerning the application of computers in education. Much of the information and services available from these sources can be obtained free or at reasonable prices. It is safe to say that the early impetus for integrating computer technology into the educational system was greatly encouraged by these organizations. In the following sections we consider some of the more prominent of these groups.

Minnesota Educational Computing Consortium The Minnesota Educational Computing Consortium (MECC) was established in 1973 as a cooperative effort of four separate educational agencies in Minnesota: the University of Minnesota, the state university system, the community college system, and the state departments of administration and education. MECC was established to provide computing services to educational institutions throughout the state. However, other educational agencies and individuals can take advantage of MECC services and products. Information about this is available from MECC.[9]

The activities of MECC can be classified into instructional computing services, management information services, and special projects.

Instructional services include running workshops, training teachers, meeting with school personnel, disseminating information to users, and operating and maintaining time-sharing services for members. In addition, MECC maintains educational network services, develops instructional materials and systems, and sells educational programs and materials and supporting documentation to educational users and institutions. MECC also maintains libraries of programs developed or contributed by its staff and by users.

MECC's *management services* include administrative and management information services for elementary, secondary, and vocational school districts in

Minnesota. As part of this function, software for record keeping and reporting has been developed. The organization supports uniform database standards to help maintain standards for record keeping and conformity to state and federal requirements. Consulting services are provided to assist in implementing regional computing centers and in developing and implementing microcomputer-based administrative applications. In addition, MECC provides assistance to state agencies and school districts for purchasing computing equipment; this includes negotiating state contracts with computer vendors to obtain significant discounts for school districts.

Special projects of MECC include providing assistance to member systems for obtaining funds for instructional computing. MECC also conducts research related to the use of computers in education. In this endeavor, it seeks support from agencies such as the National Science Foundation and the National Institute of Education. MECC's special projects also include development of new applications and technologies applied to education, and evaluation of existing systems, techniques, and products.

The Minnesota Educational Computing Consortium is a prominent and respected agency in the field of instructional computing. Its activities, products, and services have contributed significantly to the development of that field.

CONDUIT   CONDUIT[10] reviews and distributes educational software. While its major focus is higher education, much of its offerings are suitable for secondary schools. CONDUIT has converted many of its programs from mainframes and minicomputers to run on several kinds of microcomputers. The organization has produced guidelines for authors of educational software and documentation, evaluation materials, and other items for instructional computing.

Alaska's Office of Educational Technology and Telecommunications   The Office of Educational Technology and Telecommunications (OET&T) of the Alaska Department of Education has been a leader in bringing novel and effective use of microcomputers into schools.[11]

The fact that much of Alaska is rural presents a considerable challenge to education. Not only is the school population dispersed across a vast area, but the climate and terrain make transportation and communication difficult. In addition, several different cultures are represented in the population. The state of Alaska has aggressively sought to meet these challenges with a mixture of technology and creative solutions, and it has become a model of what a state department of education can do to assist its local school districts.

Among the innovative projects instituted by the state department of education was one of the first statewide administrative telecommunications networks, and a series of instructional television programs for school students and adults across the state. In addition, in its Individualized Study by Technology (IST) program, a series of computer-based secondary education programs were developed to enable students in remote areas to take courses in their local districts, and to help teachers in the cities to individualize instruction for their students. IST courses have been produced in general mathematics, developmental reading, English, American history, general science, Alaskan history, Alaskan health education, and related topics.[12] In addition, OET&T sponsors training workshops for teachers and has developed eight multimedia instructional modules to be used by local school districts in training teachers to use microcomputers. It also publishes a newsletter for teachers who use computers; assists local schools with purchase of equipment, courseware, and software; and performs other activities to encourage and support the use of technology to meet the needs of the Alaskan schools.[13]

Other state departments of education have also made initiatives in instructional computing, and these agencies are becoming important resources for educators in their states.

Resources for Evaluating Software: MicroSIFT and EPIE MicroSIFT and EPIE were discussed in detail in Chapter 7. A major service provided by these organizations is review and evaluation of educational software. In addition to reviews of instructional software, MicroSIFT provides technical assistance to teachers and schools in the northwestern United States. The focus of MicroSIFT is on computer applications for the K–12 curriculum. Information and guides for evaluating instructional software and a quarterly journal, *MicroSIFT News,* are published by MicroSIFT.

Educational Products Information Exchange (EPIE) has been reviewing educational products for many years, taking the point of view of the consumer. More recently, EPIE has teamed with Consumers Union, which publishes *Consumer Reports* and focuses on the general products and services market, to produce reviews of educational computing products. Their newsletter, *MICROgram,* is published nine times a year. *MICROgram* offers advice on choosing, purchasing, and maintaining educational computer products.

Northeast Regional Exchange The Northeast Regional Exchange (NEREX) is a cooperative nonprofit organization chartered to promote improvement in education by pooling resources within a seven-state area including the New England states and New York. One notable project in 1982, undertaken by NEREX in cooperation with Technical Education Resource Center (TERC), led to the development of *Microcomputers in Education: An Introduction,* by Adeline Naiman, a guide for novices in educational computing.[14]

Professional Groups Interested in Educational Computing

Many professional organizations involved in education support some activities that focus on educational computing, such as sessions in the programs of annual meetings, columns in newsletters, and articles in periodicals sponsored by these organizations or in other publications. The organizations listed in this section, however, generally have a more formal commitment to educational computing.

- Association for Educational Communications and Technology (AECT), 1126 Sixteenth Street, N.W., Washington, DC 20036.

People who belong to this group are usually specialists in educational media. The organization includes a group whose special interest is educational computing.

- Association for Educational Data Systems (AEDS), 1201 Sixteenth Street, N.W., Washington, DC 20036.

Members of AEDS tend to be teachers and administrators who are interested in educational computing and other applications of technology in education.

- American Educational Research Association (AERA), 1230 Seventeenth Street, N.W., Washington, DC 20036.

The American Ecucational Research Association is the primary professional association in the United States concerned with educational research. Most of its members are researchers employed by universities, research organizations, or governmental agencies. Interests range from research in curriculum design, testing, human development, and counseling to administration, policy analysis, and social and theoretical aspects of education. Many members of the association use computers in their own fields of interests. A Special Interest Group (SIG) within AERA focuses on microcomputer applications in education.

- International Council for Computers in Education (ICCE), 135 Education, University of Oregon, Eugene, OR 97403.

ICCE has individual and organizational members. It encourages communication among member organizations and within the field of educational computing by making information about activities available, developing informational brochures and training materials, and offering free advertising in its publication, *The Computer Teacher,* to member organizations. ICCE has produced booklets or monographs on computer literacy and evaluation of courseware, and teachers' and administrators' guides to educational computing. All are available at reasonable prices from ICCE.

- National Council of Teachers of Mathematics (NCTM), 1906 Association Drive, Reston, VA 22091.

NCTM has been one of the most active professional organizations promoting educational computing. It has developed a courseware evaluation guide and other publications that cite computer applications in mathematics education. It has also sponsored numerous regional workshops to assist mathematics teachers in instructional computing.

- National Science Teachers Association (NSTA), 1742 Connecticut Avenue, N.W., Washington, DC 20009.

NSTA has also been a supporter of computer education; however, as would be expected, its focus is on teaching science. Through its regular publications and at its national meetings, science teachers are exposed to ideas and applications of computer technology in science instruction.

• Society for Applied Learning Technology Systems (SALT), 50 Culpepper Street, Warrenton, VA 22186.

SALT is interested in technology applied to a broad spectrum of educational settings such as special, vocational, health, military, and industrial education.

Numerous other professional organizations support the use of computers in education through their publications, presentations at annual meetings, and occasional special-topic publications. Computers are becoming so prevalent in every aspect of education that most professional societies support some kind of computer-awareness activities for their membership.

FINDING OPPORTUNITIES FOR TRAINING

Since widespread use of computers in education is relatively new, many experienced teachers in the field would like to learn about computers through in-service training. In addition, because the field has been changing so rapidly, even those who are experienced in educational technology often feel a need to update their proficiency and knowledge. Opportunities for training in educational computing are becoming more numerous and more diverse. Such opportunities exist at many institutions of higher education and may also be found in other settings.

Currently, only a few colleges and universities offer the opportunity for teachers to develop a major concentration in educational computing.[15] However, more are recognizing the importance of this kind of training. In addition to formal courses in computers for teachers, many institutions are beginning to sponsor short courses, continuing education courses, workshops, and summer experiences for teachers who wish to upgrade their skills in computing. Many of these opportunities are advertised in newspapers, periodicals, and other public media. Another way to find out about them is to call or write to an institution of higher education.[16]

Educators should not overlook the training experiences that might be available at a professional meeting or conference. It is not at all uncommon for a workshop on educational computing to be presented at a meeting of a state education association or a similar meeting. Further, there are often software and hardware displays at such meetings.

Many local computer dealers offer courses in computer literacy, programming, and specific applications. Such courses might be made a contract condition when a school district makes a large purchase. In addition, some dealers will occasionally provide demonstrations of new products or equipment.

If enough teachers in a school district require in-service training in computers, a private consultant might be engaged to present it. Knowledgeable computer consultants who can be effective teachers and trainers are sometimes difficult to find; and poor teaching or training can have unfavorable effects on the quality of the program. The following suggestions for choosing a consultant might reduce the chances of making a poor choice:

Clearly specify goals and objectives for the training.

Look for a consultant whose background matches the training required (e.g., computers in support of mathematics education or language arts education).

Get references from others who have used the same consultant as a trainer.

Approve the training program before agreeing to use the consultant. This might involve examining a proposed agenda and some of the training materials.

Another way to obtain training is by organizing small self-help study groups. Self-help materials can help one learn about educational computing. Many self-teaching or tutorial devices are available from commercial sources. For example, the Step-by-Step package (a product of Program Design, Inc., Greenwich, CT) is a tutorial for learning to program in BASIC on the Apple II computer. Using these techniques with others can enhance the quality of learning and provide support when problems or difficulties arise. Other ways to educate oneself about computing would be to read periodicals and books, attend meetings of users' clubs, and tinker with a computer by running applications programs or developing new programs. Hands-on experience with a microcomputer can be extremely instructive.

FINDING FUNDS TO SUPPORT EDUCATIONAL COMPUTING

Schools are always in need of funds. Sources of funding to support aspects of the school program are generally welcome. Some organizations and agencies may be able to help schools obtain computers. However, for various reasons, these sources are constantly changing their priorities, their policies, and the amount of money available. Educators who are searching for funds to help defray the costs of educational computing should expect competition from other school districts. Further, it will usually take some effort to locate a fund whose criteria match those for which the grant is being proposed.

Some of the more consistent supporters of educational computing are listed below. Each should be contacted to determine its most recent criteria and the procedures for making a proposal.

• National Science Foundation (NSF). This agency usually has some funds for supporting educational activities in science and mathematics. Computer education is also one of its concerns.

• U.S. Department of Education, Division of Educational Technology. This agency is sometimes able to provide money to state departments of education to assist local schools.

• Carnegie Corporation, 437 Madison Avenue, New York, NY 10022.

- Alfred P. Sloan Foundation, 630 Fifth Avenue, New York, NY 10111.
- Apple Foundation for the Advancement of Computer-Aided Education, 20525 Mariani Avenue, Cupertino, CA 95014.
- Atari Institute for Educational Action Research, 1265 Borregas Avenue, P.O. Box 427, Sunnyvale, CA 94086.

This list is by no means complete. Educators should look for other sources in publications such as *Grants Register* and *Foundation Directory,* usually available in the reference departments of public and university libraries. In addition, the Foundation Center (888 Seventh Avenue, New York, NY 10106) maintains information about foundations that make funds available to public institutions and agencies in the United States.

Occasionally assistance in finding funds can be obtained from a nearby college, university, or research institute. These organizations maintain records of resources for funding educational activities. Sometimes a cooperative effort between a school district and an institution for higher education will allow both to qualify for funds from a particular agency where one or the other alone could not qualify.

In conclusion, when the school district seeks outside funds to support educational computing, there may be help available. However, creativity and persistence may be necessary to find these funds. In addition to the sources listed above, educators may find assistance in some of the periodicals listed in the appendix to this chapter.

SUMMARY

Many sources of assistance and support exist for the educator who becomes involved in instructional computing. These sources include users' groups; periodicals; dealers' services; professional organizations; and state, federal, and private organizations.

Users' clubs can provide a great deal of assistance and support to their members. Such clubs can provide information and help with problem solving and purchasing of equipment and supplies. Users' clubs formed in a school can bring together teachers and students to work on projects of benefit to the school and can promote development of a base of expertise within the school.

A variety of publications can help educators keep abreast of developments in hardware, software, and applications. These publications include anthologies of software and hardware, popular magaines, books, and periodicals published by professional organizations. In addition, organizations such as the Minnesota Educational Computing Consortium, ICCE, NEREX, MicroSIFT, EPIE, and SOFT-SWAP should be familiar to educators. Each provides a valuable service or services in educational conputing.

At present there are a number of ways to obtain training in educational computing. These include formal courses on university or college campuses; courses offered by local dealers; and workshops provided at meetings of professional groups, in school districts, or in other settings. Many of these training opportunities are advertised in newsletters, magazines, and publications of professional groups. Another way to obtain training is through use of tutorials and training materials that can be purchased. Whatever method of training is used, educators should recognize that the field of educational technology is constantly changing and that keeping one's knowledge up to date is a continuing challenge.

The cost of educational computing hardware and software is not as great as it once was. However, many schools may still need financial assistance to provide educational computing opportunities for their students. Such assistance may be available from a variety of public and private sources, such as the National Science Foundation, the state or federal department of education, computer companies, and private foundations. Competition for these funds may be heavy. Creativity and persistence are useful traits to have when looking for external funding support.

NOTES

1 The Electronic Grade Book program from Charles Mann & Associates (Yucca Valley, CA) is a sample of such a program; it is designed to run on the Apple II computer.

2 See: Updated book of Jobs. (1983). *Time, 121* (1), 25–27.

3 Wise, D. (1983). Users' groups are no longer the hobbyist's domain. *InfoWorld, 5*(14), 27.

4 *Computer Shopper,* P.O. Box F, 407 S. Washington Avenue, Titusville, FL 32780.

5 For more information about CAM and Mastery Management, contact: MECC, 2520 Broadway Drive, St. Paul, MN 55113.

6 Information may be obtained from: Publications C/VEG, Mail Code 236, Santa Clara Office of Education, 100 Skyport Drive, San Jose, CA 95115.

7 See, for example: *Softalk.* (1983, May). *3,* 242–245.

8 See, for example: *InfoWorld.* (1983). *5*(21), 1, 4–6, 8.

9 For information about MECC or its products and services, write to: Minnesota Educational Computing Consortium, 2520 Broadway Drive, St. Paul, MN 55113.

10 For more information about CONDUIT, write to: CONDUIT, P.O. Box 388, Iowa City, IA 52244.

11 A summary of many of the Alaska Department of Education's initiatives in educational technology can be found in: *Informational technology and its impact on American education.* (1982). Washington, DC: Report of the Office of Technology Assessment, Congress of the United States.

12 For information about obtaining instructional computing products and programs, contact: Director, Office of Educational Technology and Telecommunications, Alaska Department of Education, Pouch F, Juneau, Alaska 99811.

13 Mason, E. J., & Bramble, W. J. (1982). Evaluation of a computerized solution to delivery of education in Alaska. *AEDS Monitor, 21*(3, 4), 33–36.

14 More information about NEREX and *Microcomputers in education: An introduction* can be obtained from Northeast Regional Exchange, 101 Mill Road, Chelmsford, MA 01824.

15 No micro training available to education majors. (1982). *Electronic Education, 2*(1), 19.
16 Periodicals such as *Computing Teacher, Classroom Computing News, SOFTALK, and Electronic Learning* advertise many of these workshops and summer programs. Announcements of summer programs usually begin to appear in the issues published in the early spring.

APPENDIX: Sources of Information about Educational Computer Applications

SOFTWARE ANTHOLOGIES

• *Commodore software encyclopedia (3rd ed.).* (1983). West Chester, PA: Commodore Computer.

This publication is more than just a software directory. It also contains information on users' groups, supplies for the Commodore computers, and other items of interest. There is a section on educational software for Commodore computers, along with sections on other categories of applications including games and business.

• *Educational software sourcebook.* (1983). Radio Shack (A Division of Tandy Corporation).

Contains over 800 listings of educational software for the TRS-80 computers.

• *Skarbeks software directory: Apple computer.* (1980). Maryland Heights, MO: Skarbek.

Lists software and peripherals for the Apple II computer, with short descriptions accompanying each listing. Includes a separate section on education.

• *VanLoves Apple II/III software directory.* Overland Park, KS: Vital Information.

Focuses on two models of the Apple computer. Includes an education category.

• Stanton, J., & Wells, R. P. (Eds.). (1983). *The book of Apple software (1983).* Los Angeles, CA: Book Company. Stanton, J., Wells, R. P., & Rachowansky, S. (Eds.). (1983). *The book of ATARI software (1983).* Los Angeles, CA: Book Company.

These two volumes contain listings and evaluations of hundreds of programs written for the Apple II and Atari computers. Each includes a section on educational software.

• *Swift's educational software directory.* Austin, TX: Sterling Swift.

Includes descriptions of programs, hardware requirements, grade level, and other useful information about educational programs. Updated annually.

NATIONAL USERS' GROUPS

- Boston Computer Society, 3 Center Plaza, Boston, MA 02108.

This organization was founded in 1976 and has rapidly grown to national proportions. It has become a resource center and a consortium of computer groups. The group publishes *Computer Update* and does other activities to promote microcomputers and educate people about them.

- Computer-Using Educators (CUE), c/o Don McKell, Independence High School, 1776 Educational Park Drive, San Jose, CA 95133.

CUE is a users' organization that focuses on microcomputers. It is one of the sponsors of SOFTSWAP, the public-domain software exchange in San Mateo County (CA) schools. CUE performs a number of other functions, including publishing a newsletter and organizing conferences and programs.

- Young People's Logo Association (YPLA), 1208 Hillsdale Drive, Richardson, TX 75081.

This organization is dedicated to introducing computers and problem solving to young people through Logo. It also has an interest in using Logo with the handicapped. The organization publishes a newsletter for children and adults and serves as a software exchange. Several local chapters are affiliated with it.

PERIODICALS

The publications listed below may not be entirely devoted to computer applications, or to education. However, each has regular features, articles, or sections devoted to educational computing. A complete listing of publications relating to educational microcomputing is difficult to compile, because changes come rapidly in this field. However, the present list of publications can be considered representative of what is available.

Periodicals for a General Audience

- *BYTE.* (Monthly.) Published by Byte Publications, 70 Main Street, Peterborough, NH 03458.

This is one of the more prominent computer magazines. Each issue is usually over 500 pages. *BYTE* tends to take a technical orientation with articles on programming, design and modification of hardware, and other technical subjects. Each issue concentrates on some topic of interest, such as a particular application in business or education, one of the programming languages, game programming, or telecommunications hardware.

- *Computer Update.* (Bimonthly.) Published by Boston Computer Society, Inc., 3 Center Plaza, Boston, MA 02108.

A good general publication for the computer novice. Contains hardware and software reviews, information of interest to those who follow the computer industry, and information about the Boston Computer Society, probably the largest organization of computer users in the United States.

• *Computers and Electronics* (formerly *Popular Electronics*). (Monthly.) Published by Ziff-Davis Publishing Co., 1 Park Avenue, New York, NY 10016.

With the new name, in 1982, the editors indicated a shift in interest from the electronics hobbyist to the computer hobbyist. The publication contains reviews of equipment, articles on design of applications and equipment, and building projects for the hobbyist.

• *Creative Computing*. (Monthly.) Published by Creative Computing, P.O. Box 789-M, Morristown, NJ 07960.

Contains reviews of hardware and software, educational applications, games, programming, and other topics of interest to computer users. In the course of a year, a large number of topics will be covered, allowing readers to stay fairly well abreast of developments. Most issues focus on a particular topic but also contain discussions on a wide range of material. The articles tend to be written in a nontechnical style that would appeal to most readers.

• *Infoworld*. (Weekly.) Published by InfoWorld, 375 Cochituate Road, Box 880, Framingham, MA 01701.

A weekly publication for microcomputer users, *InfoWorld* has very timely information. New products and developments, reviews of products, industry gossip and news, people in the computer industry, and other relevant topics are covered. In late 1983 the publication changed from a newspaper to a weekly magazine format.

• *Microcomputing*. (Monthly.) Published by Microcomputing, P.O. Box 997, Farmingdale, NY 11737.

Contains practical information, program listings, reviews, and articles related to general use of microcomputers. Occasionally, articles and features of interest to educators are included.

• *Personal Computing*. (Monthly.) Published by Hayden Publishing Company, Inc., 50 Essex Street, Rochelle Park, NJ 07662.

Articles in this publication are intended for people who are getting started in microcomputing or are not interested in the technical end of the field. Features on education, software and hardware, tips, and news are regularly found in *Personal Computing*.

• *Personal Software*. (Monthly.) Published by Hayden Publishing Company, Inc., 50 Essex Street, Rochelle Park, NJ 07662.

Publishes reviews and useful advice for software purchasers. The magazine considers a variety of software, including games, educational programs, and business applications packages. Written for the nontechnical user.

• *Popular Computing*. (Monthly.) Published by BYTE Publications, 70 Main Street, Peterborough, NH 03458.

A good introduction to microcomputing for beginners without a technical orientation. The magazine covers the field with articles that are easy to read and timely.

• *Softside*. (Monthly.) Published by Softside Publications, Inc., 6 South Street, Milford, NH 03055.

Contains reviews, program listings, and articles on hardware, software, and applications. The focus is on several brands of microcomputers.

Periodicals Specifically Oriented toward Education

• *AEDS Monitor*. (Six issues per year.) Published by Association for Educational Data Systems (AEDS), 1201 Sixteenth Street, N. W., Washington, DC 20016.

Publishes articles and news of interest to members of AEDS. An issue may include articles on programming, novel applications of computers in educational settings, statewide equipment adoption plans, guidelines for educational applications, and other topics. Issues also include applied research, evaluation studies, and product reviews.

• *AEDS Journal*. (Quarterly.) Published by Association for Educational Data Systems (AEDS), 1201 Sixteenth Street, N. W., Washington, DC 20016.

This is primarily oriented toward the academic community. It contains reports of research, projects, and evaluation studies; and theoretical or speculative articles on a variety of topics relating to educational technology.

• *Education News*. (Quarterly.) Published by Apple Computer, Inc., 20525 Mariani Avenue, Cupertino, CA 95014

This publication could be more accurately called *Apple Education News,* since it focuses on applications of the products of Apple Computer Company. It is free to educators and well worth the price to anyone interested in Apple computer products. In addition to information about products and applications — and news about the company — it provides information about special purchase plans for schools, funding opportunities, and novel computer applications.

• *Classroom Computer News*. (Bimonthly.) Published by Intentional Educations, Inc., 51 Spring Street, Watertown, MA 02172.

The focus of this publication is classroom use. Among the kinds of articles found in it might be a description of a particular teacher's experience with classroom computing; discussions of specific applications in reading, mathematics, languages, or other school subjects; and software reviews.

• *Computers and Education*. (Quarterly.) Published by Pergamon Press, Fairview Park, Elmsford, NY 10523.

This is an international journal that tends to publish articles dealing with theoretical, technical, and scientific aspects of computerized education. Articles may concern programming, the psychology of problem solving with a computer, educational simulation, robotics in education, etc. This publication tends to be more concerned with secondary and higher education than with the elementary education.

• *The Computing Teacher.* (Nine issues per year.) Published by International Council for Computers in Education (ICEE), 135 Education, University of Oregon, Eugene, OR 97403.

The Computing Teacher publishes short articles on an array of topics, news, announcements of meetings and important events pertaining to educational computing, reviews, and theoretical pieces. Individual and organizational members of ICCE receive the journal as part of their membership. Although the K–12 curriculum is a major focus, training of teachers and continuing education are also major considerations.

• *Educational Technology.* (Monthly.) Published by Educational Technology, 140 Sylvan Avenue, Englewood Cliffs, NJ 07632.

This publication includes educational computing as part of its broader interest in educational technology. Periodically, issues will be prepared concentrating on a central topic. However, most issues contain articles on some aspect of computers in education. Articles and features may range from research, evaluation, comment, reviews, and theoretical presentations to new developments in educational technology.

• *Educational Computer Magazine.* (Bimonthly.) Published by Educational Computer, P.O. Box 535, Cupertino, CA 95015.

Wide-ranging interests in education are represented. Articles often go beyond classroom uses to applications in administration, special education, and other areas. This publication provides evaluations, product reviews, interviews, and classroom applications.

• *Electronic Education.* (Nine issues per year.) Published by Electronic Communications, Inc., Suite 220, 1131 Executive Center Drive, Tallahassee, FL 32301.

Articles on applications, reviews of software and books, news, and editorials are usually part of this publication. The information presented tends to be descriptive and nontechnical.

• *Journal of Educational Technology Systems.* (Quarterly.) Published by Baywood Publishing Company, 120 Marine Street, Box D, Farmingdale, NY 11735.

Readers of this publication would be primarily those interested in the technical aspects of instructional design and development. Its focus is on technology in general; but educational computing represents a major portion of its articles. Articles tend to be technical or theoretical in orientation.

• *Microcomputers in Education.* (Monthly.) Published by QUEUE, 5 Chapel Hill Drive, Fairfield, CT 06432.

This newsletter provides news, announces and reviews meetings, and gives consumer information related to educational computing. Many of the products listed are offered for sale by QUEUE. The newsletter also contains reviews of hardware and software.

• *School CourseWare Journal.* (Five issues per year.) School and Home Courseware, Inc., 1341 Building Lane, Suite C-J, Fresno, CA 93710.

Two programs per issue are provided on diskettes or cassettes, along with a printed magazine containing full documentation. In addition, the magazine often contains other information of interest to educators, such as announcements of meetings and information about computer camps. The focus is on academic subjects for the K–12 curriculum.

• *T.H.E. Journal.* (Bimonthly.) P.O. Box 992, Acton, MA 01720.

T.H.E. is short for *Technological horizons in education. T.H.E. Journal* focuses on technology in general. However, a good portion of it usually deals with educational software, hardware, and applications.

Reviews of Courseware and Educational Software

Most of the periodicals listed above have at least occasional features on educational software and courseware reviews. However, the following publications concentrate on educational computer products.

• *School Microware Reviews.* (Three issues per year.) Published by Dresden Associates, Dept TCT, P.O. Box 246, Dresden, ME 04342.

Provides about 50 reviews of educational software in each issue. Indexes reviews in other publications to help locate other reviews. Groups entries by subject and grade level.

• *Software Review.* (Two issues per year.) Published by Meckler Publishing, 520 Riverside Avenue, P.O. Box 405, Saugatuck Station, Westport, CT 06880.

This publication contains descriptive reviews of many products for microcomputers. Its orientation is toward software that would be of use in libraries and educational settings. The depth of analysis tends to be greater than that in many other published reviews.

Periodicals That Concentrate on Particular Computers

The following publications focus not on education but rather on specific computers. However, they usually have at least one feature or article on education in each issue. Further, they tend to contain the kind of technical information about equipment that teachers using computers in the classroom will find important. For example, information on how to use a computer's operating system more efficiently, or how to use graphics to generate special lettering effects, might be found in a nontechnical article in one of these publications. A magazine which focuses on one computer is a little like a users' club, in the sense that it provides much information about the machine, which a user would ordinarily have to take the time to learn by experimentation. These magazines tend to be written in a nontechnical tone and to have a wide variety of articles concerning hardware; software; applications; and many of the ethical, legal, and social implications of microcomputers as they are used in society. The list below is not intended to be complete; a complete list would be impossible, given the size of the field and the frequent changes in it.

- Apple Computers

Apple Orchard, (Bimonthly.) Published by International Apple Core, Inc., 910A George Street, Santa Clara, CA 95050.

CALL A.P.P.L.E. (Monthly.) Published by Apple Puget Sound Program Library Exchange, 304 Main Avenue, South, Reston, WA 98055.

inCIDER. (Monthly.) Published by Wayne Green, Inc., 80 Pine Street, Peterborough, NH 03458.

Nibble: The Reference for Apple Computing. (Eight issues per year.) Published by Nibble MicroSPARK, Box 325, Lincoln, MA 01773.

SOFTALK. (Monthly.) Published by Softalk Publishing Company, P.O. Box 60, North Hollywood, CA 91601.

- ATARI computers

ANTIC: The Atari Resource. (Bimonthly.) Published by Antic, 297 Missouri Street, San Francisco, CA 94107

- Commodore Computers

COMMODORE: The Microcomputer Magazine. Published by Commodore Business Machines, Inc., 487 Devon Park Drive, Wayne, PA 19087

- Health/Zenith

Sextant. (Quarterly.) 716 E Street, S.E., Washington, DC 20003

- IBM Personal Computer

PC: The Independent Guide to IBM Personal Computers. (Monthly.) Published by Software Communications, Inc., 1528 Irving Street, San Francisco, CA 91007.

Personal Computer Age. (Monthly.) P.O. Box 70725, Pasadena, CA 94122.

SOFTALK for the IBM Personal Computer. (Monthly.) 11021 Magnolia Boulevard, Box 60, North Hollywood, CA 91603.

- North Star computers

North Star Notes. (Quarterly.) Published by North Star Computers, Inc., 14440 Catalina Street, San Leandro, CA 94577.

- Radio Shack computers

Computronics Montly News Magazine for TRS-80 Owners. Published by H & E Computronics, Inc., 5 North Pasack Road, Spring Valley, NY 10977.

80 Microcomputing. (Monthly.) Published by 1001001, Inc., 80 Pine Street, Peterborough, NH 03458.

- S-100 systems

S-100 Microsystems. (Bimonthly.) Published by Microsystems, 39 East Hanover Avenue, Morris Plains, NJ 07950.

- Sinclair/Timex

SYNC. (Bimonthly.) 39 East Hanover Avenue, Morris Plains, NJ 07950.

SYNTAX. (Monthly.) Published by Harvard Group, Bolton Road, R.D. 2, Box 457, Harvard, MA 01824.

CHAPTER 9

HOW MUCH DO EDUCATORS NEED TO KNOW ABOUT COMPUTING?

CHAPTER CONTENTS

In earlier chapters, we presented considerable information that educators should know about computing. Topics such as hardware, software, and fitting computer activities into the educational program were covered. These topics are extremely complex; people can make whole careers in just one aspect of any of them. Therefore, it would be unrealistic to expect an educator to master all these areas.

Although there is no simple formula for determining how much knowledge one needs, what an educator needs to know depends, in general, upon the applications that are intended. For example, an elementary school teacher who plans to introduce computerized drill in mathematics should know how to select and operate the hardware and software and should learn techniques for integrating computer activities into the instructional program. On the other hand, a special education teacher who plans to develop a series of computer lessons for hearing-impaired students may need to learn more about instructional programming and computer graphics. In each of these situations, accomplishing an educational task requires specialized knowledge.

This chapter provides an overview of the knowledge that is required to accomplish a variety of educational tasks with a microcomputer. Our purpose here is not to provide a comprehensive course in computer science or programming, but rather to help educators determine whether they need to study a subject further or to seek the advice of others. Educators should recognize that they cannot be expected to master the whole field of computing and that expert advice might be helpful from time to time.

Our discussion will include descriptions of several of the more popular computer languages and their advantages. It will also include some aspects of programming: the reader will be given some insight into what is required for the development of instructional software, and there will also be an overview of course authoring languages. Some peripheral devices that can enhance the usefulness of a microcomputer will be presented. The discussion ends with a brief look at use of computers in the real world.

COMPUTER LANGUAGES

Without instructions, a computer is not capable of doing anything. As was mentioned in Chapter 2, a *program* is a set of instructions to a computer, written in a special language that the computer can "understand." There are probably hundreds of computer languages, each with its own symbols and rules of grammar. Many have been developed for specialized tasks, and several for educational purposes.

Why Learn about Computer Languages?

At this point it should be stressed that most teachers will have no need to learn extensive computer programming techniques. For example, a teacher who plans to use a computer to supplement regular instruction with occasional drill and practice, using commercially prepared programs, may need to learn only a little about operating a computer in a classroom.

However, there are situations where knowledge of a computer programming language might be advantageous. Following are some examples.

Alteration of a program: An educator who has a working knowledge of a programming language may be able to modify a program written in that language to meet specific needs of students.

Using the computer in problem solving: Students can be taught to write programs and use a computer to work out solutions. In writing a program, the student must break a process into separate steps and "teach" the steps to the computer, using a computer language. The National Council of Teachers of Mathematics has encouraged use of the computer for instructional problem solving.[1] In this kind of activity, knowledge of several fundamental commands and rules of grammar is usually enough to enable teachers and students to begin using the computer as a tool for solving problems.

Teaching computer programming: Another reason for a teacher to learn a computer language is to teach programming. Most computer languages are formally introduced into the curriculum in high school. However, students at the upper elementary level may be capable of learning a computer language. Even young elementary school students and preschoolers have successfully programmed computers with the Logo language.

Background knowledge and general computer literacy: Computers have become an integral part of our society. A general knowledge of computer languages can benefit any person who works with or around computer technology. Having a working knowledge of a computer language might help an educator to do a better job of teaching computer literacy.

Machine Language

As we saw in Chapter 2, computers perform their essential functions in the central processing unit (CPU). The central processing unit of a modern microcomputer consists of one large chip that contains the equivalent of thousands of transistors. The CPU works with instructions in the form of binary numbers (1s and 0s). This is machine language.

Machine language is very difficult for humans to use. However, in the early days of computing, all the instructions in a program were entered into the computer in machine language. Technicians would spend hundreds of hours inserting wires on wiring boards or flipping switches to enter thousands of binary codes. Programmers and computer technicians worked primarily with machine language up to the early 1950s. The need for programming languages that were easier to use led to the development of assembly language.

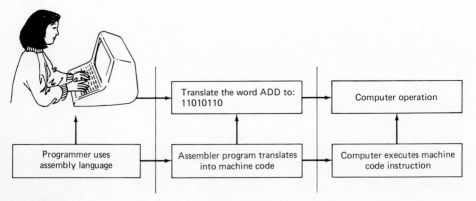

FIGURE 9.1
Assembler programs translate assembly language into machine code.

Assembly Language

To use machine language, programmers had to memorize hundreds of binary codes, each representing a specific instruction or memory location. By assigning to each of these binary codes a unique symbol (called a *mnemonic code*), programming was made somewhat easier. For example, if the binary number 11010110 is the code which tells a computer to perform an addition operation, we can substitute the symbol ADD for the binary code.

Assembly language uses mnemonic codes in place of binary codes (Figure 9.1). Clearly, it is easier for a programmer to remember and use the mnemonic codes than binary codes made up of 1s and 0s. In addition to using mnemonic codes, most assembly-language software assigns instructions to locations in computer memory; thus another laborious aspect of programming in machine language is simplified by assembly language.

While assembly language makes the task of writing computer programs easier for human beings, the computer still understands only binary codes. Therefore, assembler programs must be able to translate mnemonic symbols into machine language for the computer.

Since assembly language is easier than machine language, programmers using it tend to produce software more quickly and with fewer errors. But there is still a place for programming languages that are even easier to use. Except for very specialized applications, most classroom teachers will have little need to learn assembly-language programming.

High-Level Languages

Assembly language does not reduce the number of instructions a programmer must write, since one assembly-language instruction is required for every

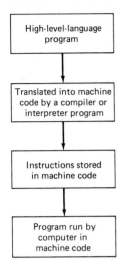

FIGURE 9.2
A compiler or interpreter program is required for using higher-level programming languages.

machine-language instruction. In order to speed up the process of programming, special assembler programs were developed, in which one assembly-language instruction stands for several machine-language instructions. The concept of a single instruction that stands for several instructions led to the development of high-level languages such as FORTRAN, COBOL, and BASIC.

Many high-level languages use English words and follow rules of grammar which are not difficult to learn. The term *high-level* is used for these languages because they are several steps away from machine language. A computer's central processing unit still requires programs (called *interpreters* or *compilers*) to translate high-level-language instructions into machine codes (Figure 9.2).

The new high-level languages are easier to use and learn than machine language or assembly language; but ease of use has been gained at the expense of speed and flexibility of execution. Speed is reduced because time is needed to compile or interpret a program. Flexibility can be reduced because only a limited number of functions may be built into a programming language. A high-level language such as BASIC is suitable for most educational applications. But it might be too slow for a complex simulation involving a graphic display of the interaction of several constantly changing variables, or for a chemistry experiment in which a microcomputer is used to measure the temperature change of a reaction 10 times per second. For such applications, a microcomputer must still be programmed in machine or assembly language.

BASIC   BASIC, an acronym for *B*eginner's *A*ll-Purpose *S*ymbolic *I*nstruction *C*ode, was introduced in 1964 at Dartmouth College by John Kemeny and Thomas Kurtz.[2] This language was developed to be easy for students to learn yet capable enough to make full use of the computer. Because it is relatively easy to learn, BASIC is the language used in most microcomputers. Today it is used by educators, scientists, engineers, and businesspeople in a broad range of applications. It has become one of the most widely used computer languages.

As in any programming language, a number of rules must be followed for statements. For example, in BASIC each line of a program is numbered (e.g., 10, 20, 30, etc.). Another rule in BASIC is that alphanumeric characters enclosed in quotation marks can be printed on the CRT screen. For example, suppose that the following line runs on a computer.

10 PRINT "TYPE A NUMBER"

In this case the words

TYPE A NUMBER

will appear on the CRT screen. A letter or word that is not enclosed in quotation marks in a PRINT statement will be treated as a variable name. When the computer encounters

70 PRINT W

the W is treated as the name of the variable W, and the value stored for that variable is printed on the screen. If no value has been previously assigned, then zero is printed.

A working knowledge of BASIC can be a valuable asset to a teacher. With such knowledge, a teacher can program a computer directly for problem solving and analysis. A thorough treatment of programming in BASIC is beyond the scope of this book; but the short program written in BASIC shown in Table 9.1

TABLE 9.1
A PROGRAM WRITTEN IN BASIC TO ADD TWO NUMBERS AND PRINT THE TOTAL

Statement	Explanation
5 REM X AND Y ARE INPUT	Remark statement, not executed
10 PRINT"TYPE A NUMBER"	TYPE A NUMBER: will be printed on CRT screen
20 INPUT X	Value of X typed at keyboard
30 PRINT"TYPE ANOTHER NUMBER"	Message appears on screen
40 INPUT Y	Value of Y typed at keyboard
50 LET W = X + Y	X and Y are added and the sum is stored as W
60 PRINT"THE SUM OF THE TWO NUMBERS IS ";W	Prints the message and the value of W

illustrates the use of several key words and commands. The reader who decides to learn more about BASIC programming is referred to the list of supplementary readings at the end of this chapter, or to other books, programs, and courses currently available from commercial sources.

As we have seen, BASIC programs operate relatively slowly on a computer, but the language is easy to learn and convenient to use. Most colleges and junior colleges teach introductory courses in BASIC. There are dozens of textbooks and manuals available in bookstores and through mail order. The language is simple enough to be self-taught, particularly with access to a computer.

Logo   Logo is a unique computer programming language. It was developed by Seymour Papert and the staff of the Artificial Intelligence Laboratory at the Massachusetts Institute of Technology.[3] Before working on Logo, Papert worked for five years with Jean Piaget, the well-known Swiss child development researcher. During that time, Papert developed a deep appreciation of how children learn about the world as they progress through several stages of development. Papert thought that a programming language should give young people an opportunity to explore the world of computers.

With Logo, the child is in charge of the computer. The child learns the language while exploring at the computer and teaching the computer to perform various tasks. This approach is in contrast to the standard drill and practice applications, in which the computer programs the child.

The young learner is introduced to Logo by a triangle shape called a *turtle* located in the center of the CRT screen (Figure 9.3). The turtle can be made to move or rotate in any direction, leaving a ''turtle track.'' For example, if the student gives the turtle a command to go forward 60 steps (FORWARD 60), the turtle will draw a line on the screen 60 steps long (Figure 9.4). (A *step* is a move of one unit on a computer screen; it can be thought of as similar to a square on a sheet of graph paper.) The command 90 RIGHT tells the turtle to rotate 90 degrees to the right. Thus, a student can draw a square on the screen (see Figure 9.5) by typing the following commands:

```
FORWARD      60

RIGHT        90

FORWARD      60

RIGHT        90

FORWARD      60

RIGHT        90

FORWARD      60

RIGHT        90
```

FIGURE 9.3
Initial position of the Logo turtle on the CRT screen.

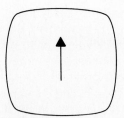

FIGURE 9.4
The turtle moves forward 60 steps at the command FORWARD 60.

Through commands, the turtle can be taught procedures. For example, to teach the turtle to draw a square, the student would type:

```
TO SQUARE

FORWARD      60

RIGHT     90

FORWARD      60

RIGHT     90

FORWARD      60

RIGHT     90

FORWARD      60

RIGHT     90

END
```

The computer has now been taught a procedure. The word SQUARE has been made a command. Whenever the command SQUARE is typed into the computer, the turtle will draw a square. (If the child had chosen to name the command CIRCLE rather than SQUARE, then the machine would produce a square every time CIRCLE was typed.) This command is unique in that the operations it

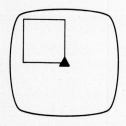

FIGURE 9.5
A square resulting from Logo commands to the turtle.

represents were created by the child. Commands can be tied together to build larger programs.

By exploring with turtle graphics, youngsters are able to discover a number of useful facts (e.g., the fact that there are 90 degrees in a right angle and that four right angles equal 360 degrees) and to solve problems such as those concerning relationships in geometry. Students can create dozens of procedures and save them on diskettes. In addition, Logo is an example of a *recursive* language. This means that a procedure can call itself (e.g., a series of squares can be drawn by placing the command SQUARE into the SQUARE program). Unlike BASIC, Logo is modular in structure and uses no line numbers.

The ease of use and flexibility of Logo have resulted in a growing worldwide interest in the language. Several different versions of Logo are available for microcomputers. Most versions require at least 64K of memory, because the language itself occupies a considerable amount of a computer's memory. An educator who will be using Logo in the classroom should plan to learn the language. Fortunately, learning Logo is not difficult.

Pascal   In 1970, Niklaus Wirth, a Swiss professor, developed Pascal, a programming language (named after the French mathematician Blaise Pascal), to help teach structured programming to his students.[4] Wirth became dissatisfied with conventional computer languages such as BASIC and FORTRAN because these languages do not require the programmer to systematically analyze and organize procedures to produce what are known as *structured programs*. As a result many young programmers were developing poor programming habits. Pascal was developed to encourage a more disciplined approach to structured programming.

Pascal contains several unique innovations. One is the operator, $:=$, which means *becomes*. Consider the following:

$$Y := Y + 1$$

should be read as

$$Y \text{ becomes } Y + 1$$

Along with BASIC and Logo, Pascal is one of the dominant languages used with microcomputers in education. Many instructors choose it for high school programming classes. Its structured design allows the student to concentrate on solving the problems rather than attending to many of the requirements imposed by the machine. Whether an educator should learn to program in Pascal really depends on individual needs.

FORTRAN   FORTRAN is an acronym for *For*mula *Trans*lator. It was developed during the 1950s for scientific and mathematical applications and was the first high-level language that allowed scientists and engineers to write their own programs.

FORTRAN has been modified since it was first introduced. Currently, several versions are used. However, FORTRAN is a fairly well standardized language. Programs written in FORTRAN can usually run on, or easily be converted to run on, a large number of computers. One of the disadvantages of FORTRAN is that it requires a larger amount of memory than other languages used on microcomputers. Computers on which FORTRAN is run are often larger than the microcomputers commonly used in schools.

Other Programming Languages

A number of other programming languages are used with microcomputers. Three are discussed briefly below so that the reader will recognize them as programming languages with particular capabilities or applications. However, they are not popular for educational uses.

COBOL   The name COBOL is an acronym for *Common Business Oriented Language*. COBOL was developed through a joint effort of business and government agencies in 1959.[5] The designers of COBOL set out to develop a business language which would be easy for nonprogrammers to understand. Programs in COBOL take a long time to write and run relatively slowly on the computer. COBOL is one of the more difficult high-level languages to learn; but, ironically, it is easy for nonprofessional programmers to read and understand a COBOL program. COBOL is widely used in business for data processing activities such as mailing lists and inventory maintenance. It will rarely be encountered in educational settings for purposes other than teaching programming to business students; and, even for this application, other languages (such as BASIC and Pascal) might be preferred.

ALGOL   ALGOL was designed by an international committee and released in the early 1960s. It is intended for scientific computations. As one of the early structured languages, ALGOL influenced the development of such languages as Pascal and Logo. ALGOL is more popular in Europe than in the United States.

Ada   Ada was designed by the U.S. Department of Defense as the standard language for all military services and activities. The language gets its name from the Countess of Lovelace, Augusta Ada Byron, who worked with Charles Babbage on mechanical calculating devices (see Chapter 1). Ada is a high-level structured language that has many capabilities built into it. Because it is relatively new (it was first introduced for general use by the armed forces in the early 1980s), the extent to which it will eventually be used is difficult to predict. However, many people are enthusiastic about it.[6] Although complete implementation of Ada requires a machine at least as large as a minicomputer, scaled-down versions for microcomputers are becoming available.[7]

PROGRAMMING

Must One Be Able to Program?

How much knowledge of computer languages and programming a teacher will need depends on the situation and individual choice. For most educational applications, previously prepared software can be used, and the teacher will not need much sophistication with programming. But some general knowledge of programming languages and how they are used will be helpful to a teacher who is introducing computer literacy to students.[8] Also, having some programming ability allows a teacher to begin using a computer with students for problem solving, and possibly to alter and adapt programs to meet specific needs. To teach programming, of course, a teacher will need extensive knowedge of at least one language and considerable familiarity with structured programming techniques. And in general, some knowledge of programming removes much of the mystery surrounding the operation of computer programs and gives a teacher greater flexibility in using the computer.

We now consider some aspects of programming as it relates to the development of instructional materials.

Elements in the Preparation of Instructional Software

Most educational microcomputers are used primarily to run instructional software. The production and marketing of educational programs has become a multimillion-dollar industry since the advent of the microcomputer. However, educational programs — often referred to as *courseware* — are expensive, and the market is cluttered with flashy instructional programs of dubious quality. Therefore, many teachers have wanted to create their own educational software. For this reason, we will now examine the process of courseware development.

Several large educational organizations — including the Minnesota Educational Computing Consortium (MECC) and the Alaska Department of Education — have implemented ambitious programs of courseware development to meet specific needs. MECC has sponsored the development of hundreds of well-documented educational programs which are made available to schools in Minnesota and elsewhere. The Alaska Department of Education has developed multimedia courses which use microcomputer technology to increase the efficiency of the educational delivery system to high schools throughout the rural areas of Alaska.[9]

Both the Minnesota project and the Alaska project resulted from a systematic analysis of needs; a substantial investment of funds; and the cooperative efforts of computer programmers, experts in curriculum content, and specialists in instructional design. The production of high-quality instructional software is a substantial undertaking, requiring a major commitment of time, funds, and expertise (Figure 9.6).

Much of the courseware on the market has not resulted from systematic

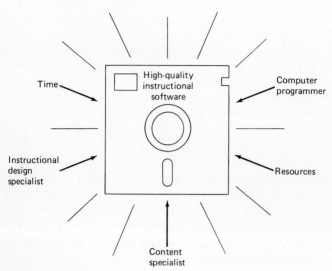

FIGURE 9.6
Resources required for developing high-quality instructional software.

developmental efforts. Often, courseware production is simply equated with programming, and little or no consideration is given to instructional design. Educators may contribute to the mediocre quality of much educational software by assuming that any lesson presented by a computer is somehow ennobled by the medium.

M. D. Roblyer has suggested that emphasis should be placed on designing an instructional system to achieve educational goals rather than on developing a particular kind of lesson (e.g., drill and practice or tutorial).[10] She further suggests that four major elements are necessary for creating high-quality courseware:

1   The courseware should be based on instructional theory — that is, on how students learn.

2   The design, the objectives of the courseware, and the sequence of skills should be detailed and documented.

3   A team approach — involving a programmer, a content expert, and an instructional designer — should be used.

4   The final product should be reviewed carefully and then tested.

Roblyer maintains that a large volume of high-quality software will not be available until systematic instructional design methods are applied to educational computing.[11]

Courseware development is normally too complex for individual educators to undertake. Programming alone can be very time-consuming and complex, and the planning and research required to produce courseware add considerably to the time needed for development. Thus, although an individual teacher may be able to produce an occasional instructional program to meet a specific need, it would not be realistic to expect teachers to produce much courseware on a regular basis.

Figure 9.7 shows some of the elements that must be part of a courseware development project. These elements are discussed below.

• *Specification of objectives:* The first step in courseware development is to determine exactly what the educational objectives are. Many of the major problems with educational products stem from unclear formulation of objectives.

• *Organization:* There are several ways to organize resources for software development. Some organizations cannot spare personnel for extended periods to work on projects and may not be able to hire additional personnel. In such a situation, the work may be done under contract with an outside source. While this minimizes the impact on the organization, it has two disadvantages. First, the sponsoring organization may have little control over the courseware as it is being developed. Second, the sponsoring organization does not gain the expe-

FIGURE 9.7
Elements of courseware development.

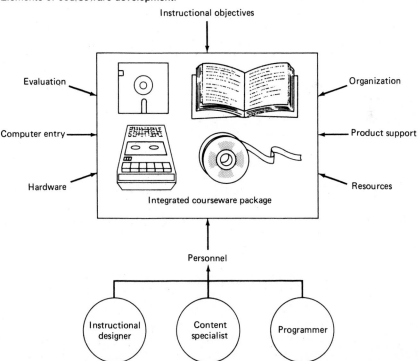

rience of having done the work. A second approach is to build a production team using people from the school organization; with this approach, employees can develop expertise. A third approach is to arrange for major portions of the development to be done by an outside source, but to assign an employee as part of the production team. This increases the input of the sponsoring organization and builds employees' expertise.

• *Resources:* Money, time, working space, and staff will be needed for the duration of the project.

• *Personnel:* People with three kinds of expertise are needed to develop good computer-assisted instruction.

Instructional designers — Instructional design usually requires a master's or doctor's degree, or comparable training and experience. An instructional designer should have a good background in educational research and instructional theory.

Content specialists — A content specialist should have considerable knowledge about the academic subject involved. Teachers tend to be the content specialists when they are part of an instructional design team.

Computer programmers — A programmer codes the written material and frequently enters it directly into the computer. The computer programmer should be considered the member of the design team who keeps the content and design experts informed of the capabilities of the hardware and programming language. However, decisions about how to accomplish an objective on the computer should not be left to the programmer but shared by the design team.

• *Hardware requirements:* Hardware includes the type of microcomputer on which the courseware will be run, the amount of memory required, and the peripherals that will be needed.

• *Computer entry:* Most instructional software for microcomputers is programmed in BASIC or machine language. In recent years, special computer programs called *authoring systems* have been developed for instructional software. For certain kinds of instruction, an authoring system can increase production and decrease costs substantially. (Authoring languages are discussed later in this chapter.)

• *Evaluation:* Good courseware requires extensive evaluation.

One kind of evaluation activity is known as *bench testing.* This involves testing each computer activity many times during the production process. Every branch and every "user option" should be tested to reveal formatting errors, misspellings, branches that go nowhere, and omissions. Bench testing is a vital part of the production process. The more effort is invested in it, the higher the quality of the product will be.

A second kind of evaluation takes place in an *instructional setting.* This type of evaluation includes tests, interviews with users, and surveys. It may be performed in a field setting during the production or development stage, or in selected schools after the courseware has been completed. (It may be done in the context of formative and summative evaluation, as discussed in Chapter 7.)

• *Product support:* Support can consist of answering inquiries about the courseware, replacing defective diskettes, correcting errors which have been discovered by users, and providing information about effective strategies for classroom use. Product support may also involve training users.

It should be evident that the development of educational software is not a simple process. It requires time, resources, and expertise. Educational software might be compared to educational textbooks. Preparing either a textbook or courseware requires thorough knowledge of the subject and a clear understanding of how to present the information to support learning. Preparing courseware requires, in addition, knowledge about computers and about how to program. Even if a teacher has all this expertise, it is not likely that normal classroom responsibilities will leave time for programming lessons. Thus (as we noted earlier), teachers should not be expected to produce extensive amounts of high-quality educational software — any more than they are expected to produce well-written textbooks on a regular basis. However, a teacher who can use a computer programming language might be able to develop small programs for problem solving and special classroom applications and help students with their programming projects.

Authoring versus Programming

Educational courseware can be produced using a computer programming language or a course authoring system. A *course authoring system* is a computer program which is designed to make production of educational programming easier. Many authoring systems allow the user to rapidly generate complex graphics that would take many hours or even days with a high-level language. An added advantage of authoring systems is that they can be used by people who are not sophisticated programmers. On the other hand, authoring systems do not have as much flexibility as programming languages.

Computer languages and authoring systems each have their own advantages and disadvantages. It is the responsibility of the instructional design team to select the mode of courseware development that is most consistent with the educational objectives. The relative advantages and disadvantages of common programming and authoring languages are summarized in Table 9.2.

Authoring Systems

An authoring system may be thought of as an instructional framework. Blank frames, or pages, are presented on the screen, and the programmer fills in the blanks with the instructional content. The major disadvantage of an authoring

TABLE 9.2

ADVANTAGES AND DISADVANTAGES OF GENERATING COURSEWARE WITH PROGRAMMING
AND AUTHORING LANGUAGES

Programming	Authoring
Advantages	
1 Allows extremely versatile use of the computer. Complex branching can be designed into the courseware. Numerical values entered by the student can be processed through complex situations.	1 Generation of courseware is 10 to 50 times faster than with computer languages.
	2 Data entry does not require highly trained personnel.
2 Machine- and assembly-language programs run rapidly, with no delays.	3 May permit relatively easy and rapid generation of graphics and nonstandard fonts.
3 More RAM is available for instructional use. Programs are not interrupted by frequent disk access.	4 Several authoring systems include student management systems for recording performance data.
	5 Integration of videotape and videodisk presentation during CAI lessons is possible with some authoring systems.
Disadvantages	
1 Requires a highly trained programmer.	1 Less RAM is available for instruction. Lessons are more frequently interrupted by the computer's accessing the disk drive.
2 Is more expensive.	
3 The process is very slow. Programming is labor-intensive.	2 Inflexibility: the courseware developer is limited to the instructional pattern designed into the system.
	3 Ability to process numerical values entered by the student is limited or nonexistent.
	4 The quality of the instructional program may not be as high as with programming language, because of limited options and features of authoring language.

system as compared with a programming language like BASIC or Pascal is flexibility. The programmer cannot change the existing design. For example, if the authoring system provides additional instruction only when the student requests it, the system will not be able to provide additional instruction under other circumstances (after two or three consecutive incorrect responses are given, for instance). Some authoring systems available for use with microcomputers are discussed below.

PILOT   PILOT stands for *P*rogrammed *I*nquiry *L*earning *o*r *T*eaching. Since its introduction in 1969, versions of PILOT have been developed for Atari, Monroe, TRS-80, Apple, and a host of other microcomputers.[12] PILOT is a language designed for creating lessons.

A lesson developed with PILOT can interact with a student. That is, as the student responds to lessons, the computer responds to the student's performance by giving directions or evaluating. Lessons in PILOT are usually written in a drill and practice or tutorial format. The system is capable of analyzing students' responses and branching to appropriate parts of the lesson. In many microcomputer versions, graphics and sound can be generated to enhance a lesson.

Lessons can be entered into the computer much more quickly with PILOT than with most programming languages. Another advantage of PILOT is that the user does not need to have extensive programming experience; a relative novice can create impressive-looking instructional software. However, proficiency with PILOT requires a large investment of time.

Several versions of PILOT provide a rudimentary record system for keeping track of students' scores and automatically saving them on a diskette when a lesson is completed. With this feature, an instructor can examine the scores at a later time.

PILOT is a reasonably easy-to-use and efficient authoring system for creating courseware. Some versions of PILOT are available for less than $100. The capacity of this authoring system and its relatively low price have made PILOT the most widely used authoring language for microcomputers.

PASS   The *P*rofessional *A*uthoring *S*oftware *S*ystem, PASS, is a high-level computer program developed by Bell and Howell for professional authoring of courseware on the Apple computer. PASS is an example of an authoring system designed to be used by large organizations and businesses to generate computerized staff training courses and instruction. It is one of the most versatile authoring systems available for a microcomputer. However, compared with other systems, it is one of the most expensive.

One of the major advantages of PASS is its interactive capability with specialized hardware devices. Computer graphics generated on a graphics tablet can be incorporated into a PASS lesson. PASS can integrate a videodisk or videotape presentation into a computer lesson, a feature which has made it appealing to users in business and industry. An optional management system which records data about students on a second disk drive is available.

Another useful feature of PASS is the ability to judge answers made by students and to interpret them in a sophisticated way. Its capabilities in this area include:

Keyword search: Searches out keywords in the learner's answer
Misspelling: Can accept misspelled responses
Prefix and suffix substitution: Accepts any word which contains a root word entered by the courseware author
Positional keyword search: Matches multiple words in a specified sequence

PASS can be purchased or rented on an annual basis from Bell & Howell.[13] PASS is usually used by large corporations, universities, and governmental agencies.

Although PASS has many useful capabilities, it also has limitations. For instance, computations cannot be performed using data entered by the learner. It also has limitations regarding the kinds of branching that can be accomplished in the learning sequence, what can be placed on the CRT screen, the number of colors that can be used, and other technical details.

A Miniauthoring System   The Minnesota Educational Computing Consortium (MECC) program diskette Teacher Utilities Volume I (initially created for use with Apple II computers) contains several utility files which together make up an inexpensive but flexible miniauthoring system. The files Review, Review Load, and Test Generator allow a teacher to create up to 200 questions for a computer drill and practice or a test. Each response by a student can be matched with up to 10 possible correct answers entered into the system by the teacher. Questions are presented randomly; questions answered incorrectly are automatically presented again. At the end of each lesson, the computer presents the student's score and makes a record of it for later review by the teacher. This authoring system requires little or no training and is exceptionally easy to use.[14]

SPECIAL EQUIPMENT: MATCHING SOFTWARE AND HARDWARE

In Chapters 3 and 4 we considered the instructional uses of computing and how to get started in educational computing. The recommended sequence was to begin by determining computing needs, go on to selecting software to meet those needs, and end by selecting hardware to match the software. As was mentioned earlier, many software packages list hardware requirements in their documentation. The most common items of hardware (e.g., the computer, disk drives, CRT and monitors, keyboards, game controllers, and printers) have been discussed in Chapters 2 and 4. In this section we will discuss additional hardware which teachers may need for some commercial software.

•   *Memory expansion:* Memory-expansion devices increase the amount of computer memory available to the user. These expansions may be available in the form of single chips; or the chips may be mounted on cards that can be plugged into slots or receptacles within the computer. Memory expansion is usually available in multiples of 8 or 16 kilobytes (16K, 32K, 64K, etc.). Simple educational programs, such as drill and practice, may require as little as 4K of memory. Programs using graphics, on the other hand, may require large amounts of memory — and graphics are an important feature of much educational programming. The capability to add a memory-expansion device should be considered a positive feature when one is shopping for a computer.

• *Graphics tablet:* Graphics tablets greatly simplify the use of computer graphics (Figure 9.8). Graphics tablets look like plastic writing surfaces, a little larger than legal-sized paper. Many are lined like graph paper. The tablet itself usually consists of a flat surface to which a special magnetic pen is connected with a cable. As the point of the pen is moved across the surface of the tablet, electronics in the tablet convert the pen's position into electronic data fed into the computer. Usually a software package supplied with the tablet converts the data into graphic commands which the computer executes, producing graphics displays on the screen.

Graphics tablets can be put to a number of uses in the classroom. For example, an art student can use a graphics tablet to create visual displays on a color screen. Engineering and mechanical-drawing students can use graphics tablets to create three-dimensional graphic displays. At a touch of the keyboard, the image may be rotated, giving the viewer a different perspective. With a graphics tablet, students in a programming class can easily integrate complex imagery into an adventure game they have created.

• *Light pens:* A light pen consists of a light-sensitive diode at the end of a pointer that is connected to the computer. When the diode detects light, it transmits an electronic signal. The computer is programmed to interpret the sig-

FIGURE 9.8
A graphics tablet can greatly reduce the difficulties of producing computer graphics.

FIGURE 9.9
The tip of the light pen can sense light on the CRT screen.

nal and formulate responses. (See Figure 9.9.) Potential applications of a light pen include the following.

Menu selection — A *menu* is a list of options offered by a computer program. These options are displayed on the CRT screen, and a character is flashed in sequence next to each option. The user can select an item by touching the pen to the character when it is next to the desired choice.

Multiple-choice testing — This application operates much like menu selection. The four or five responses to each multiple-choice question appear on the screen at one time, and the user touches the pen to the screen where the correct answer is flashing.

Problem detection or analysis — In physics, electronics, or shop classes, diagrams can be placed on the CRT screen. The student can then be requested to identify problems, omissions, or errors in the drawings; or to trace currents, patterns, or forces of energy with the light pen.

Light pens are inexpensive peripheral devices. They provide an additional way for a computer user to interact with the machine. Their usefulness as an input device for young children and the handicapped has only begun to be explored.

• *Plotters:* Plotters are specialized printers which can plot points or alphanumeric characters, often in several colors, along horizontal and vertical axes. Mechanical plotting devices have been used for military and industrial applications for several decades. Plotters can draw lines, points, arcs, circles, symbols, and marks to create high-quality printed charts, pictures, and other graphics. These devices can be used in mathematics, mechanical drawing, art, geography, science, and engineering instruction.

• *Printer buffer:* Even the fastest printer operates much more slowly than a computer, and sometimes this difference in speed can create difficulties. For example, when several pages of text must be printed, the computer is "tied up" because it can send characters to the printer only as fast as the printer can process them. As a result, the computer is not available for other uses while printing is being done. If this kind of delay presents problems, a printer buffer might be the solution. A printer buffer is a memory device, between a printer and a computer, which stores incoming data until the printer can print them. The contents of computer memory are sent to the buffer at the speed at which the computer can process them. Then the computer is ready for additional processing. Meanwhile, the printer buffer stores the data and feeds them to the printer at the printer's own processing speed.

• *Disk emulators:* Data management operations, disk copying, and programs requiring elaborate graphics are often delayed because time is required for retrieving data from the disk drive. For complex operations, such as the production of computer graphics, these delays can be as much as several seconds to a minute or more. Computer performance in this kind of application can be improved with a disk emulator (Figure 9.10). With this device, random-access memory (RAM) chips are used to provide the amount of memory normally available from a disk drive. These chips are mounted on cards that can be connected to many computers.

The emulator is often designed in the form of a card that can be mounted in the computer or connected to it in some other way. It contains random-access-memory chips that can be filled with information from disks. The emulator can act like a disk drive to the computer, with one difference: access to information is almost instantaneous. Since RAM chips are used to store the data, the contents of the card are lost when the power is turned off. However, when the

FIGURE 9.10
Disk emulator. *(Quadram Corporation.)*

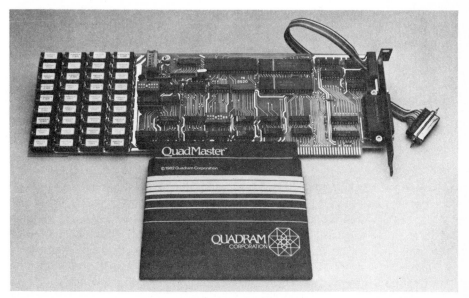

computer activity is completed, the contents of the card may be transferred back to a diskette for permanent storage.

• *Voice synthesizers:* Voice synthesizers can be used by computers to produce speech and other sounds. Synthesized speech has enormous potential in the field of educational computing. For example, visually handicapped students can interact with a computer equipped with a speech synthesizer and specialized software. A synthesized voice can add another dimension to spelling and language arts courseware. Many voice synthesizers are available for the small microcomputers commonly found in schools and educational settings. The speech produced by these devices is becoming increasingly intelligible and human-like.

• *Videotape player:* A standard ½-inch or ¾-inch videotape machine can be interfaced with a microcomputer to give highly structured tutorial lessons. For example, a student in an automobile repair course can be shown how to operate a sophisticated diagnostic machine used for locating the cause of engine malfunctions. At the appropriate point in the lesson, the videotape machine starts and the monitor screen shows a person going through the steps of operating the diagnostic machine. At the end of the sequence, the screen becomes a computer monitor again, giving more information in graphics and text.

• *Videodisks:* A videodisk is a flat record-like disk which in some versions can store over 54,000 separate pictures. The disk is read by a lasar beam or by some other electronic means.[15] The images can be shown sequentially (like a film or videotape) or one frame at a time (like individual slides or photographs). Unlike videotape, a videodisk can rapidly search out and access any individual frame. As an instructional medium, the videodisk, interfaced with a computer, is a potentially powerful educational tool. Software is available for controlling videodisk players with computers. However, technical problems and cost have slowed the widespread adoption of this technology.[16]

• *Audiotape:* Computer-controlled audiotape (sound) players can add auditory information to computerized lessons that otherwise might be primarily visual. For many students, visual and auditory modes combined are a more powerful teaching strategy than visual modes alone. This is especially true for students who have difficulty reading, and for students with visual problems.

• *Robotics:* Many people may believe that robotics is too futuristic for education; but thousands of robots are already being used in industry, and robots are beginning to have a presence in education. For example, a mechanical turtle that can be programmed in the Logo language is available for teaching young children.[17] The turtle is attached to a computer by a cable and behaves in much the same way as the Logo turtle on the CRT screen. The mechanical turtle has a "pen up" mode and a "pen down" mode which allow it to "draw" or move. Students can program the computer with procedures in Logo and watch the turtle perform the action on a flat surface.

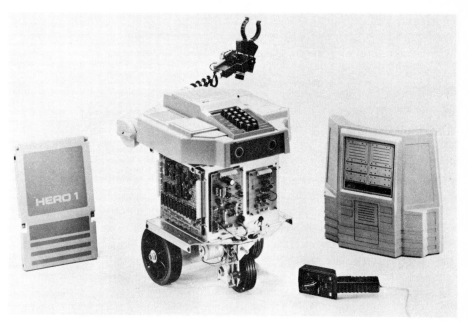

FIGURE 9.11
Educational robot, the Heath Hero I (model ET18). *(Heath.)*

By 1983, one company had introduced an educational robot (Figure 9.11). This device is controlled by an onboard programmable computer and has electronic sensors to detect light, sound, and motion. Other capabilities include a small arm, a speech synthesizer, and several artificial intelligence characteristics.[18] This teaching robot is really a computer on wheels that can be programmed to perform many of the functions of a sophisticated industrial robot.

INTERFACING COMPUTERS WITH THE REAL WORLD

Computers may use special sensory devices and programming which allow them to monitor events in the real world and control conditions and processes. For example, computers are used to monitor and control the flow of oil on the Alaska pipeline; they are also used in some home appliances and security systems. Computers can be programmed to turn lights on and off at predetermined times and maintain thermostats within a range of temperature settings.

The ability to monitor the real world has great potential in educational situations. For example, the ability to connect a computer to a temperature-sensing device that can monitor temperature changes during a laboratory experiment many times per second greatly increases the feasibility of certain kinds of research. Experiments that require long periods of observation (e.g., those involving crystal growth or photosynthesis) can be set up by the students during regular class hours. Experimental data can then be collected overnight or during a weekend by a computer. Despite the apparent usefulness of being able to connect computers to other devices, the actual interfacing may be complex if the application is not routine. Expert consultation may be required to enable a computer to communicate with another device.[19]

SUMMARY

In earlier chapters, what a teacher should know about hardware, software, and educational applications of computers was discussed. The present chapter focused on additional knowledge teachers should have about computing. Languages, programming, and hardware devices such as memory expansion, printer buffers, disk emulators, graphics tablets, and light pens were considered.

High-level programming languages allow programs to be written more efficiently than they can be with machine language. BASIC has become the computer language most commonly associated with microcomputers. When suitable commercial software is available, one can use a microcomputer very effectively without actually knowing how to program. However, some knowledge of programming is useful to increase understanding of how a computer works and to apply some existing programs in specific situations. Ability in programming is necessary for alteration or tailoring of existing programs, for developing programs to solve problems, for teaching programming, and for teaching computer literacy.

Development of high-quality educational software requires expertise of three kinds:

Instructional design
Content
Programming

Courseware production should follow a systematic instructional design process. Resources and skills in these three areas are usually beyond the scope of the classroom teacher. Further, most teachers do not have the time to produce software, and the accompanying documentation is not available to most practicing teachers. Thus, the software that teachers can produce on their own will tend to be less complex and ambitious than what is available through commercial channels.

Courseware can be authored in a computer programming language such as Pascal or BASIC, or with an authoring system like PILOT. Programming languages tend to run more quickly than authoring languages, and to permit greater flexibility. On the other hand, authoring systems allow more rapid entry of text and graphics.

Add-on features and peripheral devices can improve the performance of a computer. Additional memory is one of the least expensive ways of dramatically improving a computer's capacity. A graphics tablet allows rapid creation of high-resolution computer graphics. Microcomputers can generate speech with voice-synthesizer units. Microcomputers can also be interfaced with other educational technologies to form integrated instructional delivery systems. Videotape, videodisk, and audiotape devices can be controlled by a computer. Integration of the computer, sensory devices, artificial intelligence, and voice synthesis has resulted in teachable robots, which are potentially useful for educational applications.

Most educators do not have technical backgrounds and find themselves unprepared to deal with the rapidly expanding computer technology. No one person can become proficient in all areas of educational computing – the field is far too broad and dynamic for that. How much one needs to know is really a function of how far one needs to go beyond the basics of setting up a computer system and using it to run programs prepared by others. Many teachers will be able to use existing software effectively and will not have to become skilled at programming. A good way to expand one's knowledge of computing is to become familiar with some of the magazines, books, newsletters, and other sources that are mentioned throughout this book. Educators should begin with the applications in which they are most interested. They will find their knowledge of the technology expanding naturally.

NOTES

1 *Computers in the classroom.* (1980, October). Position statement of the National Council of Teachers of Mathematics.
2 Thompson, R. G. (1981). *BASIC: A first course.* Columbus, OH: Merrill.
3 Pines, M. (1982, November 14). Teaching kids to talk with computers. *Education Review,* 15. See also: Watt, D. (1982). Logo in the schools. *BYTE, 7*(8), 116–118, 120, 122, 126, 128, 130, 132–134.
4 Jensen, K. (1979, Fall). Why Pascal? *EDU Twenty-Five.* (A publication of Digital Equipment Corporation.)
5 Sanders, D. H. (1983). *Computers today.* New York: McGraw-Hill.
6 Gilpin, G. (1982). The countess and the language. *Creative Computing, 8*(11), 186, 188, 191–193.
7 For example: Janus/Ada Version 3.0 from RRS Software, Madison, WI. This software package is reviewed by: Mann, S. (1983). *InfoWorld, 5*(18), 59–61.
8 Some people argue that computer programming may be a necessary form of ``literacy'' in the technological age. See, for example: Luerhmann, A., & Peckham, H. (1983). *Computer literacy: A hands-on approach.* New York: McGraw-Hill. See also: Ahl, D. (1981). Pascal, Ada, and computer literacy: An interview with Arthur Luerhmann. *Creative Computing, 7*(11), 116, 118, 120–122.
9 Mason, E. J., & Bramble, W. J. (1982). Evaluation of a computerized solution to delivery of education in Alaska. *AEDS Monitor, 21*(3), 33–36.
10 Roblyer, M. D. (1981, Summer). Instructional design versus authoring of courseware: Some crucial differences. *AEDS Journal.*
11 Systematic instructional design procedures are discussed in greater detail in Chapter 10.

12 Smith, M. R. (1982). Pilot tutorial I. *Creative Computing, 8*(11), 181-182. Pilot tutorial II. *Creative Computing, 8*(12), 243-245, 249, 250, 253.

13 Information about PASS may be obtained from Bell & Howell Interactive Communications Marketing Division (Attention: Marketing Service Department), 7100 North McCormick Road, Chicago, IL 60645.

14 Information about the Teacher Utilities Volume I and other MECC software may be obtained from Minnesota Educational Computing Consortium, 2520 Broadway Drive, St. Paul, MN 55113.

15 Onsko, T. (1982). Vision of the future. *Creative Computing, 8*(1), 84, 86, 91, 92, 94, 98, 100, 102. See also: Kellner, C. (1982). V is for videodisc. *Creative Computing, 8*(1), 104-105.

16 Ahl, D. (1982). Dateline: Tomorrow . . . Videodisc manufacturers their own worst enemies. *Creative Computing, 8*(1), 6.

17 The *terrapin turtle,* available from Terrapin, Inc., Cambridge, MA, is a robot that can be used to teach programming and other concepts. It can be interfaced with many kinds of microcomputers. A less ambitious device is produced by Milton Bradley Company, Springfield, MA; it is called *Big Trak*. It can be made to move along the floor in response to simple commands. Use of this device in a classroom is discussed by: Keller, J., & Shanahan, D. (1983). Robots in kindergarten. *The Computer Teacher, 10*(9), 66-67.

18 Hero 1, an instructional robot, was designed to be used with the Heathkit Robotics and Industrial Electronics course. For information, contact Veritechnology Electronics Corporation, St. Joseph, MN, or the Heath Company, Benton Harbor, MI.

19 Witten, I. H. (1983). Welcome to the standards jungle. *BYTE, 8*(2), 146, 148, 150, 154, 158, 160, 162, 164, 166, 170, 172, 176, 178.

SUPPLEMENTARY READINGS

Barnes, B. J., & Hill, S. (1983). Should young children work with minicomputers – LOGO before Lego? *The Computer Teacher, 10*(9), 11-14.

Camuse, R. A. (1982, October). An Apple Pilot primer. *Educational Computer Magazine,* 20, 22-23.

Evans, A. (1981). BASIC beats Pascal. *Creative Computing, 7*(11), 158, 160-163.

Fox, D., & Waite, M. (1982) *Pascal primer.* Indianapolis, IN: Howard Sams.

Harvey, B. (1982). Why Logo? *BYTE, 7*(8), 163-164, 166, 170, 172, 174, 176, 178, 180, 182, 186, 188, 191, 193.

Heisermann, D. L. (1979). *How to build your own self-programming robot.* Blue Ridge Summit, PA: TAB Books

Kreuger, M. W. (1982). *Artificial reality.* Reading, MA: Addison-Wesley.

Luehrmann, A. (1981). *Apple-Pascal: A hands-on approach.* New York: McGraw-Hill.

Miller, J. M., Chaya, R. K., & Santora, D. J. (1982). *BASIC programming for the classroom teacher.* New York: Teachers College Press.

Pratt, T. W. (1975). *Programming languages, design, and implementation.* Englewood Cliffs, NJ: Prentice-Hall.

Osborne, A. (1980). *An introduction to microcomputers: Vol. 1. Basic Concepts.* Berkeley, CA: Osborne/McGraw-Hill.

Stern, R., & Stern, N. (1979). *Principles of data processing*. New York: Wiley.

Thompson, R. G. (1981). *BASIC: A first course*. Columbus, OH: Merrill.

Titus, J. S. (1981). *Apple interfacing*. Indianapolis, IN: Howard Sams.

Uffenbeck, J. E. (1982). *Hardware interfacing with the TRS-80*. Englewood Cliffs, NJ: Prentice-Hall.

Watt, M. (1982). What is Logo? *Creative Computing, 8*(10), 112, 115–116, 119–120, 124, 127, 129.

Zaks, R. (1979). Programming the 6502. Berkeley, CA: SYBEX.

Zaks, R. (1979). Programming the Z80. Berkeley, CA: SYBEX.

CHAPTER **10**

GAMES, SIMULATIONS, AND LEARNING

CHAPTER CONTENTS

242

Chapter 3 introduced various ways that educators use computers in schools. Computers were portrayed as tireless and patient workers, able to free educators from repetitious tasks. It was also pointed out that different types of computer activities engage students in different kinds of learning. For example, drill and practice activities on a computer provide repeated practice until the student gives the correct response consistently. In contrast, a computer tutorial can patiently present instructional material until it is learned by the student. In this chapter, two additional kinds of learning activities, games and simulations, are given attention.

For the purposes of this chapter, we will define a *game* as an activity in which a player must select a course of action in a competitive environment; the competition may be provided by other players or by the computer. A *simulation*, on the other hand, does not emphasize competition but is concerned primarily with representing real situations. However, this distinction may not always be clear-cut. There are simulations in which students compete and games in which the setting is very realistic.

The present chapter sets the stage for educational games and simulations by discussing the implications of cognitive levels of instructional material, instructional design, and the student's age. Then several kinds of educational games are discussed. Following this, educational simulations are discussed and some examples are given. Finally, an approach to the selection of games and simulations is presented.

WHY CONSIDER GAMES AND SIMULATIONS IN EDUCATION?

Games and simulation programs represent particularly promising uses of computers in education because of their potential for increasing motivation and bringing realism into educational experiences. They tend to make use of the ability of computers to control many interrelated variables simultaneously. Color graphics and sound may be available to increase clarity, dramatic impact, and realism. However, it should be pointed out that games and simulations which take advantage of such features can be both challenging and expensive to design and may require a considerable amount of computer memory.

With games and simulations, students can be involved in complex learning activities. When games and simulations are well designed, they promote active involvement in learning, and this leads to greater comprehension of the material. (For example, with a simulation of a nuclear power plant, the student may actually experience the operation of the plant while learning about the complex relationships involved.)

The review on the following pages of some approaches to the psychology of learning can provide a basis for understanding how to use games and simulations in instruction.

THEORETICAL APPROACHES TO LEARNING

In present-day psychology, there are two broad theoretical approaches to learning. The first focuses on behavior; it sees complex behavior as built up from small units of behavior. It is known as the *behavioral approach*. The second approach focuses more on understanding and higher-level processing in thinking, learning, and reasoning. It is known as the *cognitive approach*. A fairly extensive body of research exists to support each of these approaches.[1] A full treatment of this topic is clearly beyond the scope of this book; but elements relating to learning with games and simulations will be discussed briefly.

Reinforcement: A Behavioral Concept

Drill and practice instruction emphasizes repetition until the student can consistently give correct answers. Since giving a correct answer is a form of behavior, this form of instruction is said to represent the behavioral approach. Behaviorism emphasizes reinforcement. Any stimulus that increases the probability of a behavior which it follows is called a *reinforcer*. In drill and practice activities, the student is reinforced for giving correct responses, and this reinforcement will predispose the student to respond similarly in the future.

For example, consider the screen displays from a computerized mathematics drill shown in Figure 10.1. If the student gives a wrong answer, the computer will show the correct answer for about five seconds. If the student then gives the correct response, the display of the correct answer could be considered a reinforcer. If the student gives a correct answer, the screen will show a smiling bear's face. If the student continues to respond correctly to the problem on subsequent presentations, then the display of the bear's face would be the reinforcer.

Understanding: A Cognitive Concept

There are several different branches within cognitive psychology.[2] However, most have a common concern with relationships between newly learned and existing knowledge.[3] In the cognitive approach to learning, the student is expected to be able to do more than just give correct answers consistently. Instead, this approach emphasizes understanding — and that emphasis is particularly useful for the kind of instruction provided by many games and simulations. In the following sections some aspects of the cognitive approach are reviewed in the context of computerized instruction.

Levels of Learning   At an informal meeting of college examiners at a convention of the American Psychological Association in Boston, Massachusetts, in 1948, ways to measure different kinds of knowledge were discussed. As a result of this meeting, a hierarchy of levels of cognitive learning was developed: *Tax-*

Computer presents:

Student responds by
typing "5":

Computer responds with:

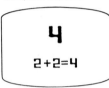

Then computer presents
item again; and if student
responds correctly, computer
displays:

FIGURE 10.1
The smiling teddy bear reinforces the child for answering the
question correctly.

onomy of Educational Objectives, edited by Benjamin S. Bloom.[4] Bloom's taxonomy forms a framework of intended behaviors of students in the cognitive domain. The cognitive domain is represented by six major classes:

1 *Knowledge:* This category includes the recall of facts, methods, processes, patterns, structures, and settings.

2 *Comprehension:* This category includes transition, interpolation, and extrapolation. It is the lowest level of understanding. At this level a student can use information that is being communicated without necessarily relating it to other material.

3 *Application:* This category includes the application of abstractions (such as generalizations, theories, rules, and methods) to concrete situations.

4 *Analysis:* This category includes the breaking down of information into its various parts and recognizing patterns of organization among the parts.

5 *Synthesis:* This category includes the assembling of parts to form a whole. This may take the form of producing a well organized communication, developing a plan, or organizing a set of abstract relationships.

6 *Evaluation:* This category includes judgment about values from internal evidence (such as perceived consistency and accuracy) and from external criteria (such as comparison with other products or standards).

Most educational objectives in the school curriculum are at the level of knowledge. Knowledge-level objectives are easiest to teach and easiest to evaluate. Therefore, teachers often overemphasize this level in the classroom, and it is often overrepresented in curriculum materials and standardized achievement tests. But evidence of the importance of instruction at the higher cognitive levels is growing. (See the discussion of computer literacy in Chapter 11, for example.)

Most teachers do not have the time or training to provide extensive feedback to students concerning their performance on higher-level cognitive tasks such as application, analysis, and synthesis. However, the developers of good-quality games or simulation programs may have been well trained to do so. Further, they should have been able to invest several hundred hours designing feedback and evaluation components into the learning activities – and designing the simulation or game to require high-level understanding or problem-solving strategies.

Effective design of instruction depends on an understanding of how different cognitive tasks require different kinds of thinking and learning. Bloom's taxonomy of cognitive tasks can help with this. However, consideration of the level of cognitive tasks alone is not enough. Instruction must also be properly organized and sequenced.

Organizing and Sequencing Instruction   The organization of a curriculum has important implications for the effectiveness of learning materials. This can be particularly true for instructional games and simulations. A structured approach to curriculum design, similar in many ways to the systems approach used widely in business and industry, can be used. A basic premise of this approach is that materials are designed to meet specified instructional objectives. In other words, the goals drive the system. Planning begins with the specification of the goals and objectives.

Following is a rough model of a systems approach to instructional design for a school:

1 Investigate instructional needs; determine goals.

2 Translate goals into curriculum. Identify target objectives for the curriculum.

3 Specify performance objectives.
4 Plan sequences of objectives.
5 Specify conditions and media for instruction.
6 Design procedures for assessment of learning.

In addition to the systematic approach to curriculum design, educators use diverse resources, instructional techniques, and media to make courses more interesting and meaningful. Gagné and Briggs advocate a series of steps for organizing and designing instruction which include the following:

Organization of content
Analysis of learning tasks
Sequencing of instruction
Instructional strategies[5]

Including these considerations in planning games and simulations can ensure that learning activities will be more effective. The teacher should also be concerned with the appropriateness of microcomputer-based games or simulations. Three questions may be addressed in this regard:

1 Is the microcomputer-based game or simulation appropriate for the objective?
2 Does the software package support the objective?
3 Where is the appropriate point in the curriculum to introduce the computerized game or simulation?

The systematic approach to instructional development ensures that the goals, various aspects of the learning situation, and instructional strategies are coordinated.

One additional concern to be addressed by the instructional designer is the student's age, and how that affects learning.

Growth and Development   Determining what types of educational materials will work best with students of different ages is a fascinating and complex study. The well-known Swiss researcher Jean Piaget has suggested that the ability to think and reason develops in concert with a child's physical development.[6] This is compatible with views of other researchers, who suggest that intellectual growth coincides with brain development.[7] Piaget described four stages of intellectual development, which are summarized in Table 10.1. As can be seen, each stage is characterized by a unique pattern of thinking and reasoning. The reader is encouraged to learn more about Piaget's fertile and provocative thoughts on education and learning.

Piaget's work suggests that children of different ages will understand instructional materials differently. For example, suppose that a 5-year-old is shown two 8-ounce glasses — one tall and slender, the other short and squat. Even after a

TABLE 10.1
PIAGET'S STAGES OF COGNITIVE DEVELOPMENT

Age range	Stage	What happens	Examples of thinking
Birth to 2 years	Sensory-motor	Basic conceptions of the material world are formed. The child begins to organize perceptions. Orientation is practical.	An object that appears can be held in memory; parts of the body are found; a woman becomes "mother"; etc.
2 to 7 years	Preoperational thought	Increased use of words as symbols for objects; increased development of grammatical structure.	The child begins to be able to think about and describe objects. Tends to focus on one aspect of a problem (this is called *centering*) and emphasizes use of language rather than the logic of what is being said (e.g., a little boy says, "I have a brother but my brother doesn't").
7 to 11 years	Concrete operations	Improvement in logical thought. The child can classify, combine, and compare objects. Tends toward literal interpretation of language.	Child can deal with hierarchies (e.g., dog, animal, living things), can do arithmetic but may not be able to apply it, or can apply ideas in problem solving but has difficulty with arithmetic.
11 to 16 years through adulthood	Formal operations	Full attainment of logical and abstract thinking. The person begins to realize the full range of possibilities. Thought becomes mature at this stage.	Can generalize from games in which problem solving is involved to similar settings in real life. Can alter and recreate conditions in thought as well as action (e.g., can plan the effects of selling properties in a game which simulates stock market activities).

child of 3 or 4 observes one of the glasses being filled with water from the other, it is not suprising to find that the child thinks that one of the glasses will hold more water because it is taller or fatter. But at a later age, the child would not make this kind of error. According to Piaget, a child cannot be expected to show mature patterns of thought before reaching the formal operations stage at about age 11 or 12.

From the perspective of developmental psychology and the work of Piaget, the educational use of games and simulations must be considered in terms of the student's age and stage of cognitive growth. Thus, while games and simulations can present students with complex problems to solve, or with an array of variables to consider, younger students will probably make the task simpler. For example, in a game of chess, a young child would tend to concentrate on the correct moves, taking turns, and so on. An older player, on the other hand, might be more aware of strategies, planning, and the notion of maintaining a good defensive position even while moving offensively. (These differences in cognitive level are not unique to computerized games and simulations. They should be considered in any learning program.)

GAMES IN EDUCATION

Children have always made games a major part of their play. Many games represent a restructuring of reality in terms that a child can understand and accept. Children learn about adult behavior by simulating adult actions in such games. Some of the games children play are produced commercially; others the children invent for themselves.

Games — whether they are played on a field, a board, or a computer — can help children learn important social concepts. For example, games can teach them how to stay within a set of rules, how to succeed, and how to accept failure.

It has been suggested that people born after the mid-1950s are inexperienced in social play, because during childhood they eventually spend 20,000 to 40,000 hours watching television. Previous generations spent this time in social play.[8] One of the fears expressed about computers in education is that they might further alienate students of the television age from one another. However, computers can be used to promote group problem solving and socialization.[9] This is especially true of programming activities and computer games. Many of the computerized educational games available today are group-oriented — that is, designed to promote group interaction.

The educational potential of games has not escaped the attention of educators. Schools have a long tradition of using games for instruction. For example, teachers have used musical games, flash-card games, spelling games, and other game techniques to improve motivation and learning.

Let us first consider how computer technology can be used to supplement and expand some traditional games. We will then consider games designed for computers.

Using the Computer with Traditional Games

Flash-Card Games   Flash cards are used to teach a wide range of basic knowledge, from letter recognition to mathematics facts. The object of a flash-card game is to respond quickly with a correct answer while a card is shown for

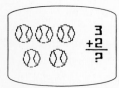

FIGURE 10.2
A screen display from the game Spaceship. (*Minnesota Educational Computing Consortium.*)

a moment. When a teacher uses flash cards as a form of competition between students or between students and a computer, then the technique becomes a competitive game. To use flash cards, a teacher, aide, or student must show the cards and provide feedback. A computer can be programmed to drill students with electronic flash cards, however, reducing the need for someone to direct the activity.

Several games using the flash-card approach have been programmed for microcomputers. For example, the diskette Elementary Volume 7 from Minnesota Educational Computing Consortium (MECC) contains a flash-card program for use with primary-level students. This program, Spaceship (see Figure 10.2), presents simple addition problems. A picture of lamps, cats, or trucks beside each numeral helps the young student to visualize the sum. When a correct answer is given, a spaceship appears on the screen. After three correct answers are given, a flying saucer appears on the screen and there is a mock battle between it and the spaceship. The spaceship and the mock battle are designed as reinforcers for correct responses. This program is a game in the sense that the student is competing with the computer to receive reinforcers. Similar game formats can be used with two or more students; the students play against each other rather than against the computer.

Flash-card games are a variation of drill and practice. As such, they are best used for promoting simple knowledge of facts. (Higher-level cognitive skills are usually not supported with these games.) Since very specific knowledge and behavior is involved, the task is developmentally appropriate for all school-age children. Presenting flash cards by computer rather than by hand provides the added advantage of freeing the teacher for other tasks and responsibilities in the classroom.

Spelling Games The spelling bee is a tradition in American schools. This game transforms the tedious task of learning to spell words into a competitive contest. It is so popular that a national spelling bee is held annually in Washington, D.C.

Most students are capable of becoming proficient spellers with practice. A variety of microcomputer software is available to increase spelling skills. For example, programs are available which flash words to be spelled on the screen for a second or two. The student must type each word correctly. The obvious disadvantage to this technique is that the student sees the word before spelling

FIGURE 10.3
A voice synthesizer for use with a microcomputer. (*Intex Micro Systems.*)

it. An alternative approach is to show a sentence with one word missing on the screen. Below the sentence, the missing word is spelled three or four different ways, only one of which is correct. The student chooses the correctly spelled word by keying the letter or number which appears next to it. This multiple-choice technique has the disadvantage that the student practices only to recognize the correct word — not to spell it.

A more advanced approach to spelling involves the use of a microcomputer with a voice synthesizer (see Figure 10.3). Such a computer can talk; in other words, it is able to take computerized electronic codes and turn them into voice-like sounds. (Early voice synthesizers were difficult to understand, but newer synthesizers are becoming capable of producing more sophisticated voices.) Optional voice synthesizers can be purchased for most of the microcomputers found in classrooms. Spelling software can be purchased to program the computer to ask in an understandable electronic voice for the student to spell words.

Most spelling games emphasize basic knowledge through drill and practice. Computers add a new dimension to the traditional ways of playing spelling games by providing the student with immediate reinforcement of correct answers. They also provide a competitor, since the student can play against the computer.

Other Games Numerous traditional games and game-like activities can be used by students. Some are played in a gymnasium or on a playground. Others involve the use of special boards, decks of cards, or paraphernalia. While some of these games are based entirely on chance and have little educational value, others do have educational value because they require problem solving, mathematical manipulation, understanding of scientific principles, memorization of facts, or other learning activities. Teachers often use games that require higher cognitive levels to increase motivation and interest.

Computer Games

Arcade Games versus Educational Games Two types of computer games are available for microcomputers: arcade games and educational games. *Arcade games* are designed for fun and often involve the player in momentary states of intense concentration. This concentration may be the result of clear goals and objectives, immediate feedback, and a sense of having one's skills tested.[10] The degree of concentration fostered by arcade games would be desirable in educational activities; but arcade games can easily become an unwanted distraction in the classroom. Also, students will hurry through their lessons in order to get a reward of several minutes of play on an arcade game. Arcade games are best left where they belong, in video arcades and on home systems.

Educational games are designed for instructional purposes. Table 10.2 shows some important differences between typical arcade and educational games. Generally, the difference between an educational game and an arcade game has to do with the purpose: instruction as opposed to amusement. Another difference is that educational games tend to deemphasize intensity of concentration on fast-moving objects and spectacular colors but tend to emphasize realism, learning, and problem solving.

TABLE 10.2
COMPARISON OF ARCADE GAMES AND EDUCATIONAL GAMES

Arcade games	Educational games
1 Designed only for fun.	Designed primarily for instruction. Generally teach or reinforce an academic or manual skill (typing). Are usually pleasurable; but fun is a secondary consideration.
2 The machine is in charge. The timing and sequence of actions are under its control. The student reacts to the machine.	The student may or may not have control over timing and sequence of events, depending on the educational purposes.
3 The central strategy is usually simple. Players must be able to comprehend the strategy within seconds. Complex strategies may be necessary to achieve high scores, but the main concept is simple.	The emphasis is on using intellectual skills rather than developing strategies or solutions.
4 Immediate reinforcement is provided to the player.	Reinforcement for learning is immediate.
5 Visual impact is usually maximized by elaborate graphics, color, computer animation, and sound effects to add to the entertainment value of the game.	Computer graphics and sound are included to enhance learning.
6 The game is nonthreatening to the player.	The game is nonthreatening to the player.
7 The player derives an immediate sense of success or failure.	Player experiences successful learning when performance is effective.
8 There is an intensity of concentration and involvement.	The educational game tends to be less intense than an arcade game.

Uses and Benefits of Educational Games   Having made a distinction between arcade and educational games, we can ask when and how educational games are best used in schools. The answer to this question must be situational. The grade level, the educational objectives, and the character of the students are all factors to consider. However, several generalizations can be made regarding the benefits of computerized educational games which would apply in most situations:

1   *Educational games motivate students.*   Although their primary purpose is educational, most computer games are fun. The motivation to learn mathematics facts, correct spelling, and rules of grammar can be increased by the proper use of educational games.

2   *Educational games can help increase a student's attention span.*   This is especially true for primary and preschool students. The movement of letters and numbers across the CRT screen can capture a youngster's attention. This powerful attention-getting device can help focus interest on the learning tasks.

3   *Games can provide drill and practice painlessly.*   Educational games are most frequently used after a student has received guided instruction through a learning task. Table 10.3 shows an appropriate placement of educational computer games in a particular instructional plan. It suggests that in this instructional sequence, games may be used in the independent practice, evaluation, and review activities.

4   *Educational games may be designed to foster the higher cognitive levels of instruction.*   In the kinds of games in which the student is required to apply

TABLE 10.3
STAGES OF INSTRUCTION IN AN INSTRUCTIONAL UNIT, SHOWING POSSIBLE PLACEMENT OF
EDUCATIONAL GAMES

Introduction	Teacher tells students the goals for the week and introduces new material.
Demonstration	Teacher demonstrates skill or material to be learned (orally or with chalkboard or book).
Guided practice	Teacher guides students through learning activity, monitoring each student carefully.
Independent practice	Students practice the skill independently, usually on a worksheet or paper or in a workbook. Computerized educational games can be very effective at this point.
Evaluation	Teacher administers a test. This can sometimes be accomplished with a suitable computerized educational game that tests the instructional objectives.
Review	Computerized educational games can sometimes be effectively utilized to provide periodic review.

academic skills, to analyze relationships between elements within the game, and to synthesize a plan to win the game, the cognitive level would be more than simple knowledge. Students usually retain more learning if they can actively use knowledge and skills in new situations. Computer games provide such situations in the classroom.

5 *Games can provide another instructional strategy for a teacher.* Important facts and skills are frequently taught in several different ways in a single curriculum, to ensure that all learning modes are covered. For example, instruction may be presented visually (e.g., demonstration, film, printed material), in auditory form (e.g., lecture, radio, cassette tape), or in a combination of auditory and visual material (e.g., sound film, television, discussion with demonstration). Some students seem to have preferred modalities for learning. Educational games that use graphics or sound can be selected for use by students with particular characteristics and preferences.

6 *Computer games can enhance cooperation among students.* The computer may be a force for bringing students together. Instead of playing instructional games individually, students can play them together to improve overall performance and give encouragement to each other.

Some Examples of Educational Games   Many computerized educational games on the market have proved to be effective learning aids. In this section, a few examples are described. This discussion is intended to be illustrative rather than comprehensive; readers are encouraged to become familiar with other instructional games that may be available.

• *MasterType – A game of skill:* MasterType (see Figure 10.4) is an educational program which has many characteristics of drill and practice but is presented in an arcade-game format. Despite its similarity to arcade games, MasterType was designed for a specific educational purpose; the program teaches typing, a manual skill which requires a high degree of concentration.

The action of the program revolves around a space station in the center of the screen. Letters or words appear in the four corners of the screen and launch

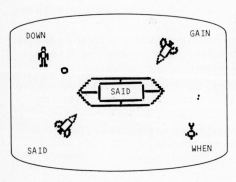

FIGURE 10.4
A screen display from MasterType.
(Lightning Software.)

missiles at the space station. The student defends the space station by correctly typing the letters or words.

Unlike a "pure" arcade game, MasterType gives the user control. There are 17 lessons, representing different levels of typing expertise. The choice of the lesson is left to the user. The user also has control over the speed at which letters or words appear on the screen. Sound effects are included, but they can be omitted if they are not wanted. The computer scores each lesson by displaying the user's typing accuracy and speed in words per minute.

MasterType is an example of a well-balanced design. It teaches a manual skill using an arcade-game format, yet it allows sufficient control by the user. MasterType could be used as a supplement to a traditional typing program, as an introduction to typing, or as an activity for people who want to refresh their typing skills.[11]

• *Hangman — A practice game:* Hangman is a popular traditional game children play in school. It can be found in dozens of computerized versions.[12] In its most frequent form, an image of a scaffold is shown on the CRT screen with blank lines representing missing letters below (Figure 10.5). The player must fill in the blanks with the appropriate letters in a given number of turns. For each incorrect answer, another part of the person being hanged is shown on the screen. If the student gives enough incorrect answers, the image of the victim is completed, and the victim is assumed to have been hanged. The game can be played by two people competing against each other or by one person competing against the machine. Computer versions of hangman are available for practice of words and phrases in several foreign languages. Some versions allow the teacher to type in the words for the game.

Hangman is an enduring and popular children's game. However, the typical computer version demonstrates a flaw in instructional practice. One of the more established principles of learning is that incorrect answers should not be reinforced. Rather, they should elicit bland or neutral responses from the computer. Reinforcing with flashy graphics, sound, or animation should be reserved for correct responses or successful completion of learning tasks. Hangman responds to a poor performance with a supposed hanging, often accompanied

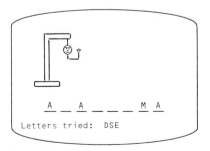

FIGURE 10.5
Sample screen from a typical hangman game.

by colorful graphics and sometimes by sound. Moreover, most computer versions provide a bland or neutral response for successful completion of the task. It is not surprising, then, for children to deliberately spell incorrectly, so that they can see the computer graphics. Hangman is included in this chapter only because it is in such widespread use.

- *Robot War — A strategy game:*

WELCOME TO THE BATTLEFIELD OF THE FUTURE! It is the year 2002. Wars still rage, but finally they have been officially declared hazardous to human health. Now, the only warriors are robots — built in secret and programmed to fight each other to the death!

This scenario introduces a programming game, Robot War.[13] The challenge to players is to program a robot that no other robot can destroy. Players do not have direct control over the robots during a battle. Instead, battle strategies are programmed beforehand into the robots' computerized intelligence, using the Robot War language. Factors under program control include radar, offensive shooting, speed, and maneuverability. The player's program controls the robot during a robot battle; the aim of the game, as we have noted, is to develop a program that will make a robot relatively invincible.

Robot War provides young computer users with an opportunity to develop skills in the logic of programming. The battle of robots is actually a graphic duel of the players' programs. The players receive the benefit of immediate feedback and the added impetus of programming in a competitive game.

- *Snooper Troops — A problem-solving game:* Snooper Troops is a package of programs designed to teach students in fifth grade or above to take notes and reason systematically.[14] The games use graphics and sound to heighten interest and realism. In each game, the object is to solve a crime. Several different cases are included on each diskette, so that the activities can be used more than once with each student. Students learn to take notes about clues and events that they encounter. Logical reasoning must be applied to solve the crimes.

Snooper Troops clearly involves the higher cognitive levels in Bloom's taxonomy. It requires students to go beyond simple knowledge and comprehension to analyze information, synthesize relationships, and evaluate hypotheses. Although the software does not teach a specific school subject, it can be utilized to enhance the learning of problem-solving techniques as these are being taught in science, mathematics, or social studies.

Games Created by Students   Young people not only play games but also invent them. Several commercial software companies have reported that some of their best programmers of computer games are teenagers. A student who has acquired knowledge of one of the high-level languages (such as BASIC or Logo) can create games with a microcomputer. Often students begin with graphics – drawing lines and creating shapes. If given the opportunity, students may go on to create games for their own amusement and to test their ideas.

This sequence of events can take place without adult direction. However, the teacher can encourage this natural inclination of students to create activities with the computer. A student who creates a computer game can be developing sophisticated skills involving the synthesis of language, mathematics, and logical reasoning. This kind of activity can often lead to opportunities for practicing such advanced skills as being able to test a hypothesis by manipulating various combinations of variables with the computer, or setting up a simulation of a real-world situation on the computer screen.

Many students enjoy creating computer games. In order to develop a game, a student must draw on a variety of academic skills. The game must begin with an idea, which should then be written down. The developer makes a diagram of the game, combines it with written text, and begins to develop the program. The procedure works best when the game can be programmed directly on a computer. The final step is to debug the program (remove problems) and add refinements. The form shown in Figure 10.6 was designed as an assignment sheet for a class in which students devise educational games on the computer.

FIGURE 10.6
Assignment sheet for developing a computerized game.

```
                          Create a Computer Game

       Name _____      Date _____

       Step 1   Describe your idea for a computer game. _____
                _____
                _____
                _____
                _____
                                  Instructor's Initial _____
       Step 2   Develop a model of the game.  Draw a diagram on a separate sheet or sheets
                of paper.  Be careful to avoid blind branches.
                                  Instructor's Initial _____

       Step 3   Write the text for the game.  Key the text to your diagram.

                                  Instructor's Initial _____

       Step 4   Write the program.

       Step 5   Debug the program and add refinements.  Demonstrate the program to
                your instructor.

                          Grade _____
```

The use of computers to develop games illustrates two fundamental characteristics of microcomputers:

1 Microcomputers are multidimensional tools which encourage *integration of learning experiences.* The student who develops a computer game uses a variety of academic skills and learning modalities.

2 Computers can help students develop *high-level cognitive skills.* In order to create a computer game, the student must develop an idea into a finished product by carrying out several sequential tasks which involve analyzing options, diagramming a model, and translating the model into a finished product.

Because higher levels of thinking are involved, students should have developed, in Piagetian terms, at least to the concrete operations stage before they can be expected to produce games with any degree of complexity. However, it has been shown that younger children can learn to program and express fairly sophisticated thoughts through programming.[15]

Two Samples of Educational Game Programs   Two samples of simple games written in Applesoft BASIC are shown in Figures 10.7 and 10.8 (pages 260–261). These games illustrate the kinds of programs students and teachers can write. They will run as shown on Apple II computers but can be easily adapted to other versions of BASIC for use on other microcomputers.

The first game (Figure 10.7) is a mathematics game in which the player must guess a number between 0 and 9. The computer advises the player if the guess is too large or too small. The object of the game is learn the principle by which the number can be identified in the fewest guesses.

The second game (Figure 10.8) is an adventure game which is like a story. The player assumes a role and has freedom to choose different courses of action as the story unfolds. Variations on this second program could be used to enhance a history unit or language arts instruction on writing short stories.

SIMULATIONS

As computers gain acceptance in schools, educators are beginning to evaluate the potential of computer simulations for classroom instruction. Most educators agree that classroom instruction can be improved by providing students with opportunities to apply their knowledge to actual situations. Computer simulations are one way of meeting this need.

Uses and Benefits of Simulations

A *simulation* is a working model of a portion of the real world, designed to run on a computer for instructional purposes. Simulations allow students to apply their knowledge and skills to real-world situations without leaving the classroom. Learners can participate in experiences that would otherwise be impossible.

Experimental variables can be manipulated without cost or risk. For example, a simulation of an air traffic control center in a busy airport challenges a student to learn to manage air traffic coming into and leaving the airfield. The student must develop a basic understanding of the layout of the airport and its traffic patterns. In the process, the student can practice trigonometric relationships, use various algebraic equations, and apply principles and rules from geometry and logic. Failure to balance the variables successfully can result in a simulated disaster.

Simulations can involve higher cognitive levels in learning. Students must apply previously acquired skills and knowledge to a new situation, analyze the conditions presented by the simulation, and synthesize data in order to formulate strategies to deal with dynamic conditions. They may also find themselves making ongoing evaluations of their solutions as they reformulate strategies to adapt to changing settings created by the program. The effectiveness of computer simulations for instruction is attested to by their use in government, business, and industry. For example, astronauts at the National Aeronautics and Space Administration (NASA) learned how to land a space shuttle from a computer simulation. Many decisions made by business and industry result from experience gained through simulations.

Realism is added to learning with simulations. The computer can control hundreds of interrelated factors. The effects of an alteration in one factor on the total system can be calculated and displayed instantly. Computer graphics and sound can heighten the realistic effects. The resulting combinations of sound, color, movement, and content can make learning with a simulation a more interesting experience than it is with textbooks or lectures.

Computer simulations (like games) can place the student in a variety of roles. For example, students may be pioneers leading a team of oxen to Oregon, or a team of seismologists attempting to locate the epicenter of an earthquake. The ability of the computer to create roles is limitless. As the sophistication of the hardware and educational software increases, the realism of the roles will increase. (A very high degree of realism has already been achieved in advanced flight simulators, which use computers to recreate the sounds, sights, and motions of flight.) Role playing in a simulated problem situation can be used to support higher cognitive levels of learning than the drill and practice methods on which many computer games are based. In simulations, many variables can be controlled in relation to each other. The complex situations that can therefore be presented to the student tend to encourage the kind of understanding necessary for successful problem solving rather than simple memorization of a set of facts.

Simulations are most effective when they are carefully integrated into a learning sequence. In most simulations, some background knowledge is required in order to understand the processes involved. A simulation occurring toward the end of a series of lessons helps to integrate the various learning experiences, and to tie together concepts and knowledge in a meaningful context.

```
10   REM   GUESS THE NUMBER
15   PRINT : PRINT : PRINT : PRINT
     : PRINT
20   HOME : VTAB 5: PRINT "HI.   I
     HAVE A GAME THAT WE CAN PLAY
     TOGETHER.   IT IS A GUESSING
     GAME."
30   VTAB 9: PRINT "I WILL THINK O
     F A NUMBER FROM 0 TO 9.   YOU
     WILL TRY TO GUESS WHAT THAT
     NUMBER IS."
40   VTAB 15: INPUT "BEFORE WE STA
     RT, PLEASE TYPE IN YOUR NAME
     .    ";D$
50   HOME : VTAB 5: PRINT "HELLO,
     ";D$;", I HAVE A NUMBER.   RE
     MEMBER THAT NUMBER IS ANYWHE
     RE FROM 0 TO 9."
60   LET X =   RND (10) * 10
70   LET X =   INT (X)
90   PRINT : PRINT : PRINT "PLEASE
     TYPE A NUMBER FROM 0 TO 9."

100   VTAB 12: INPUT E
110   IF E = X GOTO 400
120   IF E =  > X THEN   GOTO 450
130   IF E =  < X THEN   GOTO 500
400   HOME : VTAB 5: PRINT "EXCELL
      ENT.": GOSUB 1600: GOTO 600
450   HOME : VTAB 5: PRINT E" IS T
      OO LARGE.   TRY NOTHER NUMBER
      .": GOTO 90
500   HOME : VTAB 5: PRINT E" IS T
      OO SMALL.   TRY ANOTHER NUMBE
      R.": GOTO 90
600   HOME : VTAB 5: INPUT "DO YOU
      WANT TO DO IT AGAIN.? TYPE
      Y FOR YES OR N FOR NO.   ";F
      $
610   IF F$ = "Y" THEN   GOTO 60
620   HOME : VTAB 5: PRINT "IT HAS
      BEEN FUN, ";D$".   TILL NEXT
      TIME."
1600  FOR I = 1 TO 6000: NEXT I: HOME
      : RETURN
2000  END
```

FIGURE 10.7
A mathematics guessing game in Applesoft BASIC.

```
10   HOME : VTAB 5: PRINT ; TAB( 1
     5);"ADVENTURE GAME"
30   VTAB 8: PRINT ; TAB( 5);"YOU
     ARE ABOUT TO ENTER INTO A GA
     ME   OF ADVENTURE.  IN THIS
     ADVENTURE, YOU   ARE ONE OF
     THE KNIGHTS OF THE ROUND
     TABLE."
40   PRINT : PRINT ; TAB( 5);"KING
     ARTHUR HAS CHOSEN YOU TO BE
     THE KNIGHT TO RESCUE A DAMS
     EL IN DISTRESS."
50   PRINT : PRINT ; TAB( 5);"THIS
     DAMSEL HAS BEEN KIDNAPPED B
     Y AN EVIL KNIGHT AND HAS BEE
     N IMPRISONED IN A CASTLE SUR
     ROUNDED BY A DEEP MOAT.   THE
     BRIDGE IS GUARDED BY A LARG
     E TROLL."
60   PRINT : PRINT ; TAB( 5);"IN O
     RDER TO RESCUE THE DAMSEL, Y
     OU WILL NEED TO GO TO THE CA
     STLE.": GOSUB 1800
90   HOME : VTAB 5: PRINT ; TAB( 5
     );"YOU ARE NOW READY TO BEGI
     N YOUR        JOURNEY.  ALL T
     HE EQUIPMENT YOU NEED    HAS
     BEEN PACKED FOR YOU. YOU MO
     UNT       YOUR WHITE HORSE."
95   PRINT : PRINT ; TAB( 5);"YOU
     ARE ON YOUR WAY.  SOON YOU S
     EE THE CASTLE.  YOU SEE THE
     MOAT.   THE DRAWBRIDGE IS DOW
     N.  YOU SEE THE TROLL ON THE
     DRAWBRIDGE.  YOU ASK YOURSE
     LF, HOW WILL I GET PAST THE
     TROLL AND RESCUE THE DAMSEL.
     ": GOSUB 1800
100  HOME : VTAB 5: PRINT "YOU AR
     E PRESENTED WITH THE FOLLOWI
     NG        CHOICES."
110  VTAB 8: PRINT "1.   SHOULD I
     TRY CLIMBING THE WALL?"
120  PRINT : PRINT "2.   SHOULD I
     CHARGE THE TROLL?"
130  PRINT : PRINT "3.   SHOULD I
     TURN AROUND AND GO HOME?"
140  GOSUB 1200
150  IF J = 1 THEN   GOTO 300
160  IF J = 2 THEN   GOTO 310
170  IF J = 3 THEN   GOTO 1000
180  IF J =  > 3 THEN   GOSUB 1500
     : GOTO 110
300  HOME : VTAB 5: PRINT "THE WA
     LL IS TOO HIGH TO CLIMB.  PL
     EASE TRY ANOTHER CHOICE.": GOSUB
     1400: GOTO 110
310  HOME : VTAB 8: PRINT "YOU NO
     W ASK YOURSELF, HOW WILL I C
     HARGE THE TROLL."
320  VTAB 11: PRINT "1.   SHOULD I
     USE MY SWORD?"
330  PRINT : PRINT "2.   SHOULD I
     USE MY LANCE?"
340  PRINT : PRINT "3.   SHOULD I
     USE NO WEAPONS AND DIRECTLY
     CHARGE WITH MY HORSE?"
350  GOSUB 1200
360  IF J = 1 THEN   GOTO 400
370  IF J = 2 THEN   GOTO 410
380  IF J = 3 THEN   GOTO 420
390  IF J =  > 3 THEN   GOSUB 1500
     : GOTO 310

400  HOME : VTAB 5: PRINT "THE TR
     OLL WAS ABLE TO REACH YOU WI
     TH ITS LONG ARMS WHILE YOU W
     ERE TRYING TO GET THE TROLL
     WITH YOUR SWORD."
401  VTAB 10: PRINT "THE TROLL TH
     REW YOU OFF THE DRAWBRIDGE.
     YOU HAD TO SWIM BACK TO SHO
     RE AND MAKE ANOTHER DECISION
     .": GOSUB 1600: GOTO 310
410  HOME : VTAB 5: PRINT "YOU WE
     RE ABLE TO CHASE THE TROLL O
     FF THE DRAWBRIDGE INTO THE M
     OAT.  YOU NOW HAVE ACCESS TO
     THE CASTLE AS THE TROLL CAN
     ONLY DOGPADDLE BACK TO SHOR
     E."
414  PRINT : PRINT "YOU PUT YOUR
     LANCE AWAY AND FINISHED CROS
     SING THE DRAWBRIDGE.  THE CA
     STLE IS YOURS FOR THE TAKING
     .  YOU LOCATED THE DAMSEL LO
     CKED IN A ROOM.  THE KEY WAS
     NEARBY.  YOU OPENED THE DOO
     R AND YOU AND THE DAMSEL BEG
     UN YOUR JOURNEY BACK."
415  GOSUB 1800: HOME :  VTAB 5: PRINT
     "YOU HAVE SAVED THE DAMSEL.
     I HOPE THAT YOU HAVE ENJOYE
     D THIS LITTLE ADVENTURE.  IF
     YOU WANT TO SEE WHAT HAPPEN
     S WITH THE OTHER CHOICES, TY
     PE RUN.   TILL NEXT TIME.": GOSUB
     1600: GOTO 2000
420  HOME : VTAB 5: PRINT "THE TR
     OLL DODGED YOU AND YOUR HORS
     E, THEN GRABBED YOU WITH ITS
     LONG ARMS AND THREW YOU OFF
     THE DRAWBRIDGE INTO THE MOA
     T."
425  PRINT : PRINT "YOU FIND YOUR
     SELF IN THE MOAT.  YOU MUST
     SWIM BACK TO SHORE AND TRY A
     GAIN.": GOSUB 1600: GOTO 310
1000 HOME : VTAB 5: PRINT "YOU H
     AVE LEFT THE DAMSEL TO WHATE
     VER LIFE THE EVIL KNIGHT HAS
     PLANNED FOR HER."
1010 PRINT : PRINT "THIS ENDS TH
     E ADVENTURE GAME.  I HOPE YO
     U HAVE ENJOYED THE GAME.": GOSUB
     1600: GOTO 2000
1200 PRINT : PRINT : INPUT "WHIC
     H ONE OF THE THREE IS YOUR C
     HOICE?  PLEASE TYPE 1, 2 OR
     3.   ";J: RETURN
1400 FOR I = 1 TO 6000: NEXT I: HOME
     : RETURN
1500 HOME : VTAB 5: PRINT "YOU H
     AVE CHOSEN A NUMBER THAT IS
          NEITHER 1, 2 NOR 3.
     PLEASE TRY AGAIN.": FOR I =
     1 TO 4000: NEXT I: HOME : RETURN

1600 FOR I = 1 TO 6000: NEXT I: HOME
     : RETURN
1800 PRINT : INPUT "      PRESS R
     ETURN TO CONTINUE.      ";D$:
     RETURN
2000 END
```

FIGURE 10.8
An adventure game in Applesoft BASIC.

Some Examples of Simulations

The number of simulations that can be presented by computer is virtually infinite. New educational simulations are becoming available all the time. (However, high-quality simulations can be expensive to develop.) The simulations described below illustrate the versatility of the computer in presenting learning experiences.

Quakes *Quakes* is a science simulation produced by the Minnesota Educational Computing Consortium (MECC). This activity guides students through the process of locating an earthquake by calculating the time lag between the arrival of a pressure wave (*P* wave) and a secondary wave (*S* wave) following an earthquake. Students are placed in the role of seismologists obtaining seismographic readings.

This simulation effectively uses the computer's ability to simulate the performance of other machines. The computer mimics a seismograph sending data about earthquakes. Students function as seismograph operators and receive data on the CRT screen as though it were being printed out on seismic paper. At another stage of the simulation, the computer becomes a plotter to aid the operators as they locate the epicenter of the earthquake. The computer then checks the accuracy of the students' plotting and evaluates their performance.

Quakes is an effective program to use with small groups (two or three students working together). The impact of this simulation is enhanced by having students work together on problem solving, because at the same time they practice socialization and cooperation. The simulation also illustrates the fact that educational computers are at their best when integrated with other instructional media. Students doing this simulation are not merely working at a computer keyboard and screen. They may refer to a map of the western United States and may use rulers, pencils, scratch paper, and reference materials. The computer sets up the problem, adds an element of realism, and evaluates the results. The students perform tasks involving concepts and skills which they are learning.

Another important point illustrated by Quakes is that a computer simulation can be run by the same students several times. Most microcomputers can generate numbers randomly. Using this capability, variables in the simulation (such as the times of arrival of the *P* waves and *S* waves) are set at random by the computer every time the program is run. This means that, unlike paper-and-pencil simulations (in which the possibility of variation is limited), computers can present almost infinite versions of a problem. The probability that the identical situation will be presented twice to the same student is very small.

Three Mile Island Three Mile Island (see Figure 10.9) is an example of a complex simulation that makes use of computer graphics to display the inner workings of a nuclear power plant.[16] This simulation places the student in the role of

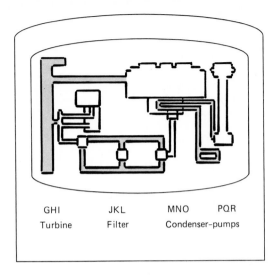

GHI   JKL   MNO   PQR

Turbine   Filter   Condenser-pumps

FIGURE 10.9
Sample screen from a Three Mile Island
implementation. *(Adapted from version
by Muse, Inc.)*

operator of the plant; the student must operate the plant safely and at a profit.

The software presents a realistic simulation of the operation of a pressurized reactor. The operator must supply electric power to customers at a reasonable rate and (as we have noted) produce a profit; failure to make a profit can result in loss of the operating license. The plant must be operated according to safety rules and a maintenance schedule must be followed, or the operator risks leaking radiation into the environment. Depending on the version of the program, the operator is initially given several options — such as viewing graphic displays of the containment building, turbines, filter and condenser, reactor core and control rods, and pump house; or viewing charts depicting costs, current operating profits, and operational status of various components.

The realism and complexity of this simulation can be impressive. In one version, as water is pumped through a filter, sludge builds up. When sludge buildup reaches a certain level, the filter is automatically taken out of operation. The operator must then flush out the sludge. Various water pressures are available to remove the sludge accumulation. The simulation includes safety features found in a real plant. For example, the operator cannot flush out a filter when the filter is online. Warnings of equipment failures may be given. The operator must make all the necessary decisions as time ticks away at the rate of one real second for each minute of simulation time.

Three Mile Island is a complex computer activity. It would be an excellent complement to the study of nuclear energy in a general science or physics course at the secondary school level. It might also be useful as a group activity in social studies classes on the political and economic ramifications of nuclear energy.

Eliza In 1966, Dr. Joseph Weizenbaum, a professor of computer science at the Massachusetts Institute of Technology (MIT), created an algorithm that allows a computer to carry on a dialog with a person at a keyboard.[17] The program which resulted, Eliza, was named after a character in George Bernard Shaw's play *Pygmalion*. Eliza simulates conversation; it is not really an instructional simulation. The reason it is included here is that it is one of the better known examples of an artificial intelligence simulation, and it suggests how certain kinds of educational simulations might look in the future. Artificial intelligence (AI) is becoming increasingly important.[18] Researchers in AI seek to program machines to solve the open-ended kind of problems that one ordinarily would expect only a human to solve. Artificial Intelligence programs have been developed to play chess, to control robot functions, and to solve a variety of problems (see Chapter 12).

The program Eliza takes on the role of a psychologist or counselor giving a kind of counseling known as *nondirective therapy*. (Figure 10.10 suggests, rather humorously, a generalized nondirective therapy situation.) A sample of a conversation between *Eliza* and a human typing at a keyboard might be:

Eliza:	May I help you?
Operator:	No. I feel good today.
Eliza:	Tell me about your family.
Operator:	My mother always tells me what to do.
Eliza:	Can you think of a specific example?
Operator:	She is always telling me to clean up my room and stand up straight.
Eliza:	Clean your room and stand up straight. That's interesting.
Operator:	It's really embarrassing when she says that in front of my friends.
Eliza:	Why do you say your friends?

FIGURE 10.10
Eliza simulates a nondirective psychotherapist.

After Eliza was made public, Dr. Weizenbaum was astounded to find that people were taking the program seriously. He pointed out that Eliza is merely a program which analyzes sentence structure and then responds without any of the feeling or comprehension of a human being. Nonetheless, the temptation seems strong to respect a computer as human when it is able to carry on a conversation.

While the educational applications for this kind of simulation have not yet been thoroughly investigated, the possibilities are intriguing. For example, it is possible to envision a computer program that will monitor a student who is doing word processing. The student might be questioned by the machine about phrasing, word usage, spelling, grammar, and syntax as the passage is being composed. The effect would be almost like having a teacher looking over the student's shoulder. Thus, it would be the teacher, not the situation, that is being simulated. An artificial intelligence approach to simulation could, therefore, result in educational simulations that are even more responsive and adaptable to students' responses than any simulations that are currently available tend to be.

Hammurabi   Hammurabi is a simulation which exists in a number of different versions, each with varying degrees of complexity. This simulation is known by several names. In its basic version, the operator is placed in the role of Hammurabi, king of ancient Sumeria. The operator is responsible for the health and welfare of the people and must make decisions to ensure that the kingdom thrives and the population increases.

Each year Hammurabi must decide how many acres of ground to plant, whether to sell land, and how much food to distribute to the people. The computer enhances the simulation by adding periodic plagues which kill part of the population and rat infestations which seem to take a percentage of each year's crop. The simplest versions of Hammurabi consist of text on the screen in black and white, occupying less than 4K of memory. More elaborate versions of this simulation include color graphics to illustrate the harvest, rat infestations, the weather, and the changes in the size of the population.

The object of the simulation is to increase the population and at the same time avoid losing any of Hammurabi's subjects through starvation. The student must apply elementary mathematics skills to determine how much land to buy, sell, and plant for each yearly cycle. In order to complete the simulation successfully, the student must learn from experience approximately how many bushels of food are necessary to support one subject for a year and how many acres must be planted for each subject.

The player gains a sense of being a ruler in charge of subjects and responsible for their well-being. The computer periodically reports to Hammurabi as if it were a humble subject: "Hammurabi, I beg to report that . . . " At the end of the simulation (some versions can go on indefinitely), the computer sums up the student's performance. A student's performance might be evaluated by a chart, or by a statement informing Hammurabi of how many subjects are plotting assassination because of the king's poor decisions. All versions keep a running account of acreage available for planting, food in storage, and the current population. The simulation includes population increases resulting from people moving into the city.

Students who know how to program can develop variations or enchancements of the program based on their own reading. For example, if the region was subject to periodic flooding and foreign invasion, this could be added to the simulation. Another possibility is to research the layout of a Sumerian city and graphically portray this on the screen. Thus, Hammurabi can be treated as a simulation in agriculture and economics involving problem solving and basic

TABLE 10.4
FORM FOR SELECTION OF COMPUTERIZED GAMES AND SIMULATIONS FOR INTEGRATION INTO AN INSTRUCTIONAL PROGRAM

Instructional unit or lesson:_____

1 What is the instructional purpose of the courseware?

2 What is the reading level? Can your students read and comprehend this activity?

3 How many students can work with this computer activity at one time?
- _____ 1
- _____ 2
- _____ 3 to 5
- _____ Other

4 How much time is necessary to complete the activity?
How many times should students run the activity? _____
How much time is required to set it up on the computer for each student? _____
How much time is required for a student to run it once? _____

5 Evaluate the cognitive level of game or simulation.
- _____ Knowledge
- _____ Comprehension
- _____ Application
- _____ Higher levels (analysis, synthesis, and evaluation)

6 Have your students functioned at this level before? Are they capable of working at this level?
- _____ Yes
- _____ No
- _____ Uncertain

algebraic relationships, as an entertaining game, or as a programming activity involving historical research and analysis.

GUIDELINES FOR USING GAMES AND SIMULATIONS

Games and simulations can be powerful tools for achieving educational goals. But if they are improperly used, they can also be distractions and sources of frustration for both students and teacher. Table 10.4 is a form that can help a teacher make decisions about integrating these activities into an instructional program. The time spent incorporating these guidelines into decisions about when and how to use simulations and games will pay dividends in terms of students' performance.

TABLE 10.4
CONTINUED

Instructional unit or lesson:_____

7 What skills need to be taught beforehand?

8 How much supervision will the students need as they are performing the activity?
      ———— Direct supervision at all times
      ———— Supervision in starting up and then occasional supervision or direction
      ———— Supervision only in starting
      ———— No supervision
      ———— Other (add comments as necessary)

9 Is the documentation adequate? Will the student need to read the documentation, or is the program self-documented?

10 Where does this activity belong in the instructional sequence?
      ———— Introduction
      ———— Guided practice
      ———— Independent practice
      ———— Testing
      ———— Review
      ———— Other (add comments as necessary)

11 Appropriate companion assignments:
    Reading_____
    Group discussion_____
    Other_____

SUMMARY

Educational games and simulations can significantly enhance an instructional program. Effective instructional simulations and games require consideration of the cognitive level of the tasks in the learning activities, the organization of the instructional program and the tasks and activities in the game or simulation, the child's level of cognitive development, and the objectives of the instructional unit. Three questions to be addressed when considering the use of an educational game or simulation are:

1   Is the microcomputer-based game or simulation appropriate for the educational objective?

2   Does the software package support the objective?

3   Where is the appropriate point in the curriculum to introduce the game or simulation?

Games and simulations work best when they are integrated into a planned sequence of learning. Computerized simulations and games must fit into the larger educational program, which includes textbooks, writing exercises, various media, and teaching strategies. In short, computerized games and simulations should be considered one more tool the teacher can use in a total instructional program.

New games and simulations for the microcomputer become available almost daily. As the quality of educational programming for microcomputers improves, simulations have great potential for enhancing instruction in complex intellectual tasks.

NOTES

1   Hilgard, E. R., & Bowers, G. H. (1966). *Theories of learning* (3rd ed.). New York: Appleton-Century-Crofts. Snelbecker, G. E. (1974). *Learning theory, instructional theory, and psychoeducational design.* New York: McGraw-Hill. Wingfield, A. (1979). *Learning and memory.* New York: Harper & Row.

2   Hill, W. F. (1977). *Learning: A survey of psychological interpretations* (3rd ed.). New York: Crowell.

3   Mayer, R. E. (1975). Information processing variables in learning to solve problems. *Review of Educational Research, 45*(4), 525–541.

4   Bloom, B. S. (Ed.). (1956). *Taxonomy of educational objectives: Cognitive domain.* New York: McKay.

5   Gagné, R. M., & Briggs, L. J. (1974). *Principles of instructional design* (2nd ed.). New York: Holt, Rinehart & Winston.

6   Kohen-Raz, R. (1977). *Psychobiological aspects of cognitive growth.* New York: Academic Press.

7   Epstein, H. (1978). Growth spurts during brain development: Implications for educational policy and practice. In J. Chall (Ed.), *Education and the brain: NSSE Yearbook.* Chicago, IL: National Society for the Study of Education.

8   Arnold, A. (1972). *The world book of children's games.* New York: World.

9   Bandelier, N. (1982). TI Logo and first-graders — A winning combination. *The Computing Teacher, 10*(3), 38–39.

10 Bowman, R. F. (1982). A "Pac-Man" theory of motivation: Tactical implications for classroom instruction. *Educational Technology, 22*(9), 14–16.

11 Bockman, F. (1982). MasterType: The typing instruction game. *Apple Journal, 1*, 18–20. The game was programmed by Bruce Zweig and is marketed by Lightning Software of Palo Alto, CA. For a discussion of learning to type with a microcomputer, see: Stares, S. (1983). Learn to touch type. *Creative Computing, 9*(4), 202, 204, 206, 208, 210, 212.

12 For example, there is a listing for a hangman game in the chapter on games in: C. Doerr. (1979). *Microcomputers and the three R's.* Rochelle Park, NJ: Hayden. Another listing can be found in: Fine, E. (1983). Hangman's noose. *InCider, 1*(10), 160, 162.

13 Robot War was programmed by Silas Warner and is marketed by Muse Software of Baltimore, MD.

14 The author of Snooper Troops is Tom Snyder, and the game is available from Spinnaker Software, Cambridge, MA.

15 Watt, D. (1982). Logo in the schools. *BYTE, 7*(6), 116–118, 120, 122, 126, 128, 130, 132–134.

16 One popular version of the Three Mile Island simulation was programmed by Richard Orban and is marketed by Muse Software of Baltimore, MD.

17 A number of versions of Eliza are on the market which are available for several microcomputers. Gnosis of Philadelphia, PA, includes a version of Eliza in its LISP programming language package for the Apple II microcomputer. Another version is available from Artificial Intelligence Research Group, Los Angeles, CA.

18 Sanders, D. H. (1983). *Computers today.* New York: McGraw-Hill.

SUPPLEMENTARY READINGS

Ahl, D. (1983). Learning can be fun. *Creative Computing, 9*(4), 98, 100, 102, 105, 106, 108, 112–114, 116, 118–119, 122, 123, 125, 130, 134, 137, 138, 143.

Bell, T. E. (1983). Learning to win. *Personal Computing, 7*(4), 134–137, 139, 141.

Crawford, C. (1982). Design techniques and ideals for computer games. *BYTE, 7*(12), 96–100, 102, 104, 106, 108.

Deken, J. (1982). *The electronic cottage.* New York: Morrow.

Gabel, D. (1983). What's in a game. *Personal Computing, 7*(4), 63–65, 67, 69, 172.

Malone, T. W. (1981). Toward a theory of intrinsically motivating instruction. *Cognitive Science, 4*, 333–369.

Piaget, J. (1980). *Experiments in contradiction* (D. Coleman, Trans.). Chicago, IL: University of Chicago Press.

Schwebel, M., & Raph, J. (Eds.). (1973). *Piaget in the classroom.* New York: Basic Books.

Stadsklev, R. (1982). *Handbook of simulation gaming in social education.* University, Alabama: Institute of Higher Education Research and Services.

Tommervik, M. C. (1983, July). The art and craft of the game. *SOFTALK, 3*, 145–148, 150, 152, 155.

Varven, J. (1983, April). When Rich Hoffman's Apple talks, children listen. *SOFTALK, 3*, 194–196, 198–199.

WHAT STUDENTS SHOULD KNOW ABOUT COMPUTERS

The prevalence of computers in society has increased dramatically in recent years. Computers are no longer limited to universities, research laboratories, and large corporations, as they were until the early 1970s, but are now routinely found in elementary school classrooms, in homes, and in consumer products, including toys, washing machines, and automobiles. Clearly, computers have become part of everyday life.

One of the most vexing questions to come out of this computer revolution concerns educating students about computers. Should education emphasize computer programming, or the chemical and electrical properties of the silicon chip, or social and environmental factors? Questions have also been raised about whether students should learn to program computers or merely to use computers for specific applications after they have been programmed by others. These issues have to do with the problem of literacy in a technological society. That is, in addition to traditional ideas of literacy — competence in language, mathematics, science, literature, and so on — many people have suggested the concept of *computer literacy.* The present chapter addresses this matter of educating students to become literate in computing.

First we will look at some of the problems, controversies, and areas of general agreement in how people think about computer literacy. We ask why computer literacy is important. Then we analyze several of the more common approaches to computer literacy programs in elementary and secondary schools and describe aspects of computer literacy programs. Finally, we discuss the practical side of setting up a computer literacy program in a school.

DEFINING COMPUTER LITERACY

Trying to define *computer literacy* is a little like trying to describe the shape of a cloud. It is reasonably easy to say, in general, what a cloud is and is not; but it is difficult, if not impossible, to say exactly what every cloud looks like. This kind of situation exists not only with computer literacy but also with traditional ideas of literacy, such as reading, writing, and mathematics. When we consider computer literacy, it can be helpful to consider traditional notions of literacy.

Traditional Concepts of Literacy

Even in the traditional sense, *literacy* is not a clearly defined concept. Many people would include in "traditional" literacy the ability to read and write, and to understand and use language. Others include some forms of mathematical and scientific knowledge, and the ability to comprehend relationships and to reason. However, most people will agree that the ability to communicate is a fundamental aspect of literacy. Definitions of literacy that emphasize basic skills and knowledge (such as grammar and spelling) have been criticized as simplistic and as neglecting the richness of concepts of valuing, experimentation, and artistic expression. Communication and understanding tend to be shallow and limited in perspective without these other aspects.[1]

According to this broader view, literacy should include rapport and depth of communication. Thus, it is one thing to be able to write a sentence with a subject and a predicate and quite another to be able to paint a picture with words as a poet does. Not all literate people can write poetry, but anyone who is considered literate should be able to recognize, understand, and appreciate metaphor, simile, and other elements of poetry. A literate person, according to this view, can use language to communicate and to receive and understand the communications of others, even when abstractions, subtleties, values, and artistic expression are involved. Thus literacy includes understanding, appreciating, and evaluating communications from others. Another dimension of literacy, stemming from the ability to communicate, is the ability to participate actively in society. Finally, the literate person is able to act on his or her own initiative and to be creative.

Computer Literacy

Ideas of "traditional" literacy provide a context for definitions of computer literacy. That is, definitions of computer literacy should emphasize communication, understanding, and the ability to participate in society.

We should begin by distinguishing between *computer literacy* and *computer awareness*. The term *computer awareness* generally refers to knowledge of the ways computers are used in society, the social and economic implications of these uses, and the effects of computers on peoples' lives. *Computer literacy* is a broader term. It includes not only the concepts usually considered part of computer awareness, but also some experience in controlling and operating computers. Generally, computer awareness has to do with studying about computers; computer literacy has to do with studying computers and includes hands-on experience.

There is some controversy among educators about whether education for computer awareness is sufficient in today's schools, or whether students need to become computer-literate.[2] And even among those who believe that today's students do require actual hands-on training with computers, there is controversy over whether education should emphasize use of prewritten software or computer languages and programming.[3]

For the purposes of this book, we will define the *computer-literate* person as one who knows about and understands computers sufficiently to

• Comprehend the social, economic, and ethical issues related to computer applications
• Operate computers as necessary
• Function and participate in an increasingly computer-based society (as Figure 11.1 suggests)

FIGURE 11.1
The citizen of tomorrow will have to learn to communicate with technology.

This definition includes computer awareness as part of computer literacy, but it does not take a position on the issue of programming versus applications packages. However, programming can be taught on many levels. As a minimum, a basic introduction to programming ought to be part of any computer literacy curriculum.

Perspectives on Computer Literacy

The problem of defining computer literacy is compounded by the different perspectives taken by people in the field.

For example, one writer makes the valid point that a computer-literate person should be able to appreciate that the role of hardware is insignificant compared with the role of software. Software is made by people; thus it reflects the skills, talents, and knowledge of the programmer. A computer will not make a mediocre teacher into a good one. A poor mathematics teacher who writes instructional software will in all likelihood write poor software.[4] This view of computer literacy stresses the ability to recognize the fundamental role that people have in a technological society. This is an interesting slant on computer literacy; most other approaches focus on the technology and its impact.

Understanding how people influence technology is expected to give citizens some control over technological applications, even if it is not direct. The term *techno/peasant* has been coined to describe individuals who do not understand technology and are at the mercy of *technocrats,* people who do understand it.[5] Knowledge of technological capabilities should lead to informed participation by citizens in decisions that will affect society. According to this view, the ability to program computers is not essential to understanding technology or to communicating in an information-based society.

Arthur Luehrmann, a well-known advocate of computer literacy training in the schools, takes another point of view: that learning a programming language is essential to attainment of computer literacy. According to Luerhmann, communication is fundamental to any concept of literacy; and to communicate with or about computers, one must know how to get computers to do things by programming them.[6]

The notion that learning a programming language should be a basic element of a computer literacy curriculum is supported by others prominent in the field. For example, David Moursund, who has written extensively on computer literacy, argues that giving students experience with a programming language is preferable to using applications software; but for him the essential element is hands-on experience.[7] On the other hand, some of the supporters of this view suggest that the real benefit to be gained from learning to program is learning to think procedurally, like a computer scientist.[8]

WHY IS COMPUTER LITERACY IMPORTANT?

The idea of literacy in computing does not have a long history. Most writers trace the beginning of interest in education for computer literacy to statements by various mathematics and science education groups in the 1970s.[9]

Two events appear to have made computer literacy imperative. First, easy access to computing was made possible by advances in microprocessor and silicon-chip technology. By the late 1970s, computers had become so reasonable in price that many people began to buy them for home use. The impressive capabilities and low prices of these machines hastened their introduction into classrooms.

Second, society now has the ability to handle tremendous amounts of information with electronic efficiency and speed. In other words, it has become oriented toward information processing. Computers are now used with large-scale data-storage devices (such as videodisks and floppy diskettes) and in electronic message transmission (as with satellites, telephones, and radios) to control many processes in manufacturing, science, finance, and industry. Computer-aided design and computer-aided manufacturing (CAD/CAM) have revolutionized engineering. The printing, publishing, and communications fields have also been profoundly affected. Business and industry need workers who are able to use these new technologies.[10] These social changes are placing pressure on the schools to produce citizens who can live and work in a technology-oriented culture.

The role of education is crucial for development of universal computer literacy and technological skills.[11] New patterns of thinking will probably emerge as emphasis on technological education increases. Evidence of new ideas can already be seen in the character of mathematics being offered to undergraduates; several colleges are beginning to emphasize discrete mathematics rather than the traditional approaches involving continuous mathematics and calculus.[12]

If education is to produce citizens for the technological society, students must have access to computers. This means that schools will need sufficient funds and resources to establish good computer literacy programs. Some people fear that only wealthy school districts will be able to make the kind of investment necessary. This raises concerns about educational equality,[13] and the possibility that children from lower socioeconomic backgrounds will lack opportunities to learn computing and will therefore lack the skills necessary for full participation in society.

APPROACHES TO TEACHING COMPUTER LITERACY

There has not been widespread vocal opposition to the idea of education for computer literacy.[14] However, there is debate over the best way to approach the teaching of technology and computing. The debate is similar to that over definitions of computer literacy.

Some people argue that the most essential part of education about computers is awareness of technology, its uses, and its impact on society. This is what we have already called *computer awareness.*

Others argue that students should learn that they can control computers rather than that computers can control them. According to this view, the relationship between communication and traditional literacy has a direct counterpart in *computer literacy.* That is, if one can receive information from a computer and give commands to make the computer perform, then one is computer-literate.

Within the second view, there are two camps. One camp emphasizes programming skills.[15] The other would be satisfied if students could use applications software to do meaningful data processing and problem solving.[16] A third way to approach this problem is to focus on needs and to consider the computer literacy curriculum as part of an integrated overall school program. Students might pursue information about computers in a science or mathematics course, or they might do a unit on word processing in language arts class. Programming would be taught in the context of problem solving. This integrated approach tends to soften the distinction between programming and using applications packages.

Figure 11.2 summarizes the different approaches. This figure is explained fur-

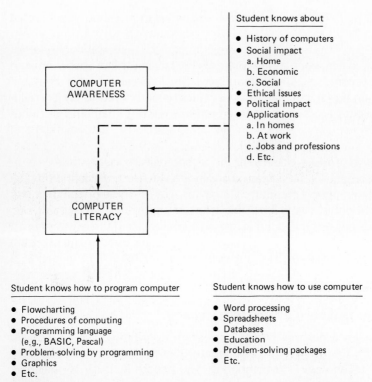

Student knows about

- History of computers
- Social impact
  a. Home
  b. Economic
  c. Social
- Ethical issues
- Political impact
- Applications
  a. In homes
  b. At work
  c. Jobs and professions
  d. Etc.

COMPUTER
AWARENESS

COMPUTER
LITERACY

Student knows how to program computer

- Flowcharting
- Procedures of computing
- Programming language
  (e.g., BASIC, Pascal)
- Problem-solving by programming
- Graphics
- Etc.

Student knows how to use computer

- Word processing
- Spreadsheets
- Databases
- Education
- Problem-solving packages
- Etc.

FIGURE 11.2
Different views of the contents of computer literacy and computer awareness
curricula.

ther below, and some samples of various kinds of computer education programs are given. (The examples are provided only for illustrative purposes; inclusion of a program should not be taken as an endorsement by the authors.)

Computer Awareness Programs

As is shown in Figure 11.2, in computer awareness programs students learn about computers and their impact on society and life. The learning objectives tend to be oriented toward understanding of computers in general rather than making computers perform certain functions.

Books Many books on the popular market are suitable computer awareness texts for use in secondary schools. The following list is representative of the kinds of books available for computer awareness programs.

- The Print Group. (1980). *The techno/peasant survival manual.* New York: Bantam Books.

This book includes chapters on microcomputers, fiber optics, lasers, genetic engineering, space exploration, satellites, nuclear energy, weapons technology, and artificial intelligence. Its goal is to acquaint citizens who are not sophisticated in technology *(techno peasants)* with technological language and concepts. It is hoped that this knowledge will enable citizens to assume greater responsibility for the effects of technology rather than leaving all decisions to the technocrats (people who are part of the technological world). The book is written in an entertaining nontechnical style. It would provide a good introduction for secondary students to concepts in technology and their political, economic, philosophical, and social consequences.

- Deken, J. (1981). *The electronic cottage.* New York: Morrow.

This book includes discussions of logic; programming concepts; interfacing of machines and people; electronic games; communications; and technology in homes, schools, businesses, and industries. It focuses on technological effects that are a little closer to home than those in *The Techno/Peasant Survival Manual.* It too is considered appropriate for secondary school students.

- Bitter, G. G. (1981). *Exploring with computers.* New York: Messner.

This short, simple book about computers can be read by students in about fourth or fifth grade. It contains an overview of computers focused primarily on hardware and does not require hands-on experience. Topics covered include the history of computers; how a computer works; applications; careers; the future; and simple activities such as flowcharting, reading a BASIC program, and reading punched cards. Books like this (and there are several of them) probably would not be considered a complete computer awareness curriculum by themselves, and the teacher would probably want to supplement them with other activities (such as field trips and problem-solving activities).

Courseware Following is an example of courseware for computer awareness.

- *Computer Discovery.* Chicago, IL: Science Research Associates.

This is a courseware package consisting of an instructor's guide, a student's workbook, and two diskettes containing interactive learning exercises (available at least for Apple and Atari computers). In some ways, this package borders on what many would consider computer literacy rather than computer awareness. However, even though hands-on experiences are included and programming concepts are part of the instruction, the level of coverage is more introductory than it would be in most formal computer literacy programs. The coverage includes a history of computers; programming concepts (algorithms, flowcharts, data definition, variables, conditional execution, syntax, etc.); computer concepts (hardware components, binary numbers, silicon chips, processing speed, etc.); and the social and vocational impact of computers. The program was designed for use in junior high school and high school classes. Workbooks were prepared at the sixth-grade and ninth-grade reading levels. As an individualized course, the publisher estimates that this book will take a student about 15 hours to complete. As a group-directed program, it would probably conform to a six-week unit on computers.

Computer Literacy Programs

As Figure 11.2 indicates, computer literacy programs tend to include consideration of the social, economic, and ethical aspects of computer technology. However, they typically place more emphasis on using computers for productive and meaningful applications. They generally include both programming and using existing software; but different programs have different degrees of emphasis. The programs listed below are examples of those that emphasize software applications or programming skills; but they have in common the idea that students should be learning to operate and control the computer. Other computer literacy programs are also available.

The Programming-Language Approach Generally, programming-language approaches to computer literacy use BASIC, Pascal, or Logo. Those that use the Logo language tend to follow the views of Seymour Papert, described in his book *Mindstorms.*[17] Basically, Papert agrees with the idea that students should be taught to control the computer rather than be controlled by it. According to Papert, Logo creates an environment in which young students can explore the computer much as they explore other aspects of their environment. Logo has been designed so that even elementary students can use it to program a computer. Some people see Logo simply as a language that can introduce students to programming early; others see it as the core of a computer literacy program.[18] (Logo is discussed with other programming languages in Chapter 9. The present discussion, however, is limited to formally constructed computer literacy curricula.)

• Luerhmann, A., & Peckham, H. (1983). *Computer Literacy: A hands-on approach.* New York: McGraw-Hill.

It is assumed that most of this text will be read while the student is seated at a computer. The student learns early in the first exercise that the idea of the course is to learn how to control computers. Lessons are laid out well, with companion software. By doing exercises, the student learns about the computer's operating system and how to write simple programs. The language taught is BASIC. Materials are geared toward the middle school or junior high school level.

• Larsen, S. G. (1980). *Computers for kids.* Morristown, NJ: Creative Computing.

This book was written to introduce elementary school children to computer programming in the BASIC language. There are editions for Apple, Atari, and TRS-80 computers. The book features large print and an easy style that students seem to enjoy. A section for parents or teachers is included, with suggestions about using the book with children. Topics include flowcharting and BASIC programming. The booklet would probably require 10 weeks to complete with weekly classes of about 45 minutes to 1 hour. There is no coverage of social issues, careers, ethics, and related issues; and coverage of problem solving is limited.

The Comprehensive Approach   The comprehensive approach differs from the programming-language approach in several ways:

It places greater emphasis on topics usually included in computer awareness programs.

It places relatively less emphasis on programming.

It places more emphasis on using computers in applications with existing software.

The examples of the comprehensive approach given below are intended for different grade levels, cover different topics, and have different underlying philosophies. However, they are similar in that they put computer literacy in the context of other subjects being studied, focus on the social issues raised by computer technology, and emphasize thinking about problems and data as a computer scientist would.[19]

• Hunter, B. (1983). *My students use computers: Comprehensive guide to computer literacy for the K–8 curriculum.* Reston, VA: Reston.

This is a K–8 computer literacy program developed with assistance from the National Science Foundation by Human Resources Research Organization (HumRRO) and the Montgomery County (Maryland) Schools. It focuses on procedural thinking. A *procedure* is defined as a set of steps that must be carried out in a particular sequence. The curriculum is developed according to sequenced objectives for each grade. Activities relate to mathematics, science, social studies, and language arts appropriate for each grade. The student begins using the computer to run programs at the lowest grade levels. However, programming is not emphasized until the seventh- to eighth-grade level. The guide includes activities for the teacher to use in the classroom and suggests software, books, and other materials to be used in conjunction with the program. The major goal of the K–8 program is thinking in terms of procedures; this includes the ability to break down tasks into their component parts. What is unique about this approach is that it presents a way of thinking, rather than knowledge or skills, as the basis of computer literacy.

• *Computer Literacy Instructional Modules* (CLIM). St. Paul, MN: Minnesota Educational Computing Consortium.

CLIM was also developed with funding from the National Science Foundation. The curriculum consists of 25 modules developed around the concept of the computer: its operation, how it works, and its applications. The modules were designed for science, mathematics, and social studies classes in secondary schools. Individualization has been built into the program so that many of the modules can be completed by students working alone. Many of the activities are computer-based. Computer science topics include introduction to micro-computers, operation of hardware, programming concepts, and word process-ing. Social studies modules include studies of computers in government, ethics and privacy, daily living, economics, crime, polls, and political science. The mathematics component includes modules on estimation, graphing, probability, prime numbers, and number systems. Science modules cover nutrition, mea-surement, microelectronics, modeling, classification, and simulations. In each module, students learn about the computer by using it with applications soft-ware or with programs that they write. However, the focus is on learning about the computer by using it rather than by programming it.

• Montana Task Force on Computer Education. (1983). *The elements of computer education: A complete program*. Helena, MT: Office of Public Instruction.

This publication is more like a curriculum guide than a curriculum; but at the same time it has a great deal of information of the kind that might be found in a computer literacy program. Thus it is very much what its title suggests: the elements of a computer literacy program. It includes survey sheets, checklists, planning guides, suggestions for staff development, lists of resources, and so on. What is significant about this publication is that (unlike the other programs listed here) it does not provide specific goals or objectives for students. The specifi-cation of the program is then left to the teacher or committee developing it.

THE COMPUTER LITERACY PROGRAM IN THE SCHOOL

Despite the lack of agreement on what computer literacy means and how it should be approached pedagogically, teachers are faced with the need to pro-vide computer literacy curricula for their students. Lack of clarity is a mixed blessing when it comes to designing a curriculum. On the one hand, without clear statements of goals, content, and sequence, the developer has consider-able freedom in designing the program and learning activities. On the other hand, lack of standardization can lead to problems in comparing the quantity and quality of training at different schools.

In the following sections, practical issues involved in providing a computer literacy program are discussed. We begin by looking at some elements that should be included in such a program, some decisions that must be made, and some facilities and equipment that will be required. Then we will turn to the training of teachers and staff that might be required to support a high-quality computer literacy program.

Curriculum

The factors to be considered in determining how a school will offer computer literacy to its students are much like those to be considered in other instructional computer implementations. Thus, many of the points made in Chapter 4 about getting started in educational computing apply equally well to setting up a computer literacy program. Specifically, determining needs and matching needs to existing systems are important in formulating goals and objectives for a curriculum. Decisions about resources and training should follow the determination of needs in the planning process.

Needs Assessment In Chapter 4, we noted that it is important to assess needs *before* determining the characteristics of a computer implementation. A needs assessment can reveal discrepancies between what is already available and what is needed. Any information that would serve to clarify needs can be used. For example, teachers', parents', and students' opinions might be surveyed; information on computer literacy can be reviewed; and existing computer literacy materials can be sampled. When this information is analyzed, expectations and needs can be compared with existing conditions. The discrepancies between what is and what ought to be can then be used as a basis for stating goals and objectives for the curriculum.

The Character of the Computer Literacy Curriculum Three aspects of a computer literacy curriculum seem to emerge as particularly important, on the basis of the current literature:

1 Integration into the school program
2 Grade level and age of the students
3 Curriculum content

Each of these is discussed below.

1 *Integration of computer literacy into the school program:* Many elementary and secondary school programs are devoted to traditional literacy. This includes the study of language arts, mathematics, science, and social studies. Although each of these subjects is taught separately from the others, they all have at least one goal in common: developing the ability to communicate and thus to participate in society. Reading and writing are certainly a part of mathematics, science, and social studies programs. Students must read textbooks and course material, write descriptions of their observations, and use language effectively to answer questions. Further, the logical and sequential reasoning fostered by science and mathematics studies is often encouraged in students' spoken and written work in other subjects. Thus, some integration of traditional school subjects already exists. A similar kind of integration would be desirable for computer literacy programs.

Placing computer literacy in the context of other school studies adds meaning to the subject. For example, integrating much of what a student needs to know about word processing with creative writing might enhance both kinds of studies. As the student becomes better at using word processing equipment, skill areas such as spelling, grammar, and vocabulary may also be improving, because of the editing features available in a good word processing program. Similar benefits can result from integrating programming exercises or problem-solving applications with science and mathematics activities. Design and use of simulations for science and social studies programs can stimulate students' thinking about how computers can be applied in those areas.[20]

2 *Grade and age level of the students:* It goes almost without saying that first- and second-grade students cannot be expected to learn the same material in the same ways as secondary school students or even older elementary school students. In addition to differences in reading ability, background experiences, general knowledge, and interests, younger students are generally not capable of working on one thing for long periods of time and cannot handle the same degree of complexity as older students. Therefore, the goals and objectives of computer literacy curricula should reflect the age of the students. For younger students, learning would be most effective when it deals with knowledge and practical activities. Secondary students are more capable of dealing with complex knowledge, comprehension of abstract concepts, and complex relationships and ideas. Younger students might be able to learn many of the major commands of the BASIC programming language or learn enough Logo to explore the behavior of a computer; but they could not be expected to produce programs that require complex structures or relationships.

3 *Curriculum content:* The contents of a schoolwide computer literacy curriculum should be flexible. All students should initially be exposed to a common core of objectives; but then they should be free to gain the kind of experience with computers that is suitable for them. The common core would consist of the fundamentals of computer operation, knowledge of component functions, and some historical, social, and ethical aspects of computer technology. This common core might be called *citizens' literacy.* The more specialized experiences with computers that students might pursue could be called *vocational literacy,* since they generally include experiences related to work or occupations.[21]

a *Citizens' literacy.* Citizen's literacy includes the kinds of knowledge that citizens in an information-based technological society will presumably need. Advanced learning experiences with computers can be based on the courses or programs in which the students are enrolled. It would also be beneficial if provision could be made for the students to pursue their own interests in computing.

Table 11.1 shows a possible outline for a core curriculum in citizens' literacy for grade levels K–12. It suggests major topics to be included and could be used in formulating goals and objectives for each grade level.

TABLE 11.1
SAMPLE OUTLINE FOR A CITIZENS' LITERACY CURRICULUM FOR ALL STUDENTS IN A SCHOOL DISTRICT

Topic	Grade level					
	K–2	3–4	5–6	7–8	9–10	11–12
Computer components	Knowledge of: Names of major components Definitions of hardware and software	K–2 Knowledge Functions of major components More components than K–2	Same as K–4, but more detail	Same as K–6 Knowledge of smaller internal components (RAM, CPU, ROM, interfaces)		
Operation of computers	Run computer with selected software Concept of giving machine commands Experimentation with Logo	Same as K–2 plus: Operation of computer for educational games, drill, simulation	Same as K–4 plus: Flow charting Entertainment software Personal applications (e.g., word processing)	Same as K–6 plus: Introduction to vocational applications Instruction in programming Binary codes	Same as K–8 plus: Programming languages Algorithms Applications programs	Same as K–10 plus: Advanced programming Assembler language Elective projects
Social and ethical studies		Applications for family use and home use	Impact of computers on world of work History of computing	Computers and personal privacy Computer security Jobs in computer field	Economics of computer technology Social interaction	Applications of artificial intelligence (AI) Robots at home Robots in the workplace
Evaluation and decision making			Comparison of different software packages to do the same application	Use of computers for various applications Problem-solving software packages Decision-making processes	Establishing criteria Comparing demands with capacities of computers	Criteria for software AI elective project

b *Vocational literacy.* Vocational literacy should emphasize technology in work settings. Specifically, the focus would be on functional knowledge and applications of computer technology in the work environment. This functional knowledge should be at a level compatible with the needs of a particular environment, and in coordination with other forms of knowledge and literacy. The kinds of training a college-bound student might require are included in this discussion.

Vocational computer literacy has six levels. Figure 11.3 shows these levels, and their inclusion in various grades. Each level is summarized below.

Level 1, the lowest level of vocational literacy, overlaps considerably (in terms of content) with citizens' literacy at the early elementary level. At level 1

FIGURE 11.3
Six levels of vocational computer literacy, to prepare people for working in a technological society.

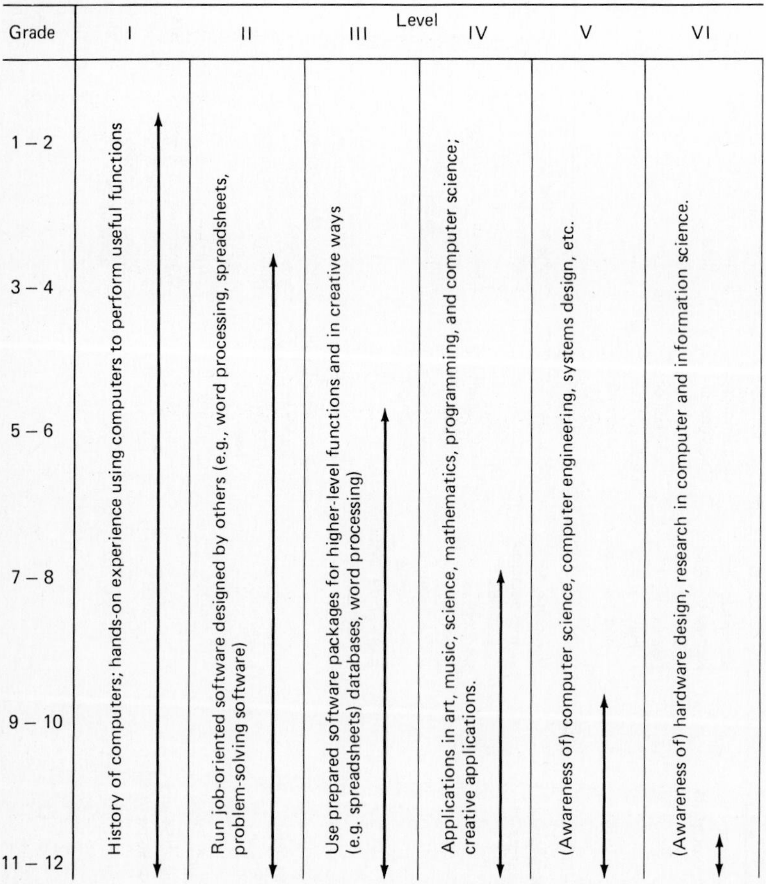

the student would learn something about the history of computers and gain some beginning-level hands-on experience in operating a computer to perform some useful functions.

At *level 2* the student learns to use job-oriented software designed by others (e.g., a computerized records system in the library, a computerized cash register with a bar code device).

At *level 3* prewritten software is used for higher-level applications (e.g., word processing, spreadsheets, problem solving). This can be done in the context of business courses or academic studies such as science, mathematics, and creative writing.

At *level 4* the student uses the computer as a tool for creating new solutions or products. This would relate to the kinds of applications found in fields such as engineering, architecture, art, and music. While students preparing for careers in such fields should have the opportunity to learn about the basics of this level in secondary school, more advanced work at this level will necessarily involve higher education.

People at *level 5* are computer professionals: data processing professionals who help others use computers to solve their problems and to meet various needs. For example, professional programmers, systems analysts, and computer technicians are found at this level. In elementary and secondary education, training at this level would primarily lead to awareness (e.g., of careers, functions, and roles).

People at *level 6* are engineers and scientists who design hardware and do research in computer-related science and technology. This is the highest level of sophistication. Training of students at level 6 would probably not be a regular, formal part of elementary or secondary education beyond basic awareness.

It is not expected that most citizens will need to go beyond level 4. Therefore, levels 5 and 6 are suggested only for awareness. For example, while students should be aware of the functions of a systems programmer, operations researcher, computer electronics engineer, etc., they cannot be expected to become expert in those areas before completing high school. Training in levels 5 and 6 would most likely take place in colleges, universities, and other post-secondary institutions and would be pursued by students interested in careers in these areas. There is some overlap between citizens' literacy and vocational literacy. The relationship between the two is shown in Figure 11.4 (page 286).

Resources

The resources needed for a computer literacy program are not necessarily more extensive than they would be for any computer-based instructional program. If a program is well integrated into the curriculum, many of the required resources may already be on hand. Although the special resources necessary for operation of a meaningful computer literacy program may not be extensive, some equip-

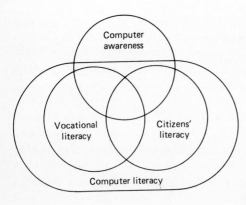

FIGURE 11.4
Relationship between computer literacy, computer awareness, citizens' literacy, and vocational literacy.

ment and facilities can be considered essential. The following sections discuss some of these essentials.

Hardware   Computer literacy involves looking at the computer as an object of study. If a school is to offer more than computer awareness to its students, enough computer equipment must be available to give students sufficient hands-on experience. The decision to provide such experience can entail a major investment for schools that are not already using instructional computers.[22] When students are using computers for problem solving or programming, they must have access to computers outside of regular classes. Providing access to computers after school or during free periods in the school day can require careful scheduling. But just as practice in reading and writing is a necessary part of becoming literate in the traditional sense, practice in operating a computer should be considered a necessary part of becoming computer-literate.

In addition to a sufficient number of computers, there should be enough different kinds of peripheral devices to acquaint students with a broad range of hardware. Young students will probably find enough to learn with small simple systems consisting of a computer, disk drive, monitor, and keyboard. A printer, game paddles, a cassette tape, and other common devices should be available when needed but would probably not be essential for every machine. Advanced students might need exposure to more sophisticated devices such as graphics tablets, modems and networking facilities, music or voice synthesizers, special interfaces for connecting computers to scientific equipment, and other devices. However, if a school has been using microcomputers in support of its instructional programs, most of the necessary equipment for offering students meaningful experiences will probably already be available.

Software   As with hardware, much of what is required for a good hands-on computer literacy program will probably be available if the school is already using instructional computers. However, as others have already noted,[23] much of the software for computer-assisted instruction (CAI), although useful in many instructional contexts, may not be suitable for computer literacy training. This is because CAI software usually implicitly communicates the idea that the computer controls the student (rather than that the student controls the computer). That is, when the student gives a correct answer, the computer *permits* the student to go on to new material. Even though the student may be gaining experience operating the computer with a CAI program, the didactic nature of much CAI does not put the student in control of the program.

Among the kinds of software which would be indispensible for a computer literacy curriculum and which might already be available are:

Word processing programs
Spreadsheet programs
Database management systems
Programming languages
Problem-solving and simulations packages for science, mathematics, and other academic subjects

Some software specifically designed for computer literacy would also be useful. For example, programs that show how a computer works or develop thought processes necessary for effective programming might be available.[24]

Other Resources In addition to the resources for general instructional computing already described (see Chapters 3, 4, 5, and 8), certain other resources would be especially valuable in a computer literacy program. These include space, library materials, and staff.

Space requirements and setting up the classroom have been discussed in Chapter 5, in the context of instructional computing. Most of this information would apply as well to implementation of a computer literacy curriculum.

Many of the periodicals, books, and other *library materials* that would be suitable for a computer literacy program were described in Chapter 8. Additional materials specifically oriented toward computer literacy are listed in the supplementary readings at the end of this chapter. The school librarian may be given responsibility for maintaining periodicals and books about computers for the computer literacy program; but other arrangements may be preferable, depending on local conditions. For example, computer literacy materials may be more conveniently kept in a resource room — or in the computer laboratory, if the school has one.

A *trained staff* is an important resource. Teachers and aides require training if they are to implement a computer literacy program successfully. Some of the kinds of training teachers might find beneficial are discussed in the next section. Administrators should also be trained to provide the necessary support for computer literacy programs in the school. In addition to knowing something about how computers are used in school administration, administrators will be in a better position to support computer literacy instruction if they understand the needs and goals of such a program. The supplementary readings listed at the end of this chapter include some material intended to enhance administrators' computer literacy.

In summary, the hardware, software, and other resources required for a comprehensive computer literacy curriculum would typically not be much more than those required for general instructional computing. Thus, a school that already has instructional computers available should be able to offer its students excellent experiences in computer literacy. But since computer literacy emphasizes that people are in control of computers, it should not be assumed that computer-assisted instruction will lead to computer literacy. Much CAI is designed to program the student to give correct responses; that is, it puts the computer in control.

Training of Teachers and Staff

As computers are woven further into the fabric of our society and its schools, training of teachers in computing will probably become more formal and widespread — with certification standards and semester-hour requirements like those now established for many other areas of education. Meanwhile, however, in the absence of established standards for training teachers to offer computer literacy instruction, it is natural to expect questions and debate about the nature of the training required.

Currently, most teachers in charge of computer literacy programs will have been trained in some area of education (e.g., elementary education, English, biology, chemistry, mathematics) but may have had little formal education in computing. The training that such teachers would require to offer effective computer literacy instruction includes:

General educational technology
History of computing
Social, ethical, and economic issues in technology
Programming languages and structured programming
Introduction to computer design and operation (e.g., central processing unit, binary numbers)
Data management techniques
Graphics applications
Operating experience with different kinds of computers
Futuristic studies in technology and its effects

It should be recognized that not all teachers need the same kind of training for teaching computer literacy. For example, computer literacy programs in elementary schools will be at a lower level than those in secondary school. Also, students in academic programs would need a computer literacy curriculum that focuses on problem solving, programming, and use of the computer in academic subjects; those in vocational programs should get more exposure to applications in workplaces such as offices and factories.

There are many ways for educators to obtain training in computer literacy. Taking college courses is only one of them. Teachers can become computer-literate through workshops, reading and self-directed study, and summer computer camps and institutes. Knowledge, skills, and understanding are important — not necessarily the ways in which training was provided. Many computer magazines and periodicals of professional organizations listed in Chapter 8 contain information about sources of training. Summer camps are often listed in early spring issues. Workshops to be offered by professional groups (such as the Association for Educational Data Systems and the American Educational Research Association) will be advertised in the publications of the organizations several months before the annual meeting. College catalogs can also be of assistance in locating suitable courses in computer literacy for teachers.

While teachers should not be expected to have an extensive background in computer science, their own computer literacy should exceed the level to which their students are being trained. That is, the teacher should be somewhat more knowledgeable than most students will be when they successfully complete the literacy program. Programming skills alone do not constitute computer literacy. Teachers should have broad knowledge of computers, so that they can discuss issues which may be raised by students in class. Further, a teacher who is well prepared to teach a subject will be more comfortable encouraging students to pursue their own interests in the field than a teacher who is not as well trained.

SUMMARY

With the inroads computer technology is making in all aspects of modern society, the need for basic computer literacy training in the schools is becoming more pronounced. *Computer literacy* is difficult to define. It can be related to definitions of traditional literacy which emphasize communication, comprehension, appreciation, and participation in society.

Computer literacy can be broken down into computer awareness and operational studies. Computer awareness includes social, ethical, economic, and historical issues. Operational literacy focuses on the practical aspects of programming and operating a computer. Some people argue that emphasis should be placed on using existing software packages for data processing and problem solving; others prefer to concentrate on actual programming of solutions.

Not every student needs the same kinds of experiences in a computer literacy program. A common core for all students would include studies of social and ethical issues, awareness of careers, and basic operational literacy. Training for vocational literacy would follow the core curriculum. Its purpose would be to prepare students for higher education or for vocational studies and careers. Vocational literacy studies would include using software packages, problem solving, and programming. Students would also learn about careers in computer technology (e.g., systems analyst, hardware programmer, and computer engineer).

Resources required for computer literacy courses are not generally much more extensive than those required for any instructional computing. The major additional needs will involve:

Giving students sufficient access to computer equipment during or after the school day, for practice

Having on hand software and reference materials designed specifically to support studying computers

Providing teachers with suitable training in computers

Computer literacy cannot replace traditional literacy. Students of the future will still need to learn, among other things, to read, write, and do basic mathematics. However, to participate in a technological society, they will also need to have knowledge, skills, and understanding of computer procedures and applications. The technological advances of the late 1970s and 1980s have produced a challenge to the schools. That challenge is to develop computer literacy in tomorrow's citizens to enable them to participate fully in a technological society.

NOTES

1 Green, M. (1982). Literacy for what? *Phi Delta Kappan, 63*(5), 326–329.
2 Varven, J. (1982). The schoolhouse Apple. *Softalk, 2*(10), 207–210.
3 Moursund, D. (1983). Computer literacy: Talking and doing. *The Computer Teacher, 10*(8), 3–4.
4 Deken, J. (1982). *The electronic cottage.* New York: Morrow.
5 The Print Project. (1980). *The techno/peasant survival manual.* New York: Bantam Books.
6 Luehrmann, A. (1983). Slicing through spaghetti code. *The Computing Teacher. 10*(8), 9–15.
7 Moursund, D. (1982). Personal computing for elementary and secondary school students. In Seidel, R., Anderson, R. E., & Hunter, B. (Eds.), *Computer literacy.* New York: Academic Press.
8 Hunter, B. (1983). *My students use computers: Comprehensive guide to computer literacy for the K-8 curriculum.* Reston, VA: Reston.
9 For example: Moursund, D. (1982). *Precollege computer literacy: A personal computing approach.* Eugene, OR: ICCE. Moursund cites the 1972 report of the Conference Board of the Mathematical Sciences Committee on Computer Education, *Recommendations regarding computers in high school education.* In addition, see: Johnson, D. C., Anderson, R. E., Hansen, T., & Klassen, D. L. (1980). *Mathematics Teacher,* 91–95. See also: National Science Foundation. (1979, July). *Technology in science education: The next ten years.* National Science Foundation. (1980, October). *Science and engineering education for the 1980s and beyond.*

10   Molnar, A. (1980). Understanding how to use machines to work smarter in an information society. *The Computing Teacher, 7*(5), 68–73.

11   For a discussion of this role, see: Molnar, A. (1982). Summary of the conference. In Seidel, R. J., Anderson, R. E., & Hunter, B. (Eds.), *Computer literacy*. New York, Academic Press.

12   Turner, J. A. (1983, June 22). "Discrete" math challenges calculus as computers alter students' needs. *Chronicle of Higher Education, 26*(17), 1, 6.

13   Hunter, B. (1980). *An approach to integrating computer literacy into the K–8 curriculum.* Unpublished paper. ERIC Doc. No. Ed 195247. Alexandria, VA: HumRRO.

14   For example, the Ad Hoc Committee on Basic Skills Education of Menlo Park, CA, sees the entry of microcomputers into the schools as an unnecessary distraction from the important business of schooling, according to its position paper of April 1982. However, this does not seem to be an opinion that enjoys wide support.

15   Luehrmann, A. (1981). Computer literacy—What should it be? *Mathematics Teacher, 74*(9), 682–686.

16   Anderson, R. E., Klassen, D. L., & Johnson, D. C. (1981). In defense of a comprehensive view of computer literacy—A reply to Luehrmann. *Mathematics Teacher, 74*(9), 687–690.

17   Papert, S. (1980). *Mindstorms: Children, computers, and powerful ideas.* New York: Basic Books.

18   Some examples of schools using Logo as a major component of computer literacy training are described in: Lemmons, P. (1982). Logo update. *BYTE, 7*(8), 334, 336–340.

19   Van Loan, C. F. (1980). Computer science and the liberal arts student. *Educational Forum, 45*(1), 29–42.

20   For example, the Minnesota Educational Computing Consortium has a set of simulations for giving elementary school students exposure to decision making in business. Students can study aspects of pricing, supply and demand, and other business concepts using the diskette the Market Place, which contains programs for selling apples, plants, bicycles, and lemonade. Another example might be an exercise in programming. Students in a mathematics class might be asked to solve an algebraic equation; or students in a science class might be assigned to draw a graph of weather data collected from the newspaper over a period of time.

21   The present discussion draws heavily from the report of a study supported by the Alaska Department of Education, entitled *Statewide computer literacy.* It was completed in January 1983.

22   Arthur Luehrmann has estimated the total cost of equipment for computer literacy for schools in the United States to be about $1 billion. See: Luerhmann, A. (1981). Computer literacy—What should it be? *Mathematics Teacher, 74*(9), 682.

23   See, for example: Taylor, R. (Ed.). (1980). *The computer in the school: Tutor, tool, tutee.* New York: Teachers College Press.

24   Existing programs that can be used for computer literacy training can be found in: Hunter, B. (1983). *My students use computers: Comprehensive guide to computer literacy for the K–8 curriculum.* Reston, VA: Reston. Guidance can also be obtained from software reviews, the Minnesota Educational Computing Consortium, computer periodicals, and other sources. Many of these resources are mentioned in Chapter 8.

SUPPLEMENTARY READINGS
AND COMPUTER LITERACY MATERIALS

The following list of readings has been compiled to assist in the preparation of elementary and secondary computer literacy programs. Readers are also encouraged to look at other references in the chapter, and at the reference notes.

Books

Abshire, G. M. (Ed.). (1980). *The impact of computers on society and ethics: A bibliography.* Morristown, NJ: Creative Computing.

Billings, K., & Moursund, D. (1979). *Are you computer literate?* Forest Grove, OR: Dilithium.

Burnett, J. D. (1982). *Logo: An introduction.* Morris Plains, NJ: Creative Computing.

Center for Learning Technologies. (1982). *Computer literacy: An introduction.* Report. Albany, NY: New York Department of Education.

Christie, L. G., & Curry, J. W. (1983). *ABC's of microcomputing.* Englewood Cliffs, NJ: Prentice-Hall.

Covvey, D., & McAlister, N. H. (1980). *Computer consciousness: Surviving the automated 80s.* Reading, MA: Addison-Wesley.

D'Ignazio, F. (1981). *The creative kid's guide to home computers.* Garden City, NY: Doubleday.

Gemignani, M. C. (1981). *Law and the computer.* Boston: CBI.

Goldstine, H. H. (1972). *The computer: From Pascal to von Neumann.* Princeton, NJ: Princeton University Press.

Hanson, D. (1982). *The new alchemists: Silicon Valley and the microelectronics revolution.* Boston: Little, Brown.

Heller, R., & Martin, C. D. (1982). *Bits 'n' bytes about computing: A computer literacy primer.* Rockville, MD: Computer Sciences.

Horn, C. E., & Poirot, J. L. (1981). *Computer literacy: Problem solving with computers.* Austin, TX: Sterling Swift.

Hyde, M. O. (1982). *Computers that think?* Hillside, NJ: Enslow.

Joiner, L. M., Vensel, G., Ross, J. D., & Silverstein, B. (1982). *Microcomputers in education.* Holms Beach, FL: Learning Publications.

Lawson, H. W. (1982). *Understanding computer systems.* Rockville, MD: Computer Sciences.

Moursund, D. (1981). *Introduction to computers in education for elementary and middle school teachers.* Eugene, OR: International Council for Computers in Education (ICCE).

Moursund, D. (1981). *School administrator's introduction to instructional use of computers.* Eugene, OR: ICCE.

Naisbitt, J. (1982). *Megatrends.* New York: Warner.

National Science Foundation and U.S. Department of Education. (1980). *Science and engineering education for the 1980s and beyond.* Washington, DC: Author.

Orwig, G. W. (1981). *The computer tutor: Learning activities for homes and schools.* Waltham, MA: Little, Brown.

Papert, S. (1980). *Mindstorms: Children, computers, and powerful ideas.* New York: Basic Books.

Rice, J., & Haley, M. (1981). *My computer dictionary*. Minneapolis, MN: Denison.

Rice, J., & O'Connor, S. (1981). *Computers are fun*. Minneapolis, MN: Denison. (This is written for young children, K–3, as a computer literacy text. It has a companion teacher's guide and an activity book.)

Richman, E. (1982). *Random House spotlight on computer literacy*. (With Teacher's Guide.) New York: Random House.

Rogers, J. (1981). *An introduction to computers and computing*. Eugene, OR: ICCE.

Seidel, R. J., Anderson, R. E., & Hunter, B. (Eds.). (1982). *Computer Literacy*. New York: Academic Press.

Taylor, R. (Ed.). (1980). *The computer in the school: Tutor, tool, tutee*. New York: Teachers College Press.

Watt, D. (1980). *Computer literacy: What schools should be doing*. Cambridge, MA: Artificial Intelligence Laboratory, M.I.T.

Multimedia Programs

Elementary computer literacy. (Kit.) (1982). Eau Claire, WI: National Business Institute. (Includes teacher's handbook, student's activity book, filmstrip, and cassette tape.)

Learning and teaching about computers. Project BEST: Association for Educational Communications and Technology, 1125 Sixteenth Street, N.W., Suite 214, Washington, DC. (Includes a 30-minute videotape produced by Project BEST, documenting the experiences of six American school districts in dealing with computer literacy, and a printed description of each of the districts.)

Microcomputers in education: A scholastic in-service training program. (Kit.) (1983). New York: Scholastic. [Includes a leader's guide, a participant's handbook, 277 35mm slides, and the magazine *Electronic Learning*. Basic tutorials and a computer literacy textbook are optional. The textbook is: Horn, C. E., & Poirot, J. L. (1981). *Computer literacy: Problem solving with computers*. Austin, TX: Sterling Swift.]

CHAPTER 12

THE FUTURE OF COMPUTERS IN EDUCATION

CHAPTER CONTENTS

Previous chapters presented the current status of computing in education; this chapter examines the future. Two major themes are woven into this final chapter. One is the idea that we are entering a new era, which has the potential to bring about social changes as great as those wrought by the industrial revolution. The second is that it is extremely important for educators to plan rationally for use of the new technologies. These technologies should be used to achieve redefined educational goals reflecting the changes that have taken place in society.

The chapter begins with a look at the development of educational computing and at some aspects of life in the information age. We then examine future trends in educational computers: hardware, software, and courseware. Finally, the changing character of schools in the information age is explored.

FOUR PHASES OF EDUCATIONAL COMPUTING

The mid-1980s might be considered part of the second phase of educational computing in the United States.

The *first phase* can be called the *experimental* phase. It began in the early 1960s when a small number of university educators were starting to explore computer-aided (or computer-assisted) instruction (CAI) on large mainframe computers. High costs, primitive software, and cumbersome equipment limited the adoption of computer-assisted instruction during this first phase.

The *second phase* can be characterized by the *popularization* of educational computing. It began in the late 1970s. During this phase, the first generation of commercially produced microcomputers were introduced, and the computer came to be popularly accepted as an educational tool. The early microcomputers in this second phase were designed for computer hobbyists and had relatively small memory and storage capacity, but they were relatively inexpensive in terms of what they could do. The courseware of the second phase was dominated by single-lesson packages, much of it drill and practice of dubious quality. However, the potential of the microcomputer has seemed obvious, even from the available applications, so that educators have remained enthusiastic and accepting during this phase.

The *third phase* of educational computing, which we will call the *transition* phase, begins in the mid-1980s, as educators are becoming increasingly computer-literate and are applying more critical standards to hardware and software designed for education. The trivial educational uses which characterized the second phase are giving way to high-level instructional applications. Networking systems that run large, integrated software packages are becoming more widely used in schools and school districts. The introduction of small, inexpensive, portable computers with large memories increases the possibility of bringing educational computing to each student in school and at home. Also, universities are starting to offer more work in educational computing as a part of teacher training programs, and educational computing is beginning to be recognized as a new educational specialty. During the third phase of educational computing, microcomputers are beginning to be used to perform educational tasks which were impossible in the past.

The *fourth phase,* which we shall call the *infusion* phase, will probably begin around the turn of the century. By this time the computer will no longer be a supplemental tool but will have become an integral part of educational procedures. In the fourth phase, most common machines (automobiles, washing machines, printing presses, etc.) will be equipped with more sophisticated microprocessors and electronic memory devices to perform various operational and control functions for the user. The increased utilization of advanced hardware and software systems will surely have an important influence on the content and methods of education; and technological awareness will be crucial for the average citizen.

The four phases are listed in Table 12.1. (The dates in Table 12.1 should be considered approximate.) In thinking about phases of educational computing, we must remember that local situations can influence developments significantly. For example, many school systems are only now entering the popularization phase, while others are well into the transition phase. Such differences between school systems can be attributed to availability of funds, awareness of technology, and community interest, among other factors. As we noted earlier, much of educational computing to date falls into phase 2. Recent changes in hardware, software, social attitudes, and public awareness affect what happens in phase 3, the transition phase. Educators, and particularly educational planners, should therefore have a perspective on the transition phase as society, along with education, moves toward the information age.

ASPECTS OF THE INFORMATION AGE

There is no doubt that society is undergoing fundamental transformations as a result of rapid technological advances. The meaning or impact of these changes is more a matter of speculation than of precise knowledge at present. Although some of the changes appear to be fundamental, their effects often seem more subtle. This new era has been given many names, among them the *global economy,* the *electronic era,* and the *third wave.*[1] We will call it the *information age.*

Although American education must adjust to this new era and prepare young people to live and work in the society of the future, the means to do this are not at all clear.[2] Before deciding how education should adapt to meet the challenges of the new era, it would be a good idea to step back and consider the transformations taking place within society. The following sections look at how nations are starting to relate to each other economically, how the world of work will change, and how education will develop in the information age.

TABLE 12.1
THE FOUR PHASES OF EDUCATIONAL COMPUTING

Phase 1: Experimentation 1960–1976	CAI research and demonstration projects; results are inconclusive. Methods and terminology are developed.
	Time-sharing CAI systems are developed using large computers and remote terminals. High operating costs prevent widespread adoption.
Phase 2: Popularization 1977–1985	Inexpensive computers are introduced. Public education enthusiastically adopts the computer.
	Courseware packages lack scope. Low-level drill and practice prevails. Quality is marginal. Major publishers refrain from entering the software market.
	Teacher training consists mainly of in-service workshops.
Phase 3: Transition 1985–2000	Computer systems become available that are designed to be used on a school-building level.
	Major publishers increase their involvement in the courseware market. Large-scale courseware packages with management systems become available.
	Preservice training programs become available. Educational computing is recognized as a new discipline. Advanced degree programs are developed.
	Educational networks are widely used, and the dynabook is introduced.
	Computers change teaching techniques and redefine the curriculum.
Phase 4: Infusion 2001–?	The computer becomes an integral part of the curriculum.
	Most machines are equipped with microcircuitry and memory.
	Mental training expands students' achievement. Artificial intelligence programs are widely used in education.
	Brain-wave input is introduced.
	An English-language operating system is developed.

The Economy

Before World War II, the foreign policy of the United States tended to be isolationist. Its geographical separation from Europe and its abundant resources seemed to justify isolationism; moreover, relatively few American jobs depended on foreign trade (as late as 1950, foreign trade accounted for only 2 percent of the gross national product).[3] The American educational system reflected this insular heritage; for example, foreign-language studies were not widely encouraged in the public schools. The major thrust of the public education system was to provide at least the skills deemed appropriate for survival in American society.

Today, ideas of what society needs from its schools are no longer determined by the politics of economic plenty and isolation. During the 1970s, the fuel crisis and the inability of many American products to compete on the world market taught the United States that it could no longer rely on its own resources and ignore what the rest of the world was doing. In addition, economic relationships between nations have become more complex. Nations rely on each other for raw materials, manufactured goods, technical skills, and financing. To take a more active role in life, citizens today must be educated to take a world perspective. Education is beginning to be seen as a necessity for national economic survival.[4]

The World of Work

Two fundamental changes are presently under way in the workplace. The first has to do with what *types of jobs* exist in the economy. The rapid spread of high technology in industry and business is causing economic displacement among workers. Many jobs, especially in heavy industry, are now being done by machines and robots. At the same time, entirely new jobs are being created by technology, such as industrial robot designer, builder, and programmer. The second change has to do with the *way we work*. New styles of working seem to be emerging, such as flexible time scheduling, working at home, job sharing, and working on production teams.

Advances in technology have made the future of industrial employment uncertain. It has been estimated that General Motors alone will install 20,000 robots which could displace 40,000 to 50,000 workers in the next 10 years.[5] Projections for other industries are similar. Robotics are not a matter of choice: American industry must either adopt robotics or lose markets to foreign competition because of inability to compete in terms of quality or price.

Technology is also beginning to cause economic dislocation in white-collar work. Computers are commonly used in libraries, offices, hospitals, and businesses of all sorts for much clerical work that was previously done by hand: indexing, filing, billing, retrieving data, and so on. Even in the more skilled professions, computers are beginning to be used; for example, expert systems have been developed that can provide sophisticated consulting services entirely by computer.[6]

Rapid introduction of new technology can cause economic dislocation for millions of workers. The situation today may be analogous to the displacement of workers by the introduction of power looms in the English textile industry during the early days of the industrial revolution.

On the other hand, technological advances can bring some good news for workers: technology is a marvelous creator of entirely new kinds of jobs. The new field of artificial intelligence provides an example. *Artificial intelligence* refers to design of machines to function intelligently — that is, to respond to the environment, adapt, and solve problems, using a knowledge base and logical procedures analogous to human thought. There are artificial intelligence programs that play chess and other games; and some sophisticated programs have been developed for industrial and professional applications. (For example, one artificial intelligence program, PROSPECTOR, asks questions about the geology of a region and predicts where valuable minerals are most likely to be found. This program has been used successfully to accurately locate valuable mineral deposits.[7]) Business, industry, government, and a variety of professions will eventually rely heavily on artificial intelligence programs to make decisions. These programs will mean that fewer workers will be needed in many technical fields; but at the same time a new industry will be built around the development, programming, and use of artificial intelligence programs. Furthermore, the output of artificial intelligence programs will result in many new jobs: geology programs which locate minerals may result in mining activity; medical and scientific programs may create new areas for research, development, and clinical services.

Education: Changing Roles

Education will be an extremely important part of any plan to meet future demands for personnel. The displaced workers of the industrial revolution were uneducated or poorly educated, had little understanding of the economic forces acting on them, and had no hope of being retrained. By contrast, the modern educational system should be able to produce enlightened citizens who think of learning as a lifelong experience and recognize the need for continuous upgrading of training and learning of new skills to respond to changing technology.

Thus, there is a distinct possibility that education will emerge as a vital part of the new society. For this to happen, however, the education profession must rethink many of its goals and methods. It must advance from the role of a system serving the industrial age to that of one serving the information age. Table 12.2 suggests some contrasts that can be drawn between the two roles.

The decision to use computers in education as an object of study and as a way to deliver instruction has placed educators on the path to the information age. As the third phase of educational computing continues, the computer will permanently alter the methods and content of education. This process of alteration will take place in several ways. Changes will take place in textbooks and how they are used. The role of computers in the curriculum will also change. Further, ideas of basic skills will begin to include fundamental concepts in using

TABLE 12.2
EDUCATION IN THE INDUSTRIAL AGE AND INFORMATION AGE

Industrial age	Information age
1 Promotes uniformity while stressing self-reliance.	1 Promotes individual variation while stressing a more collective responsibility.
2 Defines the *core* of education as knowledge of a set of basic mathematics and communication skills necessary for minimal economic survival in an industrial society.	2 Stresses training of the mind in high-level cognitive skills and acquisition of knowledge. The term *to know* is redefined to include being able to locate facts, interrelate data, and evaluate.
3 Education is primarily for individual benefit.	3 Education is a national economic imperative.
4 Insular in outlook.	4 Stresses a global perspective.
5 Promotes linear, sequential thinking.	5 Promotes nonlinear, multidimensional thought.
6 Textbook-oriented.	6 Multimedia, experiential approaches to education.
7 Promotes rigid hierarchies among students and staff in schools.	7 Hierarchical relationships are deemphasized.
8 The teacher is the purveyor of knowledge.	8 The teacher is a resource manager and guide.
9 The teacher tends to deal with people in groups and categories.	9 The teacher deals with group and individual characteristics and needs.
10 Views the outcome of education as a set of knowledge. The school is conceived of in industrial terms as the production center for a product that can be measured with standardized tests.	10 Views the outcomes of education as a process. The results of education are indirectly observed and inferred.
11 Education terminates at graduation.	11 Education is a lifelong experience.
12 Education creates individual and social mobility.	12 Education creates national wealth.

technology. Finally, learning as a lifelong endeavor and training in thinking and reasoning will receive greater emphasis. We now consider each of these points in more detail.

Textbooks and Other Media It has been observed that a large proportion of the time teachers and students spend in the classroom is structured around printed instructional material. Several reasons for this have been suggested. First, some teachers are not well prepared to teach certain subjects and consequently rely heavily on texts. Second, many teachers believe that texts are based on scientific principles and research. Third, school administrators may expect teachers to rely heavily on texts and other printed materials.[8] There may, of course, be other reasons; but whatever the reasons, most teachers appear to act — and to have been trained — as textbook technicians. Textbooks have been, and probably will continue to be, important teaching tools; but teachers in the information age should be more flexible about how they present material. They should be able to adapt the curriculum to meet students' needs.

One possible benefit of educational computing might be to make the concept of alternative instructional media more acceptable to teachers. As educational courseware becomes more sophisticated and computers become more powerful and versatile, properly trained teachers will be able to draw upon this powerful instructional instrument. The technology may encourage educators to become more adept at selecting alternative instructional devices; and teachers may begin to recognize that the textbook is only one of many ways to present instruction. Further, they may become more attuned to the practical value of the idea that the proper way to present instruction is the way which produces the best learning.

The Curriculum and the Computer   There may be a gradual rethinking of many assumptions about curriculum as a consequence of use of computers in education. In any instructional program, the medium of delivery and the content have a dynamic relationship; they are not separate entities. As the third phase of educational computing progresses, pressure for redefinition of the curriculum will be created by situations outside the educational community, such as the need for technological sophistication in the work force. And as teachers become more experienced in using computers for group and individual instruction, certain long-held assumptions will probably come into question — such as the age at which certain things should be learned and the sequencing of objectives in a curriculum. As students naturally raise questions and explore the environment, possibilities of alternative sequences and patterns of instruction will emerge.

To gain another perspective on how computers will change the curriculum, consider the teaching of penmanship. Two hundred years ago, many teachers specialized in this manual art. Legal documents, bills of sale, and business correspondence were all written by hand; and neat, clear penmanship was vital to the economy. A good "hand" could win an aspiring clerk a position. However, as the industrial age produced machines to prepare legal documents, bills of sale, and correspondence, the importance of penmanship declined. Today, children are still taught handwriting and penmanship, but with far less emphasis than was given in the past. We have come to rely on mechanical means to produce most of our important written communications.

The same principle applies to mathematics and other areas of the curriculum during the transformation from the industrial age to the information age. For example, many mathematics teachers argue that calculators make it appropriate to shift the emphasis of mathematics instruction from accuracy in mathematical operations to understanding of mathematical procedures.

As education shifts gears to meet a new set of conditions imposed by the needs of society, teachers are being asked to leave behind the ways they were taught. This will probably not be an easy thing for teachers (or for training institutions) to do.

Redefinition of Basic Skills   Another consequence of using instructional computers may be a redefinition of basic skills. The traditional basic skills — reading, writing, and arithmetic — are already undergoing reconceptualization, and the notion of basic literacy in computing is being proposed.[9] As we discussed in Chapter 11, there is some debate about what constitutes computer literacy; but most definitions include operational skill with a computer, ability to use a computer to solve problems, and knowledge of the kinds of procedures a computer performs. Further, integrating computer studies with science, mathematics, language arts, social studies, and other academic subjects may lead to new ways to explore and understand those subjects.

In fact, the idea of education in basic skills may itself become obsolete in the future. It has been suggested that the meaning of the verb *to know* has already changed: it once meant, essentially, to have information memorized; it is coming to mean being able to gain access to information.[10] The ability to find information, interrelate facts, and evaluate the relative significance of different items of information may become far more important than committing facts to memory. However, the "three R's" (reading, 'riting, and 'rithmetic) will probably not go out of style; they will remain prerequisites for this higher level of knowing.

Lifelong Learning   The total accumulation of human knowledge is increasing geometrically. No one person can be fully knowledgeable in even one discipline; there is simply too much to learn. Moreover, what a person has to know to function within a discipline is changing rapidly. Consequently, a commitment to lifelong learning is developing within many professions. (For example, without ongoing training, electrical engineers will find that their skills become out of date in less than a decade; and certainly no one would want to be treated by a doctor whose expertise is 15 years behind the times.) Fortunately, the same technology that is responsible for the fast pace of change also makes lifelong learning more feasible. Computer networks are already in existence that can help professionals keep abreast of new developments in their field. (One of the most successful is located at the Magnetic Fusion Energy Computer Center at the Lawrence Livermore National Laboratory. The center allows researchers in fusion energy to communicate with Livermore through 13 service centers across the United States.[11]) Computer networks allow professionals to keep in touch with each other, share results rapidly, and receive immediate consultations.

If lifelong education is to become a reality, education must be recognized as an infinite and continuous process. In the past, graduating from school gave one a sense of completion of studies and the beginning of work. In the future, a degree or diploma will be considered a license to begin lifelong professionally or vocationally oriented studies.[12]

The Training of the Mind   In the rush to fill each student's mind with basic facts and skills, the importance of learning to reason and think tends to be overlooked. Teachers are conditioned to think in industrial terms: their product tends to be a fact committed to memory, a concept learned, or a behavior mastered. Teacher training institutions have tended to foster the teacher's role as a purveyor of knowledge. In the future, as the dynamic nature of knowledge is recognized, mental training will probably become as important as other kinds of training. The industrial age has not demanded a high level of intellectual performance from many citizens. This will not be true of the information age.

COMING CHANGES IN EDUCATIONAL COMPUTERS

The immediate future will bring rapid advances in educational computers and computing. In this section, current trends are projected into the future. Technological improvements which are at present in the design or development stages are noted; these form the basis for speculations about forthcoming innovations. Further, the impact of these changes is considered in each case.

Microcomputer Hardware

Microcomputers in education will generally become more specialized in the future. Microprocessors and memory will be built into other devices and programmed to produce "smart" machines capable of recognizing changing conditions and adapting their functions accordingly. The videodisk will be merged with the microcomputer to create a programmable, intelligent videodisk machine, capable of complex interaction with a student. Input-output technology will probably change considerably in the years to come. Voice input devices are currently under development. Voice output is currently available, but prices are rather high for routine use in schools. In addition, some changes in the physical appearance of microcomputers can be expected in the third phase of educational computing. For example, innovations in robotics, screen displays, and memory storage devices can be expected; these will affect the way computers are packaged.

Many of the innovations in hardware can be expected to have particular impact on the education of handicapped persons. Figure 12.1, for instance, shows a prosthetic limb that operates on signals from the brain and uses microprocessor technology to assist the wearer in controlling it. Such devices should make education more accessible and remove some of the obstacles to providing education for the handicapped. Other kinds of prosthetic devices — devices that hear, see, speak, or even think — are becoming possible for the future.

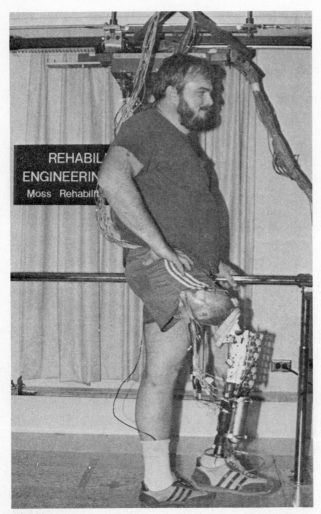

FIGURE 12.1
Microprocessor-controlled artificial limb. (*Courtesy of Professor Gordon Moskowitz, Drexel University.*)

Storage

Microcomputer storage capacity is increasing dramatically as the third phase of educational computing progresses. The standard 5¼-inch disk will be displaced by new recording techniques that will increase storage capacity by as much as a factor of ten.[13] In addition, development of several new kinds of storage devices is probable.[14] Soon microcomputer systems that exceed the storage capacities of many mainframe systems which were available only a few years ago will become economically feasible for schools.

Visual Displays

Screen resolution of microcomputer CRT displays will increase. High-resolution graphics and text display will improve dramatically, to the point where CRT displays will appear as clear as high-quality photographs. Screen technology will allow a flatter design for microcomputers, so that they will be more portable and compact.

Schoolwide Networking

The third phase of educational computing will probably see the proliferation of computer networks within school buildings and school districts. These computer networks will probably be connected to terminals in classrooms and offices and will possess enough storage capacity for an exchange of information between various functions within a school. Networking systems are now available (and have been for several years); but they have not been widely accepted, because of their cost and the greater appeal of general-purpose microcomputers. A major factor in the increased use of networking will be the introduction of large courseware packages. Initially, many schools will probably locate their terminals in computer labs. Later, it will become more usual to place the terminals in classrooms.

The single microcomputer will continue to dominate educational computing; but the use of larger systems will have a profound influence on its future. Eventually, a merging of microcomputers and larger educational computer systems is to be expected. Students will be able to download assignments from a school's large educational computer to their own microcomputers. They will then be able to work on assignments at home and upload completed assignments to the main computer the next morning for the teacher (or a properly programmed computer) to evaluate and grade.

Costs

The price of a computer is determined more by developmental costs than by production costs. Many manufacturers invest substantial amounts of money in designing and testing, as well as producing, their machines. After a sufficient number of machines of a particular model have been sold to pay off the development costs, the manufacturer may choose to lower the price. Sales volume is another factor that affects price. Higher sales volume frequently brings about lower costs.

Also, older models of microcomputers are often discounted when new models are introduced. Many of these older models will be entirely capable of handling a school's computer needs if the necessary software and maintenance services are available. Schools may therefore see these machines as a cost-effective way to expand their computing capacity. However, it should be recognized that newer machines will have more capabilities.

The fast pace of technological development produces another type of price reduction: manufacturers may introduce improvements in an existing product without increasing its price. When more memory, improved input devices, or other enhancements become available at no added cost, that is really a form of price reduction.

Courseware: A Change in Emphasis

As more sophisticated and specialized hardware is developed, new forms of courseware will appear in the educational market. Courseware of the second phase of educational computing tends to have the following characteristics:

Single-application packages dominate. The teacher has had to fit courseware into the learning sequence on a case-by-case basis. The difficulty of managing and using these small courseware packages has been one of the factors inhibiting the effective use of educational microcomputers.

Most software takes the drill and practice approach. While drill and practice has its place, it is limited in the kinds of learning it fosters, and it does not fully utilize the capabilities of the computer.

Small companies have produced most of the software. Quality has varied from excellent to unusable, and has often been disappointing.

Many software packages have been difficult for new users to operate. This has been especially true for management and utility software. In many cases, documentation has been poorly written and difficult to understand.

With the coming of the third phase of educational computing, economic forces will dictate many changes in courseware and in the market for it. Larger companies with more resources to invest in development are already beginning to enter the courseware business. Educators are becoming more sophisticated in their judgments about courseware and are beginning to expect better quality.

Some developments in courseware that might become part of the third phase of educational computing are listed below:

Full-course instructional packages will become available as major publishing companies and hardware manufacturers enter the courseware market. As of the mid-1980s, software to accompany full-course textbooks had begun to appear. The next major step will probably be for large courseware packages to become available for general-purpose microcomputers and multiterminal systems.

The quality of courseware will improve. There will be much less emphasis on drill and practice. More software for tutoring simulations, demonstrations, and other kinds of instruction will become available. The larger courseware packages will include learning management systems which allow the teacher to monitor progress and alter lessons on the basis of individual students' progress and learning styles.

Utility and management software will become more user-friendly. Most utility programs will be menu-driven. Documentation will be easier to understand, will "forgive" errors, and will help the user to correct errors.

More courseware will be developed that can be run on several different brands of microcomputers. The industry will probably not adopt a standardized operating system for the educational market in the foreseeable future; but there is already a discernable trend toward more standardization and portability of programs.[15] This means that a program written for one brand of microcomputer or operating system may in the future be compatible with several other microcomputers or systems.

Other changes in courseware are also inevitable during the third phase of educational computing. For example, more emphasis on problem-solving activities in instructional packages is expected. Educators and courseware developers will also probably begin to recognize ways that computers can change the content and sequence of education. Use of computers will lead to the development of instructional strategies which may challenge many of our traditional assumptions and practices. (The next section of this chapter describes the views of some people who have written about these challenges to society and education.)

COMING CHANGES IN EDUCATION

What Do the Futurists Say about Education?

Recent years have seen a great deal of futuristic literature. This section presents a sampling of what several futurists have predicted for education.

Christopher Evans   Christopher Evans (who died in 1979) was a psychologist and computer scientist. In his book *The Micro-Millenium,* Evans said that he expected educational computing to be inhibited by the inexactness of education as a science, by its tendency to emphasize drill and practice, and by the unwillingness of producers to develop large-scale courseware packages of high quality (such packages do not initially yield large profits). However, Evans predicted the development of a small portable educational computer which students could carry around with them, and with which they could do much of their schoolwork. He also predicted that future teaching computers would be capable of complex interaction with students. Evans expected that a true science of education would begin to emerge by the middle to late 1980s and would be based on research in how people think and learn.[16]

Alvin Toffler   The publication of *Future Shock* in 1970 established Alvin Toffler as one of the leading futurist writers in the United States. *The Third Wave,* published 10 years later, is a further examination of the future. Toffler's premise is that a powerful tide is now surging across the world; this is what he means by the *third wave*. The first wave was the agricultural revolution which began 10,000 years ago. The second wave was the industrial revolution. The third wave is the arrival of the supertechnological age.

Toffler predicts that the basic raw material of the third wave will be information. The mass media will be restructured to provide the enormous flow of information necessary to sustain society. Parents will take a larger role in the education of children and will have more influence on the schools. More learning will occur outside the classroom. Compulsory education will become more condensed; but education in general will become a lifelong process. Toffler believes that educators need to devote more time to exploring the changing structure of society.[17]

Seymour Papert Seymour Papert is internationally known for his work in the development of the Logo programming language. He was a student of the child development researcher Jean Piaget and a professor at the Massachusetts Institute of Technology. Papert has been an outspoken proponent of natural teaching methods which utilize computers. In his book *Mindstorms,* Papert describes children as builders of their own intellectual structures.[18] He describes the computer as a powerful means of giving students symbolic objects with which to think. He argues against using the computer to program the child; rather, he says that the child should be in control, programming the computer.

Papert has offered many provocative thoughts on education and educational computing. Many of his views have been discussed elsewhere in this book (see, for example, Chapters 9 and 11).

Alfred Bork As director of the Educational Technology Center at the University of California, Irvine, Alfred Bork has been in the forefront of the computer revolution. He believes that the ultimate value of the computer will depend on whether educators can develop a clear view of what education should be. He believes that the next 20 years will be among the most exciting in the history of education.

Bork maintains that institutions of higher learning have not contributed significantly to the development of computer learning materials. On the far horizon, he sees education making use of developments in artificial intelligence and long-distance learning. He predicts that educational computers of the future will have increased capabilities, including voice input, voice output, and even brain-wave input.[19]

Schools in the Information Age

How will schools actually appear in the information age? On the surface they probably will look much as they do now and much as they have looked for a long time. One obvious difference will be the presence of many computers and terminals in the schools. However, the important differences will be subtle ones, such as a focus on new patterns of thinking, new ways of conceptualizing curriculum, and the idea of lifelong learning.

The following examples were developed to illustrate how three different kinds of educational settings might look after the third, or transition phase, of educational computing has progressed further. Each example is set in the mid-1990s.

• *Example 1 — A rural high school:* A small isolated Alaskan community survives the perils of wind and weather on the northwestern seacoast. It occupies several acres of flatland near the mouth of a small river. Most of the buildings are single-family dwellings. The school building stands out from the others because of its size (see Figure 12.2). The nearest town is nearly 50 miles down the coast, but there are no connecting roads.

Twenty-three students attend the high school, which has a staff of three full-time teachers and one aide. Despite its size, the school offers a complete academic and vocational education program, and the range of subjects available to

FIGURE 12.2
The rural school of the information age does not appear very different from its predecessors.

the students is fairly complete. There are three main rooms — one for vocational education, one a regular classroom, and the last a large multipurpose room. The large room is used as an academic classroom and as a gymnasium for physical education, sports events, and community activities. The appearance of the school has not changed since the building was constructed in 1975.

At any given time, students are engaged in a variety of learning activities throughout the building. One student works vigorously at a microcomputer console on an ancient history lesson. Suddenly he sits back in his chair as a documentary about early Egyptian architecture is shown on the CRT screen. At precisely the right point in the student's studies, the computer automatically connects to a film library by a telephone and satellite communication system, and informs the larger computer to send the program. The classroom instructional computing system has several videodisks connected to it and can make a variety of similar programs available to students. However, the program on Egyptian architecture was a special request from the student and was not available in the classroom.

Another student is using a word processor to prepare an article she hopes to submit to the regional newspaper. When she is finished writing the article, it will be sent directly to the newspaper over the telephone. The newspaper regularly gets news articles from people in the community, submitted over its telephone system into its computer.

Two boys are working on a simulation of a chemistry experiment with the assistance of a microcomputer connected to a videodisk machine. The students actually set up their apparatus on the computer's CRT screen. They then "run" the experiment — providing chemical reagents and controlling heat and other conditions — just as if the experiment were really being done in the classroom. They can change conditions and observe the results. This kind of simulation permits students to perform laboratory studies that previously could have been done only in large well-equipped laboratories.

Although there are no foreign-language teachers in the school, several students are able to study Japanese, German, Russian, or French by communicating with a language-media laboratory in a distant city. Long-distance language instruction is accomplished by means of presentations on the state's educational telecommunications satellite network, printed workbooks and texts, cassette audiotapes, computer activities, and regularly scheduled telephone conversations with a foreign-language teacher.

Many students in the room are engaged in traditional classroom activities such as reading, writing in workbooks, and studying. The traditional forms of literacy will continue to be important for functioning in modern society. Thus, the changes in the rural classroom have to do primarily with how education is delivered. Modern technology will increase the efficiency of education and expand the scope and depth of the curriculum.

• *Example 2 — An urban elementary school:* At first glance, a sixth-grade classroom in this urban school of more than 600 students looks much like any traditional classroom — with chalkboards, geography charts, students' desks arranged in clusters, and so on. However, much of the students' work is done on word processors and computers of various kinds. For example, special graphics software, graphics tablets, and multicolor printers are used in art classes to study concepts in design, form, structure, and symmetry much more systematically than ever before. This kind of equipment is also applied in mathematics and science, enabling students to "see" relationships that once could only be talked about.

Each desk in the classroom has a small plug-in jack for headphones and a microcomputer. Each study carrel in the back of the room houses a large monitor with several controls. The teacher's desk is equipped with a small flat screen and a microcomputer. A detachable keyboard fits into a recess in the desk. A mass storage device for recording data on management of students' progress is mounted in a drawer in the teacher's desk.

Once a week, a music teacher comes to the class to work with the children on their synthesizers. The children learn music appreciation and elementary composition. In the course of a class session, the music teacher works briefly with each student and downloads exercises for the students to work on during the week. The synthesizer is used similarly by the speech teacher and the reading teachers during their visits to the class to work with selected children.

Students do much of their work with a small device, about the size of a textbook, called a *dynabook*.[20] This device consists of a small screen, a keyboard, output ports, and several hundred kilobytes of long-term memory storage. (See Figure 12.3.) With this device, a number of input techniques can be used, includ-

FIGURE 12.3
Student working with a dynabook
connected to a computer terminal.

ing a pencil-like instrument that writes on the CRT screen, a small hand-held box with wheels on the bottom (called a *mouse*), and voice-recognition devices that can interpret spoken language and convert it into symbols a computer can recognize. The student is able to store large amounts of data in the dynabook. This data might be collected from electronic databases, or it might consist of drawings, essays, and other work the student has done on computers in the classroom. Further, the student can access the library, the audiovisual center, and other services within the school with the dynabook.[21]

Being a teacher in this kind of classroom requires a high level of sophistication in the technology of teaching. This includes knowledge of how to blend learning and instructional research with individual, small-group, and large-group instructional methods. In addition, familiarity with modern computerized education is necessary. Consequently, certification requirements are more demanding, and teachers need to know more than they ever did before. However, this additional knowledge increases the teacher's effectiveness.

- *Example 3 — Teacher training at a state university:* At this state university, five years of training are required for students who will become high school mathematics teachers. During the first few days at the university, each new student is issued a personal computer and a portable printer. The personal computer has a full keyboard and an 8-inch CRT screen that folds flat against the top of the cabinet when the computer is not being used. A condensor microphone and a voice synthesizer allow vocal interaction with the unit. The device is equipped with over 20 megabytes of long-term memory and a 32-bit microprocessor, giving it the power of a mainframe computer of less than 20 years earlier.

Orientation at the university helps first-year students to make good use of their computers by acquainting them with the various information networks they can access from almost anywhere on the campus. The services from the resource networks are extensive. For example, students can perform information searches from their dormitory rooms and download the information into their own computers. Hundreds of tutorial programs are available, and assignments can be transmitted to instructors through the networks.

Students can use their computers as word processors, information access and storage devices, personal notebooks, and tutors. In a science laboratory, the computer becomes an electronic lab book in which sophisticated drawings of experiments can be made and results can be quantified and analyzed statistically.

Students who need assistance with their studies can enter the local network and request either a tutorial program or help from another student. The local network also provides students with a chance to meet other students who may have similar interests. Students in each academic area must become thoroughly familiar with the appropriate networks for their specialties. Education students must learn about EDU/CAT-NET because they will use it extensively when they become teachers. EDU/CAT-NET is the national educational database. It contains information about teaching by subject area, research on learning and child development, instructional theory, school law, school administration, sites where novel programs are being tried, and other matters related to education.

In addition to learning about computers and their academic specialty areas, students in education study the technology of teaching to a greater degree than their predecessors did in earlier generations. Included in their studies are topics such as how students learn different kinds of material, how to foster thinking, how to impart reasoning and problem-solving skills, how to manage group and individual instruction, and how to integrate diverse instructional strategies and media into an educational program. Teacher training is oriented toward a dynamic concept of knowledge in which education is seen as a lifelong process. The teacher training program emphasizes skills in instructional design and the structure and organization of instruction, so that teachers can be flexible in modifying and applying a curriculum in the classroom.

Although our three examples are set in the 1990s, most of the hardware described exists or is being developed now. High-technology educational delivery systems are bringing new opportunities to all students. Small hand-held educational computers, the precursors of the *dynabook,* are currently under development. Many universities are giving their students access to a variety of computer networks.[22] The home will play a more active role in education in the information age, partially because so much can be done at home with small hand-held computers that interact with networks and databases. The lifelong continuing education of adult citizens in the work force will be facilitated by these innovations.

SUMMARY

Four phases of educational computing, spanning the period from the early 1960s to the beginning of the twenty-first century, have been described. The first phase (experimentation) began with computer-assisted instruction presented on large, expensive mainframe computers at universities. The second phase (popularization) came in the mid-1970s with the introduction of the microcomputer. Although the machines of this phase were small, inexpensive, and able to perform many useful functions, the software tended to emphasize drill and practice and was often of poor instructional quality. The third phase, beginning in the mid-1980s, is the transition phase. In this phase, educators are becoming more sophisticated about how to use computers in education, are demanding better software and courseware, and are moving toward networking systems. The fourth phase (infusion) will probably begin around the year 2000. By then, computers will be an integral part of the educational delivery system.

The educational system is moving out of the industrial age and into the information age. This shift requires recognition of the national and international character of the economy, the constantly changing needs and methods of the world of work, and the increasingly important role of modern technology in general and artificial intelligence in particular.

Technology is affecting how things are done. It is also beginning to affect thinking. For example, the concept of *knowledge* is changing from *memorized information* to *ability to access information* as it is needed. The school curriculum is also being affected by the new technology of computing. Present trends suggest that there will be more emphasis on knowing how to think and solve problems in the basic skill areas. Computers are being introduced into the school curriculum in various ways. Learning is beginning to be seen as a lifelong endeavor. Networks and systems are being developed in various vocational and professional areas to help people continue their training.

It is expected that educational computers and computing will change somewhat in the near future. Equipment that provides alternatives to the keyboard for input (such as light pens and voice input devices) will become popular for educational computing. Alternative devices for output will also appear. Networking will probably become more widespread in schools, as will educational databases that serve as depositories of school records and contain a wide array of instructional resources for students and teachers. Costs of computers and computer storage devices should also be reduced as advances are made in hardware technology.

Courseware development will be more ambitious and of higher quality in the third phase of educational computing than it has been in the past. Larger publishers with more resources will become active in courseware development. Some standardization of operating systems should make software more transportable from one kind of computer to another. Courseware will probably become more accommodating to various classroom needs and will be easier to operate.

In physical appearance, schools may not change very much in the third phase. However, in more subtle ways they will be drastically different. For example, there will be increased emphasis on selecting the best instructional techniques and strategies for a given situation, and on the use of electronic instructional devices. Further, knowledge will be seen as dynamic and process-oriented rather than static and fact-oriented; and thinking and reasoning skills will become a greater concern. Learning will become more of a lifelong endeavor. Computer literacy will be added to the fundamental programs that schools offer. All these influences will make the schools very different institutions during the third phase.

The ability of education to lay aside outdated assumptions, adopt new approaches, and enter a new era is an extremely important issue. The first important step toward the information age was taken by many schools when a decision to incorporate computers into the teaching process was made. Once computers are integrated into education, changes in curriculum and teaching methods are inevitable.

The reader should be aware that the technology is already available for many of the future events and innovations that were described in this chapter. In a sense, technological development has outpaced the ability of education and society to adapt to it. Indeed, the phrase "The future is now" has never had more meaning. This is an exciting time to be an educator.

NOTES

1 Toffler, A. (1980). *The third wave.* New York: Morrow. See also: Deken, J. (1981). *The electronic cottage.* New York: Morrow. And also: *Mechanics Illustrated — Home Services Series No. 2. Personal Computers,* 12–16, 26.

2 National Commission on Excellence in Education. (1983, April). *A report to the nation and the secretary of education.* United States Department of Education, Washington, DC: U.S. Government Printing Office.

3 Education Commission of the States. (1983, June). *Action for excellence.* Report on Education for Economic Growth.

4 Molnar, A. R. (1980). Understanding how to use machines to work smarter in an information society. *The Computing Teacher, 7* (5), 68. A similar situation is developing in Europe, where a combination of factors have contributed to rather slow adaption of technological development. See: The decline of Europe. (1984, April 9). *Newsweek,* 10–16, 17–18.

5 Stein, K. (1983, April). Robo-shock. *Omni,* 46.

6 Duda, R., & Shortliffe, E. H. (1983). Expert systems research. *Science, 220,* 261–268.

7 Reboh, R. (1979). Knowledge acquisition system: A computer-based consultant for mineral exploration. In R. Duda (Ed.), *Final Report: SRI Project 6415.* Artificial Intelligence Center, Menlo Park, CA: SRI International.

8 A classic communications gap? Why teachers rely on textbooks. (1983). *EPIEgram, 11*(7/8).

9 Molnar, A. R. (1978). The next great crisis in American education: Computer literacy. *Journal of Educational Technology Systems, 7*(3), 275–285.

10 Fiske, E. (1983). Computer education update '83. *Popular Computing 2*(1), 142.

11 Physicist's dream about a computer network. (1981). *Science,* 211, 1151.

12 Naisbett, J. (1982). *Megatrends: Ten new directions transforming our lives.* New York: Warner.

13 Johnson, C. E. (1983). The promise of perpendicular magnetic recording. *BYTE, 8*(3), 56, 58, 60, 62, 64.

14 Sarisky, L. (1983). Will removable hard disks replace the floppy? *BYTE, 8*(3) 110, 112–116, 118.

15 The race to develop the microcomputer industry's most popular operating system was described in: Information processing. (1983, February 21). *Business Week,* 96, 98.

16 Evans, C. (1979). *The Micro-millennium.* New York: Washington Square Press.

17 Toffler, A. (1980). *The third wave.* New York: Morrow.

18 Papert, S. (1980). *Mindstorms: Children, computers and powerful ideas.* New York: Basic Books.

19 See, for example: Bork, A., & Franklin, S. D. (1979). The role of personal computer systems in education. *AEDS Journal, 13*(1), 17–30.

20 Kay, A. C., & Goldberg, A. (1977). Person dynamic media. *Computer, 10*(3), 31–41. Also discusseed in: Bartimo, J. (1984). A "real" computer in your lap? *InfoWorld, 6*(19), 91–94.

21 Carter, R. (1982). Schooldays 1991. *Classroom Computer News, 2*(3), 17–19.

22 Several descriptions of computer networks at universities are given in: Information processing. (1982, April 26). *Business Week, 68, 71.*

SUPPLEMENTARY READINGS

An Educational Technology interview with Mary Alice White: Into the electronic learning era – Implications for education and psychological research. (1981). *Educational Technology, 21*(10), 9–13.

Bork, A. (1981–1982). Educational technology and the future. *Journal of Educational Technology Systems, 10*(1), 3–20.

Garson, J. W. (1980). Far futures of computers in education. *The Computing Teacher, 7*(5), 36–40.

Hamrin, R. D. (1981). The information society: Its effect on education. *Education Digest, 47*(4), 46–47.

Jacobson, R. L. (1983, March 30). Colleges struggling to cope with the computer age. *Chronicle of Higher Education, 26*(5), 1, 6–10.

Postman, N. (1983). Engaging students in the great conversation. *Phi Delta Kappan, 64*(5), 310–316.

Rosenblatt, R. (1983, May 3). The mind in the machine. *Time,* 58–59.

Watt, D. (1983). Lifelong education. *Popular Computing, 2*(7), 62, 64, 67, 68.

GLOSSARY

abacus   An early computing device which consists of several rows of rods or wires and small beads, used for manual calculation. The abacus is widely used throughout Asia.

Ada   A high-level computer language designed by the U.S. Department of Defense as the standard language for all military services.

ALGOL   (ALGOrithmic Language.) A high-level computer language designed for scientific computations.

artificial intelligence (AI)   The field of computer science that is concerned with developing the capability of machines to solve problems in ways previously thought to be possible only for humans.

ASCII   (American Standard Code for Information Interchange.) A binary code established by the American National Standards Institute which is used to transmit information between computers. (ASCII is pronounced *ask-key*.)

assembly language   A low-level programming language which consists of mnemonic codes to represent binary machine instructions.

authoring   The process of developing programming on a computer using an authoring system.

authoring system   (Also called *authoring language*.) A specialized program or language developed specifically for the purpose of simplifying the creation of computer programs. Some authoring systems (such as PASS and PILOT) have been expressly developed to simplify the development of courseware and instructional programs.

BASIC   (Beginners All-Purpose Symbolic Instruction Code.) A high-level computer language which is used in most microcomputers. BASIC is easy to learn but contains advanced features for handling character strings and mathematical formulas.

binary   A term referring to the base-2 number system, in which the digits 0 and 1 are used to express numerical values.

bit A contraction of b*inary digit*. A bit is the smallest unit of memory storage in a computer (0 or 1). (See also *byte*.)

branch A point in a program where at least two alternative paths can be followed.

buffer A storage device which temporarily holds data being transferred from one device to another. Buffers are used to compensate for the difference in the rate in which computers, printers, and other devices can process data.

bulletin board A type of communications network which allows users to enter and store messages for other users.

bus Connections that provide pathways for communication between components of a computer.

byte A group of bits which form a unit of memory storage in a computer. A byte usually consists of 8 bits in most microcomputers. (See also *kilobyte*.)

calculating The application of addition, subtraction, multiplication, and division processes to data.

central processing unit (CPU) That part of a computer where instructions are decoded and executed. The central processing unit also controls the overall activity of the computer.

chip A small silicon slice containing integrated minute electronic circuitry.

COBOL (COmmon Business-Oriented Language.) A high-level computer language which is widely used for business applications.

coding The process of assigning codes to classes of information according to rules; also, programming.

communicating The process of transferring and receiving data from one location to another.

computer-assisted instruction (CAI) A method of instruction in which the computer provides educational activities leading to the achievement of instructional goals. (Also called *computer-aided instruction*.)

computer-managed instruction (CMI) The use of the computer for management of learning activities, such as keeping students' records, providing prescriptions, scheduling, and monitoring students' progress.

CP/M (Control Program for Microcomputers.) An operating system designed primarily for the Intel 8080 and Zilog family of 8-bit microprocessors.

CRT (Cathode-ray tube.) A tube with a screen (similar to a TV screen) upon which information is displayed. See *monitor*.

cursor A symbol that indicates the location on the monitor screen of the next character to be entered from the keyboard.

daisy wheel A printing device consisting of a wheel with letters at the end of each spoke. Daisy-wheel printers generally print typewriter-like characters and are often referred to as *letter-quality printers*.

data processing The application of data processing operations (such as sorting, summarizing, and classifying) to make data more useful.

database A large collection of information that is related by topic or application.

database management system The software which controls the storage, retrieval, and maintenance of a database.

debug To locate and correct errors in a computer program.

disk drive A peripheral device which reads information stored on a disk and writes information on a disk.

disk emulator A memory storage card which is capable of storing the information contained on a diskette in random-access memory and providing almost instantaneous access to the data.

dot matrix   A type of print in which characters are formed by dots on paper. Dot-matrix printers type more quickly and cost less than letter-quality (daisy-wheel) printers, but the image quality is inferior.

drill and practice   A type of computer-assisted instruction that involves the repeated presentation of questions and the provision of feedback to the responses.

dynabook   A term proposed by Alan C. Kay for the small, book-sized educational computer of the future.

educational game   (1) Any game-like activity which is designed or used to help achieve an educational outcome. (2) A computerized game which is utilized primarily for its educational value rather than for entertainment.

ENIAC   (Electronic Numerical Integration and Calculator.) A first-generation computer developed at the University of Pennsylvania in the early 1940s.

EPIE   (Educational Products Information Exchange.) A nonprofit organization which provides in-depth evaluations of educational computing products.

floppy disk   A disk made of a thin flexible sheet of Mylar which is usually 3, 5¼, or 8 inches in diameter. Floppy disks are used with microcomputers to store information.

flowchart   A chart using specific symbols that shows the sequence and branches of a procedure. Frequently used in developing programs for computers.

formative evaluation   Evaluation of the parts of an educational program conducted as the program is undergoing development. See also *summative evaluation.*

FORTRAN   (FORmula TRANslator.) A high-level computer language developed in the late 1950s for scientific and mathematical applications.

friction feed   A method of advancing paper in a printer by sheets. See also *tractor feed.*

full duplex   The transmission of data between terminals in two directions at the same time. See also *simplex, half duplex.*

graphics tablet   A device which utilizes a flat tablet and a stylus for entering graphic data into computer memory. An image drawn on the tablet can be displayed on the computer screen, saved on a diskette, or printed out on a printer.

half duplex   The transmission of data from one terminal to another in one direction at a time. See also *simplex, full duplex.*

hard copy   Information generated from a computer which is printed on paper by a printer.

hard disk   A memory storage device made of a rigid aluminum or ceramic base coated with magnetic material. Hard disks can store many times more than a floppy disk.

hardware   Computer equipment such as the central processing unit, the keyboard, and peripheral devices. See also *software.*

input   (1) Data or programs entered into a computer. (2) The act of entering data or a program into a computer.

integrated circuit   A silicon chip containing electrical electronic circuitry which might control the equivalent of thousands of transistors. Integrated circuits are less costly, consume less power, and are more reliable than individual circuits found in older computers.

joystick   An input device which is commonly used for playing computer games.

kilobyte (K) 2^{10}, or 1024, bytes of memory. For example, 64K means 65,536 bytes. Kilobyte is abbreviated K.

light pen   A light-sensitive stylus which allows the user to interact with the computer through the monitor.

Logo   A computer language developed at MIT as an educational tool for young children.

mainframe   A large computer which is capable of storing and processing large amounts of data. See also *minicomputer* and *microcomputer.*

MECC   (Minnesota Educational Computing Consortium.) An educational computing service organization which distributes computer courseware and training materials to member organizations and provides services.

microcomputer   A small computer, comparable in size to a portable typewriter. Also called a *personal computer.* (See also *mainframe, minicomputer.*)

microprocessing unit (MPU)   See *central processing unit (CPU).*

MicroSIFT   A network disseminating evaluations of and information about educational software. MicroSIFT was established by the Northwest Regional Educational Laboratory in Portland, Oregon.

minicomputer   An intermediate-size computer which operates several times faster than a microcomputer, has more storage capacity, and generally supports several high-level languages such as COBOL and FORTRAN. Minicomputers are widely used in government, business, and industry. (See also *mainframe, microcomputer.*)

modem   (An acronym for *mo*dulator-*dem*odulator.) A communications device which modulates and demodulates signals between computers and telephones.

monitor   The screen of a cathode-ray tube, commonly used to display output from a computer.

network   A communications system consisting of one or more computers, terminals, modems, and related devices for the transmission and reception of data.

output   Information which results from computer operation.

Pascal   A high-level computer language originally developed in 1970 by Niklaus Wirth to help teach structured programming. Pascal is frequently taught as the first programming language in high school.

PASS   (Professional Authoring Software System.) An authoring system developed by Bell and Howell for professional authoring of courseware on the Apple Computer.

peripheral   An input or output device, such as a disk drive or printer, which is connected to and under the control of the central processing unit.

PILOT   (Programmed Inquiry Learning or Teaching.) A popular authoring language for writing drill and practice and tutorial courseware. Numerous versions of PILOT are available for a variety of microcomputers.

PLATO   (Programmed Logic for Automatic Teaching Operation.) A computer-assisted instruction project begun at the University of Illinois in 1959 and currently supported by Control Data Corporation.

plotter   A specialized printer which can print points or alphanumeric characters along horizontal and vertical axes. Plotters are widely used in mapping and in scientific and engineering applications.

problem solving   An educational activity in which students solve problems. Problem solving may involve students in programming a computer in a language such as BASIC, or it may involve the use of utility programs such as spreadsheets and database management software to help reach solutions.

program   (1) A set of instructions fed into a computer. A program is written in a specialized code known as a *computer language.* (2) The act of writing a set of coded instructions for a computer.

random-access memory (RAM)   Memory storage in which any location can be erased or changed.

read-only memory (ROM)   A memory chip that is programmed at the time of manufacture. ROM chips store permanent program instructions or data used in the microprocessor. ROM chips cannot be reprogrammed by the computer user.

recording   The transfer of data to another medium, as in typing information into computer memory or transferring it onto a floppy disk.

relational structure   The storing of information in a database in tables which contain data in the form of relations.

retrieving   The process of locating and displaying information which has been stored.

robotics   The design, production, and utilization of robots.

simplex   One-way transmission of data from a computer terminal to another terminal. (See also *half duplex, full duplex.*)

simulation   A type of computer-assisted instruction in which the computer presents a simulated version of a real-life situation.

software   The programs which run on a computer. The term may also include the medium on which programs are stored. (See also *hardware.*)

sorting   The process of arranging data in an order or in groups according to a plan.

spreadsheet   A multicolumned ledger sheet that is used to record and calculate quantified data. A computerized spreadsheet provides considerable benefit over one that is kept on a page of paper (e. g., general formula entry, variable length and width).

storing   Placing data in orderly form on storage media such as floppy disks, punch cards, magnetic tape, and printed paper.

summative evaluation   The final testing and evaluation of a finished educational product. (See also *formative evaluation.*)

template   The format for a document or form which has been stored on a disk. Templates are frequently used with word processing, spreadsheets, and database management programs.

time sharing   A system of computer operation which allows two or more users to access the same hardware. Rapid program execution allows multiple users to utilize the equipment for a variety of purposes with a minimum of delay.

tractor feed   A method of advancing paper in a printer which uses sprockets that fit into holes in the paper. Tractor feed results in more precise paper alignment than friction feed. See also *friction feed.*

tutorial   A type of computer-assisted instruction in which the computer introduces new material to the student in an interactive fashion.

user-friendly   A term describing computer software or hardware which is easy to use.

videodisk   A flat, record-like storage device which can hold an enormous amount of separate pictures or pages of information. Some videodisks are useful for rapid search and information access and for displaying graphics.

voice synthesizer   A device which produces speech-like sounds by interpreting digital data. Voice synthesizers are used in a variety of interactive computer games and educational programs. There are also synthesizers capable of reproducing music and other sounds.

volatile   A term describing computer memory which is erased when the power supply is disconnected. Random-access memory (RAM) is volatile.

word processing   Data processing operations performed on words and text. Word processing programs are available for most microcomputers.

INDEXES

NAME INDEX

SUBJECT INDEX

9821